Every effort has been made to ensure that the information given in this guide is accurate and up-to-date as possible at the time of going to press. Details do change, however, and the publisher cannot accept responsibility for any consequences arising from the use of this book. If you come across an incorrect detail that we could amend for next year, please let us know.

IF YOU EVER WANTED TO KNOW WHO?

STANLEY MATHEWS

GASCOIGNE

Jack Charlton

Kevin Keegan

BUTCHER

BOBBY MOORE

BERGKAMP

Wright

Tosback

Jackie Milburn

Alan Shearer

LORIMER

RUSH

THE KICK OFF TEAM

Editor
Mike Ivey
Contributing Editors
Bobby Robson
David Pleat
John Motson
Trevor Brooking
Bob Harris
Editorial Secretary
Nikki Collins
Art Director
Atam Sandhu
Designers
Ian Bull
Nick Thornton
Steven Clifford
Wendy Martin
Statistics Programmers
Karim Biria
Linden Davis
Publisher
Simon Rosen

NB: The statistics relate to league matches only.

Repro: Colour Origination

SIDANPRESS

Sidan Press Ltd
7 Denbigh Mews, Denbigh Street, London SW1V 2HQ
Tel: 0171 630 6446 Fax: 0171 630 5836
ISDN: 0171 828 5686
Email: sidanpress@dial.pipex.com
Registered in England No: 3174984

Peter Leaver QC
Chief Executive of the FA Premier League

We witnessed some wonderful action in The FA Premier League last season and I am confident that we can look forward to another thrilling season in 1998/99. Congratulations go to Arsenal for winning the Premier League for the first time as well as for completing "The Double" by winning the FA Cup, and also for The FA Premier Youth League. Congratulations are also extended to Chelsea for winning the Cup Winners Cup and Coca-Cola Cup.

With more and more world class stars now playing in the Premiership, our League is now rightly regarded as one of the most dynamic and competitive in the world.

There is no better barometer of the health of the game than the number of people coming through the turnstiles and figures published in May 1998 showed that Premier League attendances last season topped 11 million for the first time since we reduced to 20 clubs. This represented 94% of total capacity across the Premiership and an increase in our average attendance of 38% since our first season.

Our fourth annual (and most comprehensive) survey of fans was published in February 1998 and showed beyond doubt that we have made great strides since The F.A. Premier League was formed. As a five year progress report, it gives us a positive boost as well as helping us to understand some of the issues that need to be addressed over the next five years. Some particularly encouraging results included:

- the increasing number of female fans, particularly among new supporters
- the growing interest across families in Premiership football
- the spread of fans across social and income groups
- the further increase in the number of new fans
- the continuing fall in hooliganism and threatening behaviour
- the approval rating given to our stadia, the business/football balance, our TV arrangements, the current size of the Premiership and the influx of top international stars.

All of this suggests we are getting something right.

However, there can be no room for complacency and we still have work to do. We want to increase the number of fans from ethnic minority backgrounds, to strive further to eradicate racism and to improve the atmosphere at some of our grounds.

In addition, I think that all those involved in football agree that there is a need to build on our investment in youth development and in grassroots activities inside and outside The F.A. Premier League. That is why I am excited by our plans to develop, through the course of this season and over time, football academies at every Premiership club. I am confident that this development will have a positive and long-lasting impact on the quality of football played at both domestic and international level.

Other initiatives and developments that occurred through the course of last season which, I believe, demonstrate our desire to progress include:

- our role in the reform and re-launch of the Football Trust
- the appointment of Philip Don as our first ever Referees Officer
- the launch of the study support centres initiative in co-operation with the Department for Education and Employment
- the launch of the "watch your language" campaign
- the continued development of the supporter panel initiative

With England's positive performance in the World Cup '98 giving a further boost to English football, I am confident of more success for our clubs in the season ahead.

Here's to another great season in the Premiership and good luck to all our fans.

Peter Leaver QC

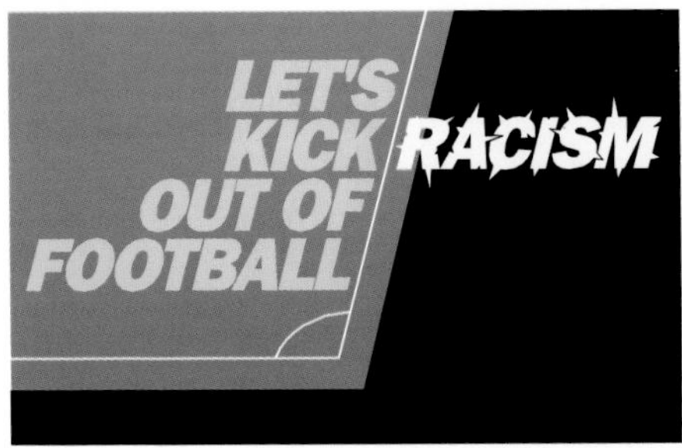

The Premier League is one of the major sponsors of Kick It Out, the independent organisation set up to run the Let's Kick Racism Out of Football campaign. During the past season the partnership between the Premier League and Kick It Out has grown from strength to strength and both parties are looking forward to developing this initiative.

Clubs and supporters from across the country are now joining the campaign in pro-active work to ensure that football is free from racism.

During the coming season Kick It Out are keen to establish links with more Clubs and supporters groups to initiate new campaigns at local levels. It is important that all supporters understand that racism is not welcome in football today and that the Premier League and Kick It Out will be working to ensure that our national game will be enjoyed by everyone regardless of the colour of their skin.

Should you wish to receive further information on the campaign or would like to get involved please write to:

Kick It Out
The Business Design Centre
52 Upper Street, London, N1 0QH
Fax: 0171-288-6042

The Champions

FA CARLING PREMIERSHIP CHAMPIONS

1997 - 1998	**Arsenal**
1996 - 1997	**Manchester United**
1995 - 1996	**Manchester United**
1994 - 1995	**Blackburn Rovers**
1993 - 1994	**Manchester United**
1992 - 1993	**Manchester United**

THE CARLING PREMIERSHIP FIXTURE LIST

CARLING F.A. PREMIERSHIP	Arsenal	Aston Villa	Blackburn	Charlton	Chelsea	Coventry	Derby	Everton	Leeds Utd	Leicester	Liverpool	Man Utd	Middlesbrough	Newcastle	Notts Forest	Sheff Wed	Southampton	Tottenham	West Ham	Wimbledon
Arsenal		16/5	6/4	29/8	30/1	20/3	1/5	7/11	20/12	20/2	9/1	20/9	29/11	4/10	17/8	6/3	17/10	14/11	26/12	17/4
Aston Villa	12/12		6/2	8/5	20/3	27/2	26/9	16/1	13/2	24/10	21/11	5/12	23/8	9/9	24/4	28/12	10/4	7/11	3/4	12/9
Blackburn Rovers	25/10	26/12		5/12	21/9	7/11	15/8	5/3	9/1	29/8	24/4	10/4	3/4	12/12	8/5	20/2	21/11	30/1	3/10	20/3
Charlton	28/12	21/12	1/5		3/4	26/9	12/9	28/11	17/4	7/11	13/2	30/1	14/11	16/1	27/2	16/5	22/8	20/3	24/10	6/2
Chelsea	9/9	31/10	13/2	17/10		16/1	16/5	1/5	5/4	17/4	27/2	29/12	26/9	22/8	12/9	28/11	6/2	19/12	13/3	14/11
Coventry City	31/10	3/10	13/3	6/3	15/8		19/12	15/11	16/5	28/11	30/1	20/2	17/4	19/9	9/1	18/10	5/4	26/12	29/8	1/5
Derby County	5/12	6/3	16/1	20/2	12/12	8/5		6/2	31/10	19/9	13/3	24/10	28/12	3/4	10/4	9/9	24/4	3/10	22/11	22/8
Everton	13/3	15/8	26/9	24/4	5/12	11/4	26/12		12/9	9/1	17/10	31/10	13/2	23/11	30/1	5/4	12/12	29/8	8/5	27/2
Leeds United	8/5	19/9	24/6	21/11	25/10	14/12	20/3	20/2		3/10	10/4	24/4	16/1	6/2	3/4	8/11	8/9	6/3	5/12	29/12
Leicester City	12/9	6/4	28/12	13/3	21/11	24/4	13/2	22/8	27/2		31/10	16/1	9/9	8/5	12/12	6/2	5/12	19/10	10/4	27/9
Liverpool	22/8	17/4	29/11	19/9	4/10	9/9	7/11	3/4	14/11	20/3		6/3	6/2	28/12	24/10	19/12	16/1	1/5	20/2	16/5
Manchester United	13/2	1/5	14/11	9/9	16/12	12/9	5/4	20/3	28/11	15/8	26/9		19/12	8/11	26/12	17/4	27/2	16/5	9/1	17/10
Middlesbrough	24/4	9/1	17/10	10/4	6/3	21/11	29/8	19/9	15/8	30/1	26/12	8/5		6/12	1/11	3/10	13/3	20/2	12/12	5/4
Newcastle United	27/2	30/1	16/5	15/8	9/1	13/2	17/10	17/4	26/12	19/12	30/8	13/3	1/5		26/9	14/11	12/9	5/4	31/10	28/11
Nottingham Forset	16/1	28/11	19/12	3/10	20/2	22/8	16/11	8/9	17/10	16/5	5/4	6/2	20/3	6/3		1/5	28/12	17/4	19/9	7/11
Sheffield Wednesday	26/9	29/8	12/9	12/12	24/4	3/4	30/1	24/10	13/3	26/12	8/5	21/11	27/2	10/4	7/12		31/10	9/1	15/8	13/2
Southampton	3/4	14/11	17/4	9/1	26/12	24/10	28/11	16/5	30/1	1/5	16/8	3/10	7/11	20/2	29/8	20/3		19/9	6/3	19/12
Tottenham Hotspur	10/4	13/3	9/9	2/11	8/5	6/2	27/2	28/12	26/9	3/4	5/12	12/12	13/9	24/10	21/11	22/8	13/2		24/4	16/1
West Ham United	6/2	17/10	27/2	5/4	8/11	28/12	17/4	19/12	1/5	14/11	12/9	22/8	16/5	20/3	13/2	16/1	28/9	28/11		9/9
Wimbledon	21/11	20/2	23/10	26/12	10/4	5/12	9/1	3/10	29/8	6/3	13/12	3/4	24/10	24/4	13/3	19/9	8/5	15/8	30-1	

Arsenal FC

Arsenal FC
Arsenal Stadium
Avenell Road, Highbury
London N5 1BU

Club No:	0171·704·4000
Fax No:	0171·704·4001
Tickets:	0171·704·4040
Dial A Ticket:	0171·413·3366
Internet:	www.arsenal.co.uk

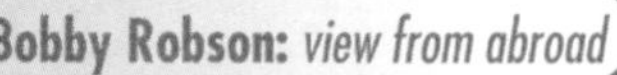

Bobby Robson: *view from abroad*

One of the pedigree clubs in the world. The staff, the manager, administration, reputation, all are of the highest level. But they know that to retain their championship they will have to play 10% better because everyone will try to knock them off their perch. Some of the faces have changed but they will still be solid in defence giving little away. They don't give away presents. Europe is a different battlefield that requires alternative qualities and styles to the Premiership. Arsenal will relish the challenge.

Bob Harris: *view in England*

The team to chase and the team to beat. Produced stunning, attractive football to overhaul Manchester United to win the Premiership and then went on to take the double by beating Newcastle United in the FA Cup. The last thing you could call the Gunner's was "lucky" last season as they suffered their share of injuries and suspensions. Indeed some claim it was the day that Footballer of the Year Dennis Bergkamp was sent off that proved to be the catalyst to the season, bringing the team close together and establishing youngsters like Anelka. They could be even better this season!

INFORMATION HOTLINES

ClubCall:	0891·20·20·20*
Ticket & Prizeline:	0891·20·20·21*

**Calls cost min of 50p per minute at all times*
Club Call, Avalon House, 57-63 Scrutton St, London, EC2A 4PJ

CLUB SHOPS

The Gunners Shop
Located by East Stand

Opening Times:
Monday-Friday: 9.30am-5.00pm
Match Saturdays: 10.00am-5.30pm
Match Sundays: 10.30am-6.30pm
Match Evenings: 9.30am-10.30pm
Tel: 0171·704·4120
Mail Order Service: 0171·704·2020

ARSENAL WORLD OF SPORT
Finsbury Park Station

Opening Times:
Monday-Saturday: 9.30am-6.00pm
Match Sundays: 10.00am-6.00pm
Match Evenings: 9.30am-10.30pm
Tel: 0171·272·1000
Fax: 0171·272·4124
Mail Order Service: 0171·704·2020

BOOKING INFORMATION

General Enquiries:	0171·704·4040
Credit Card Bookings:	0171·413·3366
Travel Club:	0171·704·4150
Recorded Info:	0171·704·4242
Junior Gunners:	0171·704·4160

CATERING

FOOD

Double Burger Meal Dea	£3.50
Regular Quater Pouner	£2.10
Breaded Chicken Burger	£2.20
Chips	£1.00
Jumbo Hot Dog	£1.80
Pies	£1.80
Spicy Beanburger	£2.00
Chilli Dog	£2.20
Nachos	£1.90
Crisps	£0.60

BAR

Lager (Pint)	£2.20
Bitter (Pint)	£2.00
Coke (16oz)	£1.00
Tea/Coffee	£1.00

MISCELLANEOUS

Stadium Tours
Contact Iain Cook - Tel: 0171·704·4000
£4 Adults, £2 Children, £1 Junior Gunners

Corporate Hospitality
Contact Yvette Brown - Tel: 0171·704·4100
Matchday hospitality packages, match ball sponsorship and private glass fronted lounge available for between 2 and 200 guests.

Literature
Programme price £2, Official Arsenal Magazine £2.50

Pre Match & Half Time Entertainment
Museum open to North Bank supporters. 2 giant screens show highlights of previous games, plus an interview with the manager who announces the team.
Half Time - Highlights of 1st Half
Full Time - Highlights of game

Sports Centre
The South Stand boasts a sports centre with indoor football pitch and gymnasium. For details call 0171·704·4140

John Motson: *one to watch*

NICOLAS ANELKA

Anelka was only 17 when Arsene Wenger brought him to Highbury from Paris St. Germain, but the startling progress he made last season was climaxed by his goal in the F.A. Cup final which confirmed Arsenal's second double. That assures him of a place in their history, but at 19 he still has virtually the whole of his career in front of him. He has added poise and purpose to his blistering pace, a ready-made successor to Ian Wright.

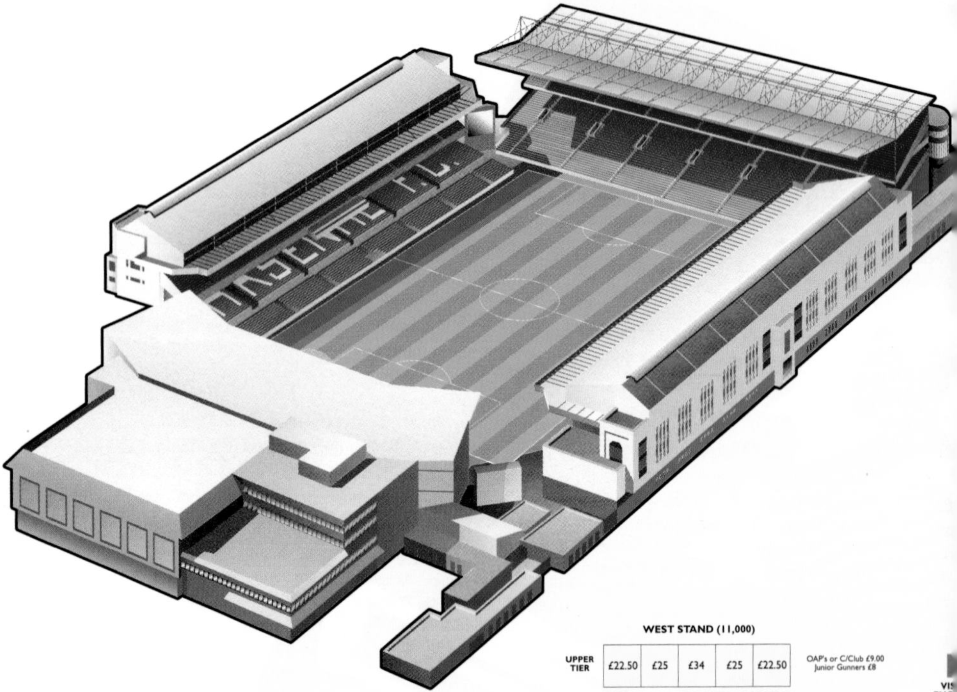

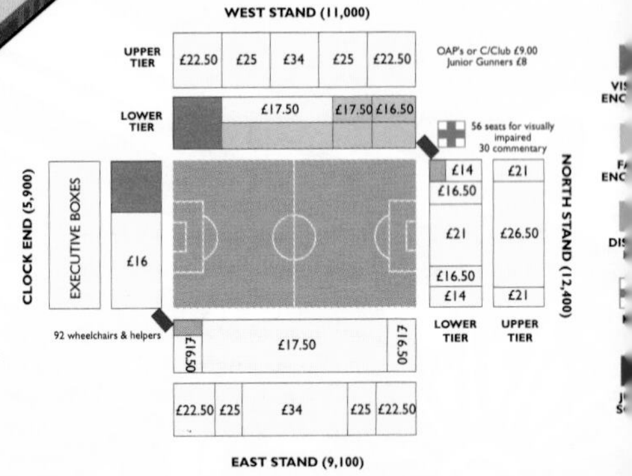

WEST STAND (11,000)

UPPER TIER: £22.50 | £25 | £34 | £25 | £22.50

OAP's or C/Club £9.00
Junior Gunners £8

LOWER TIER: £17.50 | £17.50 | £16.50

56 seats for visually impaired
30 commentary

CLOCK END (5,900)

EXECUTIVE BOXES

£16

92 wheelchairs & helpers

NORTH STAND (12,400)

LOWER TIER: £14 | £16.50 | £21 | £16.50 | £14

UPPER TIER: £21 | £26.50 | £21

£16.50 | £17.50 | £16.50

£22.50 | £25 | £34 | £25 | £22.50

EAST STAND (9,100)

97/98 season points and league position by month

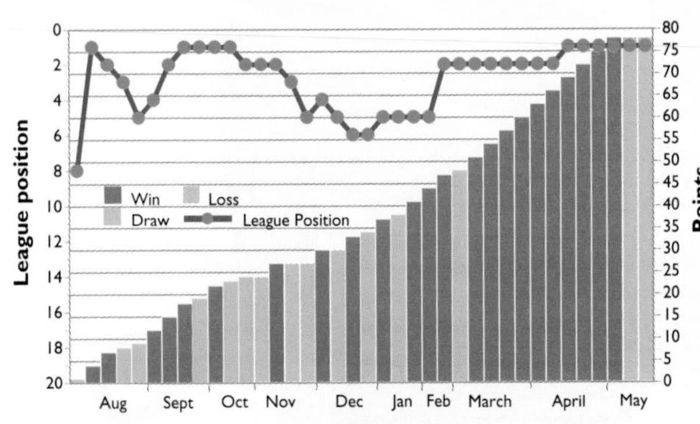

Goals for and against seasons 92/3 to 97/8

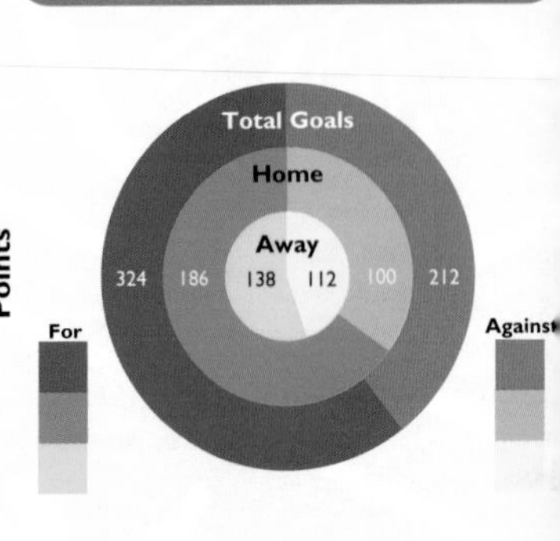

Goals scored by position by season

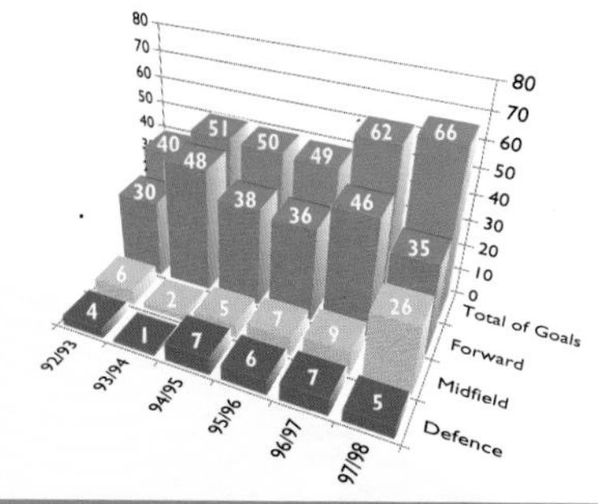

Bookings by position by season

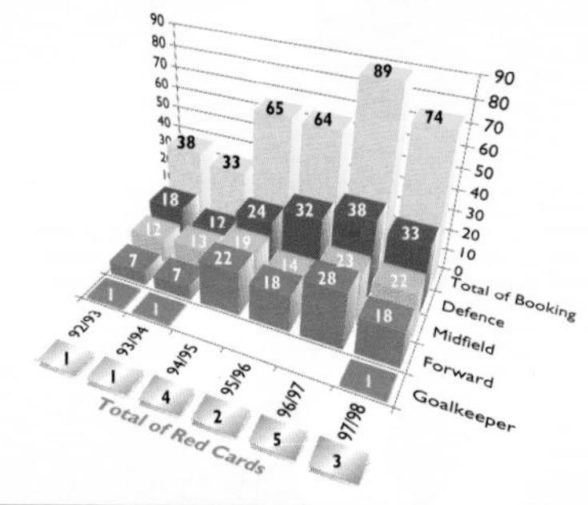

Goals scored by position by month 97/98

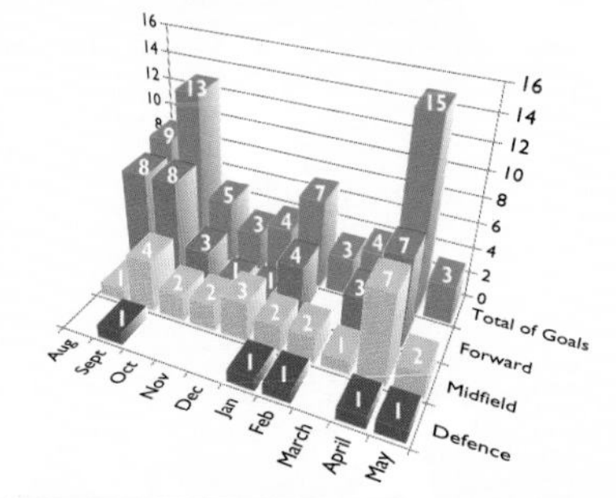

Final league position by season

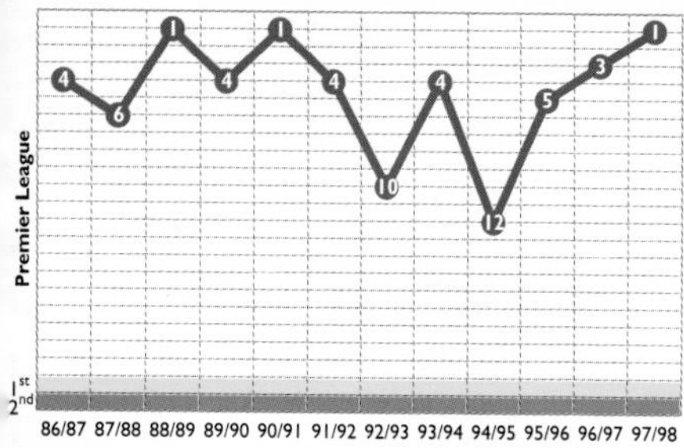

THE CARLING PREMIERSHIP FIXTURE LIST

HOME MATCH
AWAY MATCH
LAST SEASON: WIN
LAST SEASON: DRAW
LAST SEASON: LOSS

Opponent	Date	Last season
NOTTINGHAM FOREST	17/8	N/A
LIVERPOOL	22/8	0-4
CHARLTON	29/8	N/A
CHELSEA	9/9	3-2
LEICESTER CITY	12/9	3-3
MANCHESTER UNITED	20/9	3-2
SHEFFIELD WEDNESDAY	26/9	0-2
NEWCASTLE UNITED	4/10	3-1
SOUTHAMPTON	17/10	3-0
BLACKBURN ROVERS	25/10	4-1
COVENTRY CITY	31/10	2-2
EVERTON	7/11	4-0
TOTTENHAM H	14/11	0-0
WIMBLEDON	21/11	1-0
MIDDLESBROUGH	29/11	N/A
DERBY COUNTY	5/12	0-3
ASTON VILLA	12/12	0-1
LEEDS UNITED	20/12	2-1
WEST HAM UTD	26/12	4-0
CHARLTON ATHLETIC	26/12	N/A
LIVERPOOL	9/1	0-1
NOTTINGHAM FOREST	16/1	N/A
CHELSEA	30/1	2-0
WEST HAM UNITED	6/2	0-0
MANCHESTER UNITED	13/2	1-0
LEICESTER CITY	20/2	2-1
NEWCASTLE UNITED	27/2	1-0
SHEFFIELD WEDNESDAY	6/3	1-0
EVERTON	13/3	2-2
COVENTRY CITY	20/3	2-0
SOUTHAMPTON	3/4	3-1
BLACKBURN ROVERS	5/4	1-3
TOTTENHAM H	10/4	1-1
WIMBLEDON	17/4	5-0
MIDDLESBROUGH	24/4	N/A
DERBY COUNTY	1/5	1-0
LEEDS UNITED	8/5	1-1
ASTON VILLA	16/5	0-0

THE SQUAD

Goalkeeper · Defender · Midfield · Forward · No of goals · No of clean sheets · No of yellow cards · No of red cards

Player	Position	Goals / Clean sheets	Yellow cards	Red cards
A. Manninger	Goalkeeper	6		
D. Seaman	Goalkeeper	13	1	
J. Lukic	Goalkeeper			
G. Grimandi	Defender	1	5	
M. Upson	Defender			
R. Garde	Defender		3	
L. Dixon	Defender		4	
M. Keown	Defender		2	1
N. Winterburn	Defender	1	3	
S. Bould	Defender		9	
T. Adams	Defender	3	5	
D. Grondin	Defender			
R. Parlour	Midfield	5	5	
A. Mendez	Midfield			
S. Hughes	Midfield	2		
E. Petit	Midfield	2	3	1
P. Vernazza	Midfield			
M. Overmars	Midfield	12		
P. Vieira	Midfield	2	8	1
L. Boa Morte	Midfield		2	
N. Anelka	Forward	6	3	
D. Bergkamp	Forward	16	7	
C. Wreh	Forward	3		

Transfers after 15 July 1998:

David Pleat: *on the manager*

ARSENE WENGER

Thoughtful and incisive. He has learnt quickly, has bought well and has an immaculate way of coping with difficult questions from the media. There is no reason why he and the club shouldn't remain in one of the highest positions in the League this season.

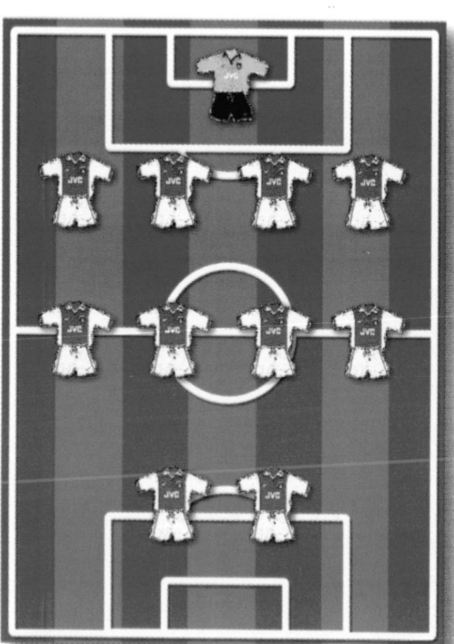

Trevor Brooking: *tactics*

Their main problem is how to improve on last season! Reverted to a solid 4-4-2 system which had that wealth of experience at the back, and the superb French duo of Emmanuel Petit and Patrick Vieira protecting them in central midfield. The emerging pace of Marc Overmars and Nicolas Anelka was vital in the closing months of the season.

Arsenal is situated in North London. Parking near the ground is difficult during a match as restrictions come into force. Travel by tube.

DIRECTIONS

From the North:

From the M1 exit at the A1 turn-off - Junction 2/3. The A1 merges for a stretch with the A406. Keep to the A1, soon called Archway Road and then Holloway Road. Turn left onto the A503 Seven Sisters Road and after 1 mile right onto the A1201 Blackstock Road which becomes Highbury Park. Turn right into Aubert Park and right again into Avenell Road.

From the North West:

From the M40 at Junction 1 stay on the A40 for 13 miles and on the A40(M). At Paddington turn onto the A501. When the A501 becomes Pentonville Road turn left onto Baron Street, signposted as the route for the A1. Take the first right Lion Street and turn left onto the A1. At the Highbury and Islington roundabout, turn right onto St Pauls Road and then left onto the A1201 Highbury Grove. Turn left into Aubert Park and right into Avenell Road.

From the West:

Approaching on the M4 turn left onto the A406 Gunnersbury Avenue at Junction 2. At Hangar Lane turn right onto the A40. Then as route for North West.

From the South West:

Stay on the M3 to end and continue on A316 to Hammersmith. Turn right onto A4 for 1 1/4 miles, left onto the A3220 Warwick Road and then onto the M41. At end turn onto A40(M) and then as route for North West.

From the East:

From the M11 turn off onto the A406 at Junction 4, and then onto the A503. After Tottenham Hale tube station, turn left into Broad Lane and then back onto the A503 Seven Sisters Road. Turn left onto the A1201 Blackstock Road and then as route for North.

Arsenal is the nearest Tube Station.

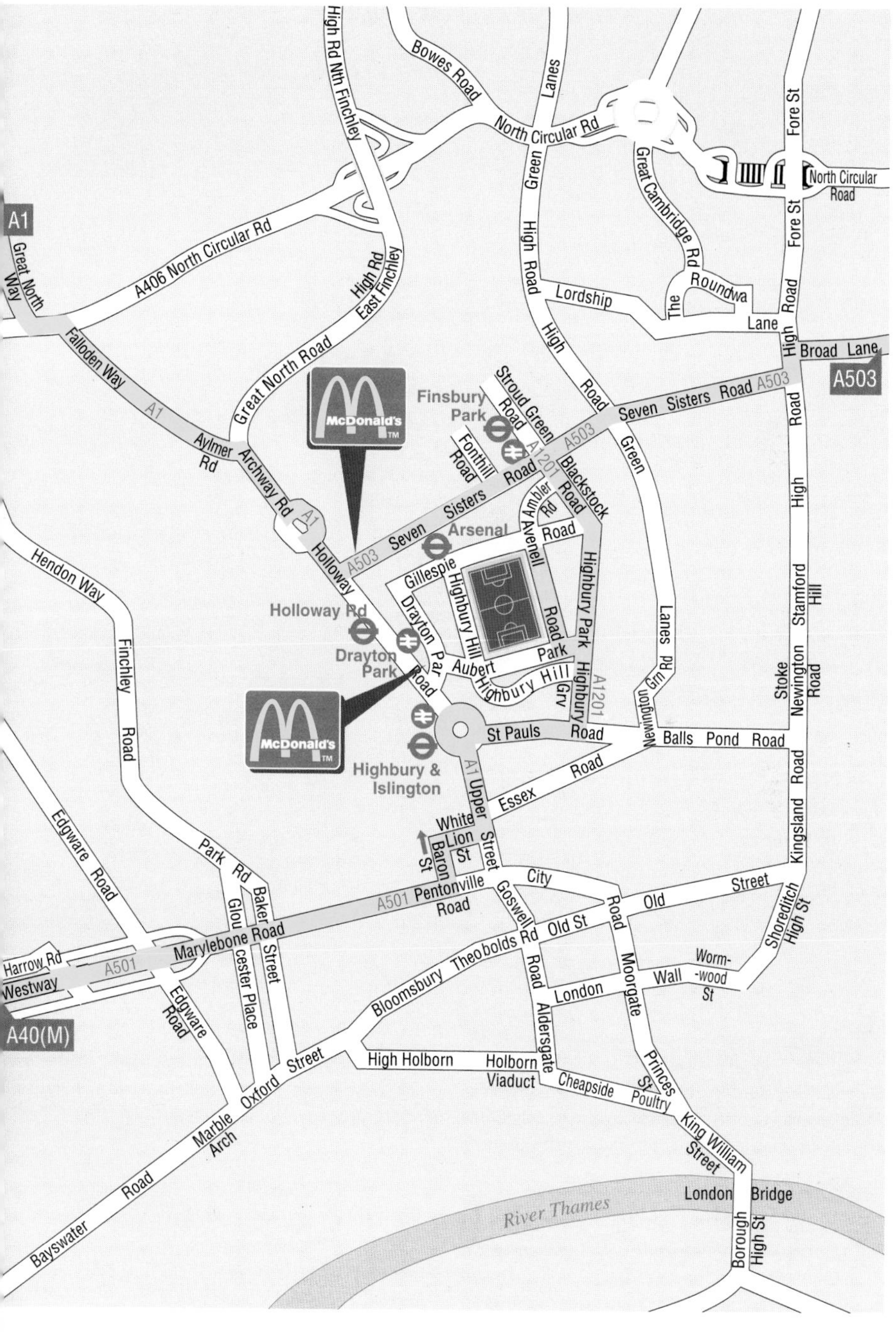

McDonald's™ 13-15 Seven Sisters Road, Holloway, London N7 6AJ
McDonald's™ 280 Holloway Road, London N7

Aston Villa FC

Aston Villa FC
Villa Park
Trinity Road
Birmingham, B6 6HE

Club No.	0121·327·2299
Fax No.	0121·322·2107
Tickets:	0121·327·5353
Dial A Ticket:	0121·607·8000
Internet:	www.astonvilla-fc.co.uk

Bobby Robson: *view from abroad*

Should always be looking for a place in Europe. A big club with big ambitions. Signing of Alan Thompson a good sign, underlining the fact that they are one of the top half a dozen clubs in the country, something they will wish to emphasise this season not only in the Premiership but again in Europe where they excelled last time around.

Bob Harris: *view in England*

Will be hoping for a much more stabilised season this time around. They began as an outside bet for the title, slipped towards relegation despite a fine run in Europe and then, under new manager John Gregory, staged a magnificent recovery which saw them clinch a place back in Europe. Personnel changes during the summer will see a different looking team this time around but with that same commitment and passion demanded by Gregory.

INFORMATION HOTLINES

ClubCall: 0891·12·11·48*

Recorded ticket Information: 0891·12·18·48*

Calls cost 50p per minute at all times
Club Call, Avalon House, 57-63 Scrutton St, London, EC2A 4PJ

CLUB SHOPS

VILLA VILLAGE
Villa Park, Aston, Birmingham B6 6TA

Opening Times:
Monday-Saturday: 9.30am-5.00pm
Match Saturdays: 9.30am-3.00pm, 4.45pm-5.30pm
Match Sundays: 10.00am-4.00pm.
Midweek Matchdays: 9.30am-7.30pm, 9.15pm-10.15pm

Free car parking for up to 400 cars (non matchdays only)

HOLTE END STAND
Beneath Holte Pub on Witton Lane

Matchdays Only:
Saturday Matchdays: 12.00a.m.-3.00p.m, 4.45p.m.-5.15p.m.
Sunday Matchdays: 1.00p.m.-4.00p.m, 5.45p.m-6.15p.m.
Midweek Matchdays: 6.00pm-8.00p.m, 9.45p.m.-10.15p.m.

Mail Order Service: 0121·327·5963/2800
Fax: 0121·327·7227
Email: merchdept@astonvilla-fc.co.uk

BOOKING INFORMATION

General Enquiries:	0121·327·5353
Credit Card Bookings:	0121·607·8000
Recorded Info:	0891·12·18·48*
Official British & European Travel Club:	0121·328·3322
Promotions/fundraising & development:	0121·328·2246

CATERING

FOOD

Hot Dogs	£2.10
Burgers	£2.10
Pasties	£1.60
Pies	£1.50
Soup	£0.80

BAR

Coke/Diet	£1.10
Ribena	£0.90
Crisps	£0.50
Tea	£0.70
Coffee	£0.80
Bovril	£0.85
Hot Chocolate	£0.80

MISCELLANEOUS

Stadium Tours
Contact Pam Bridgewater - Tel: 0121·327·2299 Ext 283
Free at 10.30 and 1.30 on weekdays.
Corporate Hospitality
Contact Abdul Rashid - Tel: 0121·327·5399,
Fax: 0121·328·2099
A wide range of corporate hospitality, matchball and match sponsorship available.
Catering from 4 to 4000.
McGregors: Licensed for weddings (seats 150).
Holte Suite: New banqueting facility for 650 diners, 12,000 sq ft exhibition space, on-site catering 3 suites, 24hr security. Tel: 0121·327·0388.
Corner Flag: Themed restaurant, open every lunchtime. Tel: 0121·326·1519
Call sales and marketing 0121·327·5308.
Literature
Programme price £2.00, Claret & Blue (bi-monthly) £2.50.
Pre Match & Half Time Entertainment
Varied/Video Screens

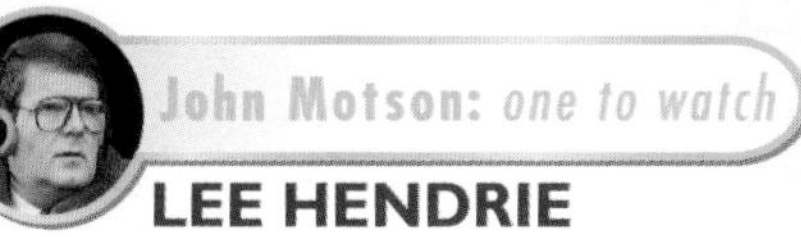

LEE HENDRIE

Birmingham born Hendrie celebrated his 21st birthday at the end of last season, by which time he was already a favourite with the Villa fans. His progress as a left-sided attacker was reflected in the whirlwind finish to the season under John Gregory which means Hendrie and Villa will play in Europe this season. Lee's father and cousin have both played league football and he looks set to further the family tradition.

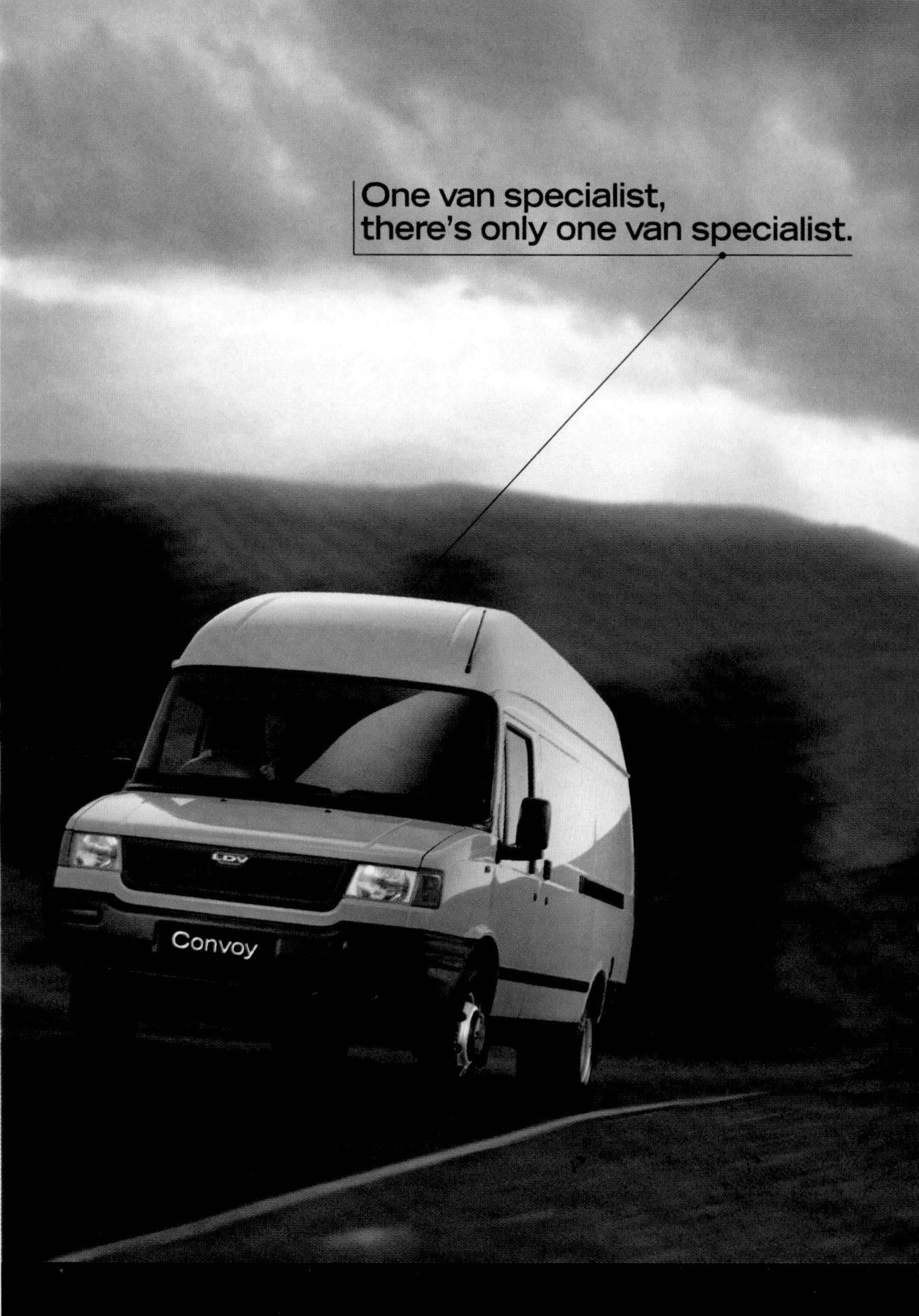
One van specialist, there's only one van specialist.
LDV
Convoy
No, seriously, there is only one van specialist. At LDV, we put all our experience, resources and people into vans. And with over 160 dealers, it's what's known as total support. For more information, call **0800 400407.**
LDV

ASTON VILLA FC

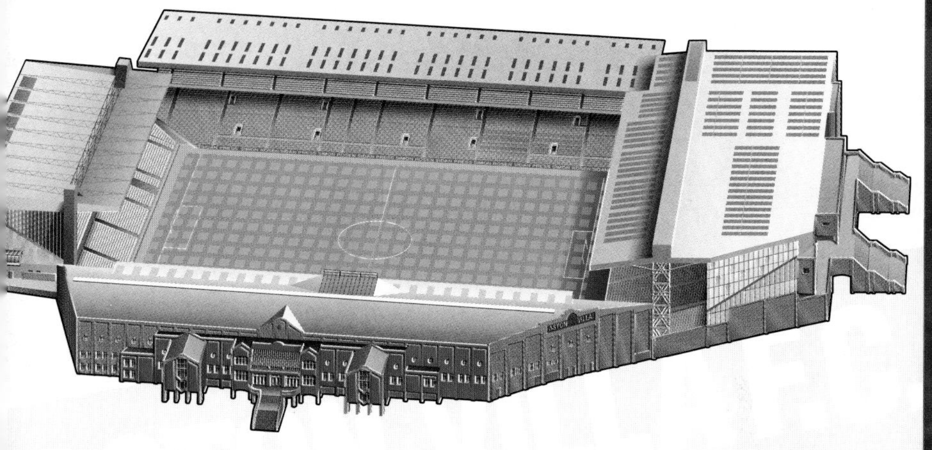

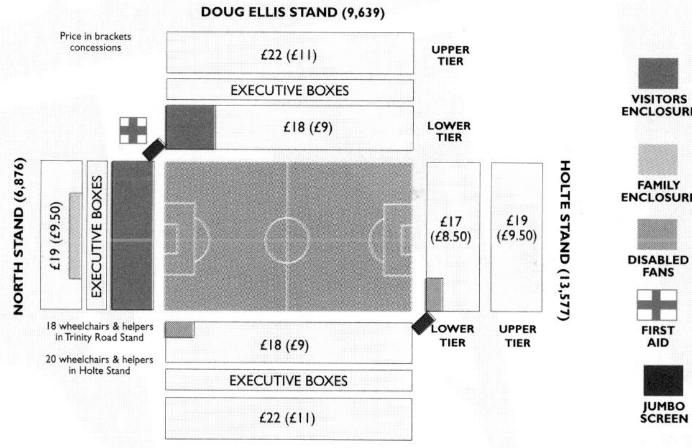

97/98 season points and league position by month

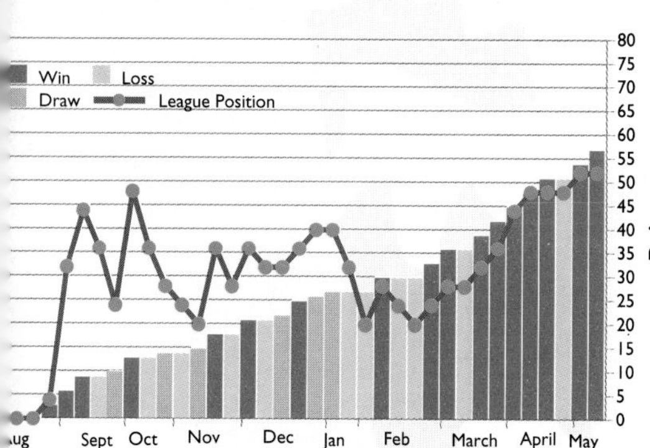

Goals for and against seasons 92/3 to 97/8

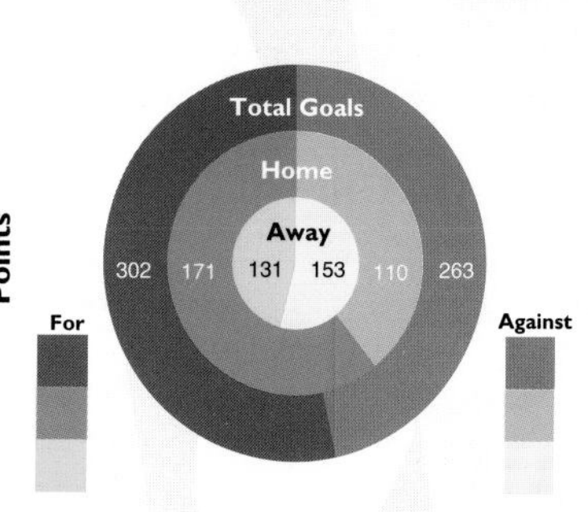

Running shoe technology changes constantly.
In our case, after every step.
Reebok
DMX. Air that moves.

Goals scored by position by season

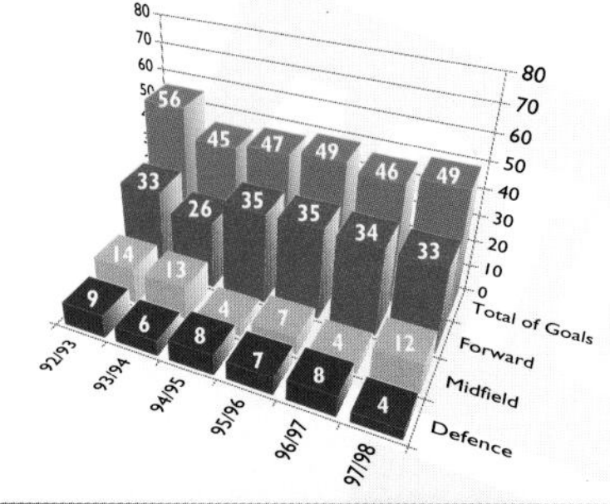

Bookings by position by season

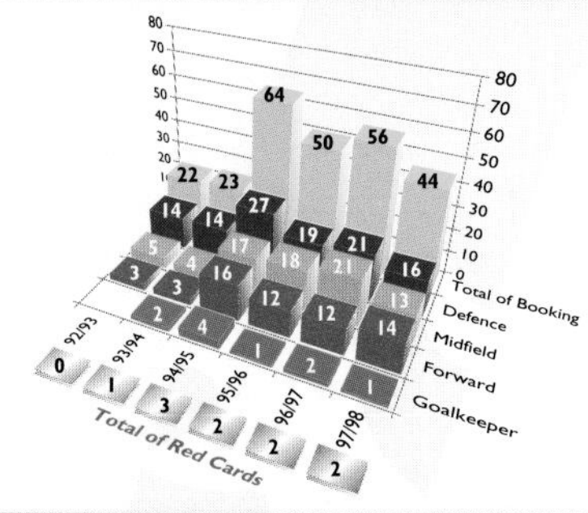

Goals scored by position by month 97/98

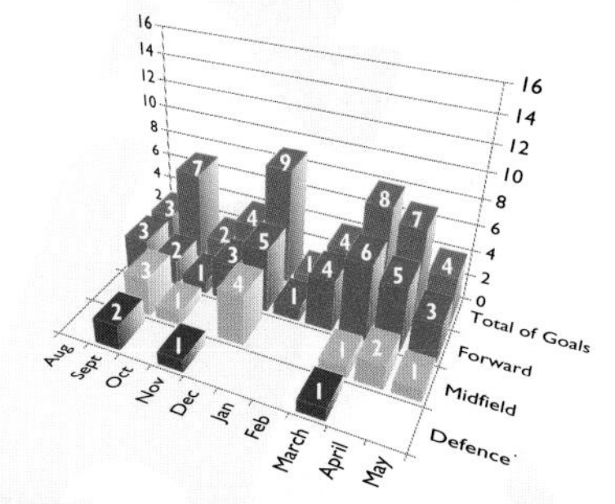

Final league position by season

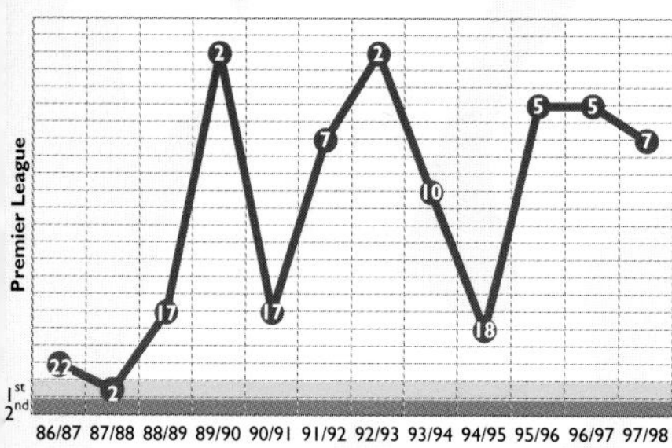

THE CARLING PREMIERSHIP FIXTURE LIST

HOME MATCH
AWAY MATCH
LAST SEASON: WIN
LAST SEASON: DRAW
LAST SEASON: LOSS

Opponent	Date	Last season
EVERTON	15/8	4-1
MIDDLESBROUGH	22/8	N/A
SHEFF WED	29/8	3-1
NEWCASTLE	9/9	0-1
WIMBLEDON	12/9	1-2
LEEDS	19/9	1-1
DERBY	26/9	2-1
COVENTRY	3/10	2-1
WEST HAM	17/10	1-2
LEICESTER	24/10	1-1
CHELSEA	31/10	1-0
TOTTENHAM	7/11	4-1
SOUTHAMPTON	14/11	2-1
LIVERPOOL	21/11	2-1
NOTTM FOREST	28/11	N/A
MAN UTD	5/12	0-2
ARSENAL	12/12	1-0
CHARLTON	19/12	N/A
BLACKBURN	26/12	0-5
SHEFF WED	28/12	2-2
MIDDLESBROUGH	9/1	N/A
EVERTON	16/1	2-1
NEWCASTLE	30/1	0-1
BLACKBURN	6/2	0-4
LEEDS	13/2	1-0
WIMBLEDON	20/2	1-2
COVENTRY	27/2	3-0
DERBY	6/3	1-0
TOTTENHAM	13/3	2-3
CHELSEA	20/3	0-2
WEST HAM	3/4	2-0
LEICESTER	5/4	0-1
SOUTHAMPTON	10/4	1-1
LIVERPOOL	17/4	0-3
NOTTM FOREST	24/4	N/A
MAN UTD	1/5	0-1
CHARLTON	8/5	N/A
ARSENAL	16/5	0-0

IF YOU EVER WANTED TO KNOW WHEN?

1991 FA CUP FINAL
Coca Cola Cup
1979
1935
CHARITY SHIELD
EUROPEAN CUP FINAL
1981
League Champions
1901
LEAGUE CUP FINAL
RUMBELOWS FINAL
1961
1984
1998

THE SQUAD

Key: Goalkeeper (GK) · Defender (D) · Midfield (M) · Forward (F) · No of goals · No of clean sheets · No of yellow cards · No of red cards

Player	Position	Goals / Clean sheets	Yellow cards	Red cards
M. Bosnich	Goalkeeper	9	1	
M. Oakes	Goalkeeper			
M. Ghent	Goalkeeper			
A. Rachel	Goalkeeper			
U. Ehiogu	Defender	2	4	1
G. Southgate	Defender			3
A. Wright	Defender		1	
G. Charles	Defender	1		1
R. Scimeca	Defender			
D. Hughes	Defender			
D. Curtolo	Defender			
R. Hazell	Defender			
M. Ridley	Defender			
T. Jaszczun	Midfield			
B. Petty	Midfield			
M. Standing	Midfield			
L. Collins	Midfield			
G. Barry	Midfield			
S. Grayson	Midfield		2	
M. Draper	Midfield	3	4	
A. Thompson	Midfield			
L. Hendrie	Midfield	3	1	
I. Taylor	Midfield	6	6	
F. Ferraresi	Midfield			
M. Blackwood	Midfield			
A. Lescott	Midfield			
D. Middleton	Midfield			
J. Joachim	Forward	8		
S. Collymore	Forward	6	2	1
D. Yorke	Forward	12	5	
A. Lee	Forward			
D. Byfield	Forward			1
R. Walker	Forward			
D. Vassell	Forward			

Transfers after 15 July 1998:

David Pleat: *on the manager*

JOHN GREGORY

Has moved confidently, smoothly and maybe, a little surprisingly into a major role with a big club. Ambitions at the club are high and have not been fulfilled and John will be determined to keep the right side of his decisive chairman. He will look to follow up on his excellent start, which carried Villa into Europe where he will be further tested. John exudes confidence; he is determined and will fight his battles. Smart and stylish he will be more in tune with his chairman than the previous incumbent.

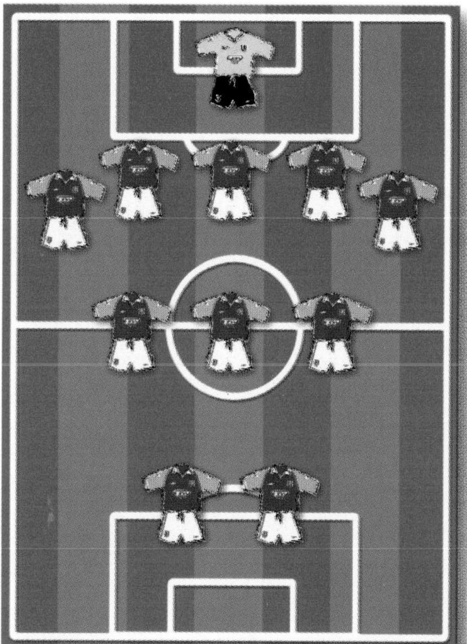

Trevor Brooking: *tactics*

John Gregory transformed Villa when taking over from Brian Little, and once again they find themselves in Europe's UEFA Cup. They have always been solid defensively, and their three central defensive system was extremely difficult to break down. Must offer more of an attacking threat if they are to take the next step forward. The signing of Alan Thompson should help.

Villa Park is 2 miles north of Birmingham City Centre. Please use car parks. Do not park in the streets surrounding Villa Park.

DIRECTIONS

From The North:
Leave M42 junction 7 onto M6. Exit M6 at junction 6 onto the A38 (M) Aston Expressway. Take first exit right onto Victoria Road. At roundabout take right exit into Witton Road for Villa Park

From The South:
Take M1 to junction 19, then M6. At junction 6 turn onto the A38 (M). Then as route for North.

From The East:
Approaching on the M42, turn off at Junction 8 and get onto the M6 heading towards Birmingham. Then as route for South.

It is a 2 minute walk to the ground from Witton Station.

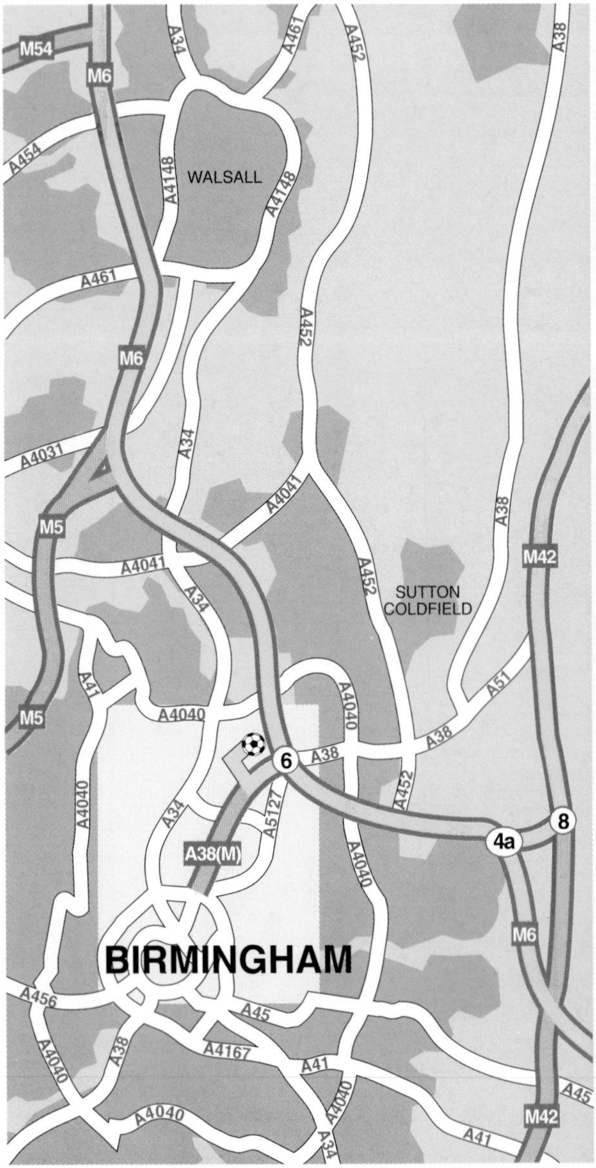

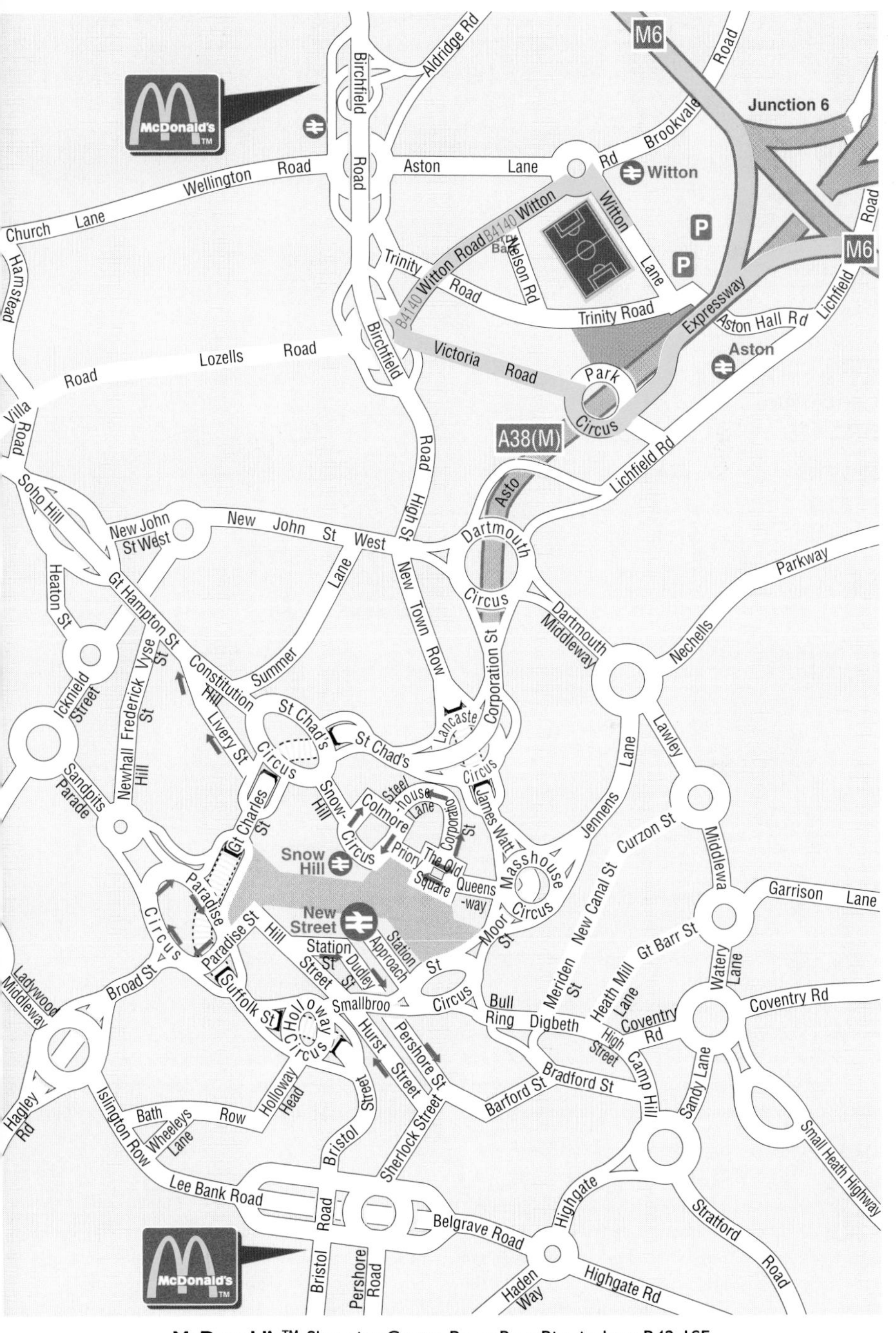

McDonald's™ Shopping Centre Perry Barr, Birmingham B42 1SF
McDonald's™ 5 Bristol Road, Birmingham B5 7TT

Blackburn Rovers FC

Blackburn Rovers FC
Ewood Park
Blackburn
Lancashire
BB2 4JF

Club No: 01254·698888
Fax No: 01254·671042
Tickets: *0321 one nil one nil one nil
*Freephone
Internet: www.rovers.co.uk

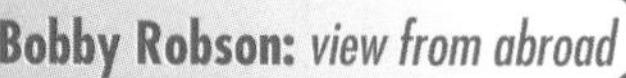

Bobby Robson: *view from abroad*

Famous old club where Dalglish did a miracle against the big clubs to win the title. How many of the smaller Premier clubs would love a benefactor as generous as Jack Walker. Kenny spent sensibly and now they have brought in Roy Hodgson who has worked abroad and come home with good ideas. I think he had a great first season and his brave gamble in buying Davies makes them worth watching next season. A measure of their strength is that they can hold onto their top players even when not winning trophies. I look forward to seeing Roy taking his side into the familiar territory of Europe.

Bob Harris: *view in England*

Looked to be the business at the start of the season but they suffered two poor spells and eventually were grateful to slip into a place in the UEFA Cup at the end of the season. Manager Roy Hodgson will be looking for this talented team to take a step upwards and forwards this season. They should improve on sixth place, especially with the powerful strike force of Sutton, Gallacher and new boy Davies all supported by the promising Duff. Overdue for a good run in one of the domestic cups if their challenge for the big prize fails to materialise.

INFORMATION HOTLINES

ClubCall: 0891·12·11·79*

*Calls cost 50p per minute at all times
Club Call, Avalon House, 57-63 Scrutton St, London, EC2A 4PJ

CLUB SHOPS

THE ROVERSTORE
Ewood Park Stadium

Opening Times:

Monday-Saturday: 9.00am-5.30pm
Match Saturdays: 9.00am - Kick off
Match Sundays: 10.00am - Kick off
Match Evenings: 9.00am - Kick off

Tel: 01254·672333
Fax: 01254·671042
Mail Order Service: *0321 two nil two nil two nil
*Freephone

THE ROVERSTORE II
Ainsworth Mall, Blackburn Shopping Centre

Opening Times:
Open 9.00am - 5.30pm

Tel: 01254·699160

BOOKING INFORMATION

General Enquiries: 01254·671666

Credit Card Bookings: *0321one nil one nil one nil
*Freephone

Travel Club: 01254·698888

Junior Rovers: 01254·698888

E-mail: www.rovers.co.uk

CATERING

FOOD

Pies	£tba
Pasties	£tba
Burgers	£tba
Hot Dogs	£tba
Chicken & Chips	£tba
Chips	£tba
Crisps	£tba

BAR

Tea	£tba
Coffee	£tba
Bovril	£tba
Drinking Chocolate	£tba
Lager	£tba
Bitter	£tba
Spirits	£tba
Soft Drinks	£tba

MISCELLANEOUS

Stadium Tours
Contact Laura Cancelliere - Tel: 01254·671888.
Mon-Fri 10am&2pm, non-match Sat 10am&1pm, Sun 11am&1pm.
Corporate Hospitality
James Cubbon, Linda McSharry - Tel: 01254·690909.
Advertising & Sponsorship
Sharon Lambert - Tel: 01254·690909.
Restaurant with varied menu 12-2pm Mon-Fri & Sun non matchdays - Tel: 01254·697900.
Literature
Programme price £2.00
Pre Match & Half Time Entertainment
Radio Rovers (1404am) with player interviews, match views/commentary and traffic updates.
Within stadium large screen and Rovers T.V.

John Motson: *one to watch*

DAMIEN DUFF

At the tender age of 19, the fair haired Irishman has already done enough to suggest he will be a fixture in the Blackburn and Republic line-up for years to come. Unnerved by the big occasion, he has fitted comfortably into Roy Hodgson's team on the left flank, although he can also operate on the right. Strong on the ball with a powerful shot, his capacity to go past opponents also appeals to Mick McCarthy. Duff will be testing his potential against European opponents for both club and country this season.

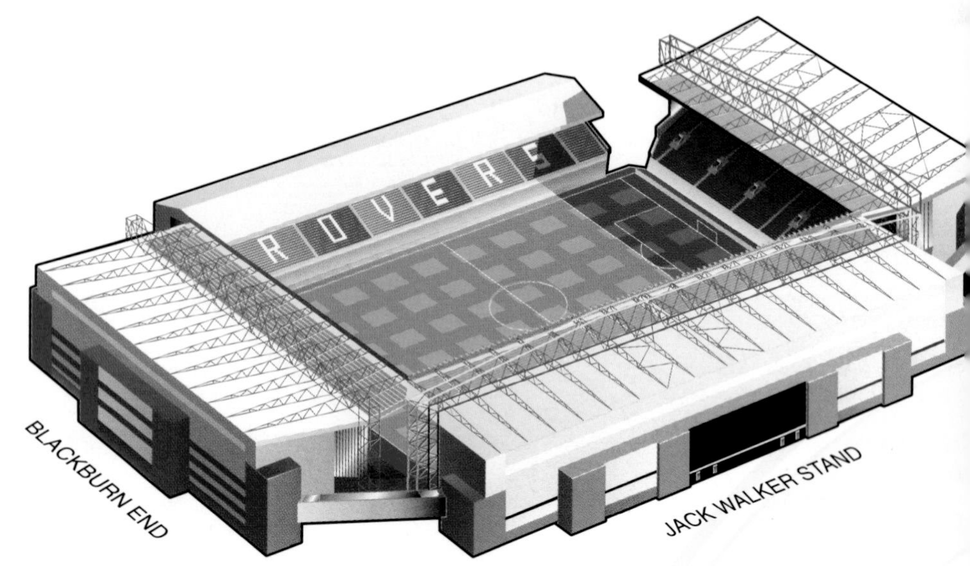

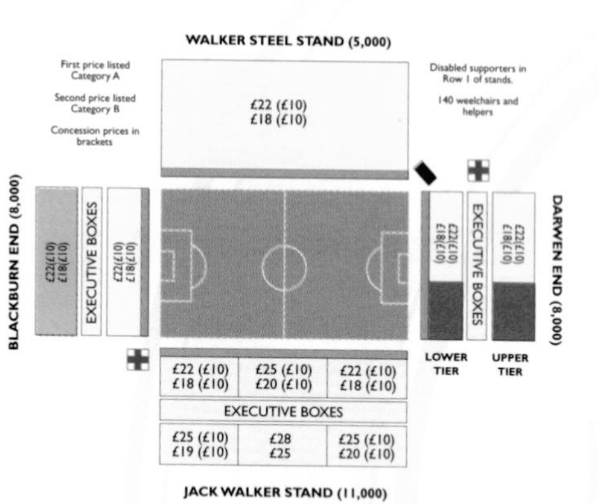

97/98 season points and league position by month

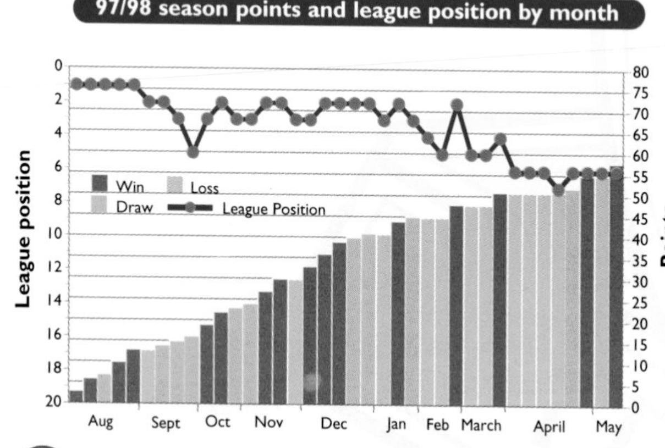

Goals for and against seasons 92/3 to 97/8

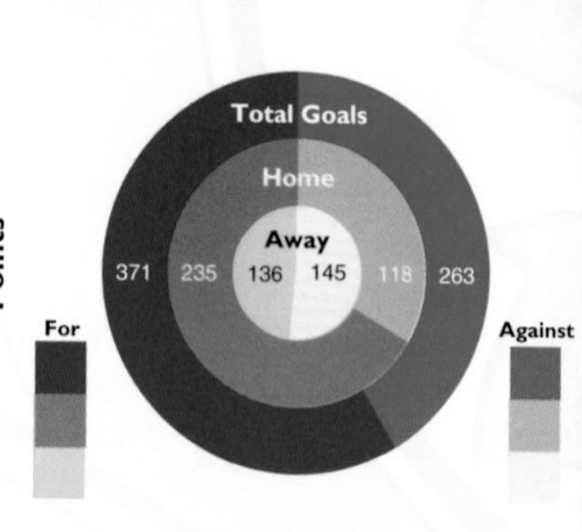

Goals scored by position by season

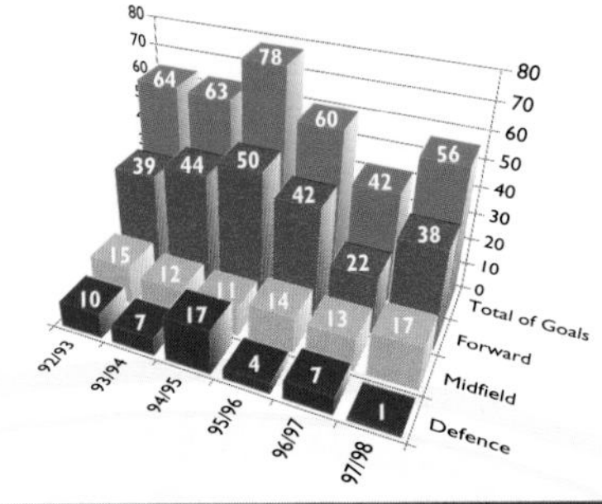

Bookings by position by season

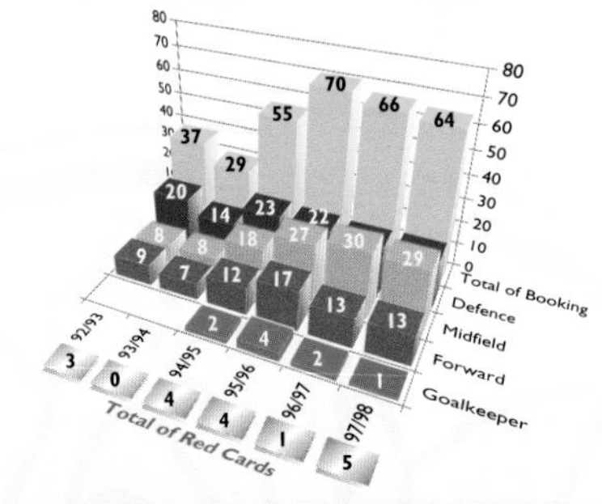

Goals scored by position by month 97/98

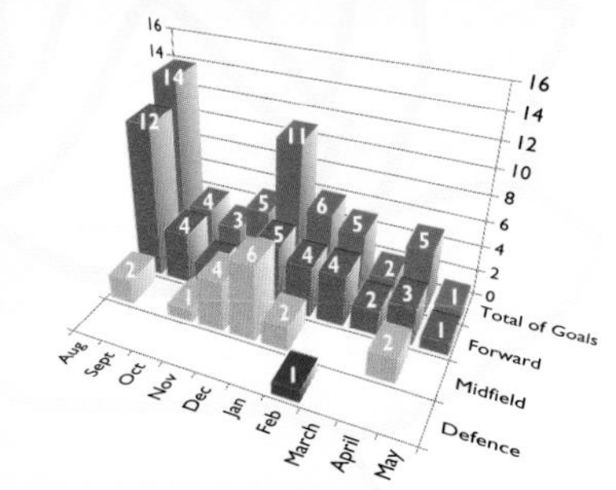

Final league position by season

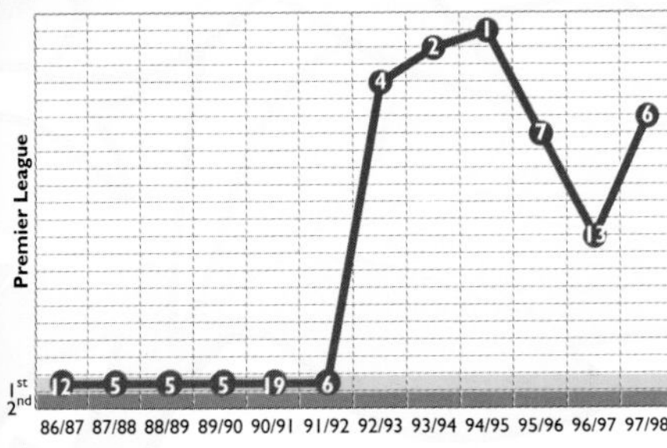

THE CARLING PREMIERSHIP FIXTURE LIST

HOME MATCH
AWAY MATCH
LAST SEASON: WIN
LAST SEASON: DRAW
LAST SEASON: LOSS

DERBY	15/8	1-0
LEEDS	22/8	0-4
LEICESTER	29/8	5-3
TOTTENHAM	9/9	0-0
SHEFF WED	12/9	0-0
CHELSEA	19/9	1-0
EVERTON	26/9	0-1
WEST HAM	3/10	3-0
MIDDLESBROUGH	17/10	N/A
ARSENAL	24/10	1-4
WIMBLEDON	31/10	1-0
COVENTRY	7/11	0-0
MAN UTD	14/11	0-4
SOUTHAMPTON	21/11	1-0
LIVERPOOL	28/11	0-0
CHARLTON	5/12	N/A
NEWCASTLE	12/12	1-0
NOTTM FOREST	19/12	N/A
ASTON VILLA	26/12	5-0
LEICESTER	28/12	1-1
LEEDS	9/1	3-4
DERBY	16/1	1-3
TOTTENHAM	30/1	0-3
ASTON VILLA	6/2	4-0
CHELSEA	13/2	1-0
SHEFF WED	20/2	7-2
WEST HAM	27/2	1-2
EVERTON	6/3	3-2
COVENTRY	13/3	0-2
WIMBLEDON	20/3	0-0
MIDDLESBROUGH	3/4	N/A
ARSENAL	5/4	3-1
MAN UTD	10/4	1-3
SOUTHAMPTON	17/4	0-3
LIVERPOOL	24/4	1-1
CHARLTON	1/5	N/A
NOTTM FOREST	8/5	N/A
NEWCASTLE	16/5	1-1

THE SQUAD

- Goalkeeper
- Defender
- Midfield
- Forward
- No of goals
- No of clean sheets
- No of yellow cards
- No of red cards

Player	Position	Goals / Clean sheets	Yellow cards	Red cards
T. Flowers	Goalkeeper	9		1
A .Fettis	Goalkeeper	1		
J. Filan	Goalkeeper	4		
J. Kenna	Defender		2	
P. Valery	Defender		3	1
C. Hendry	Defender	1	7	
S. Henchoz	Defender		6	
D. Peacock	Defender			
T. Pedersen	Defender			
M. Broomes	Defender		1	
G. Croft	Defender	1	1	
C. Davidson	Defender			
A. Andersson	Midfield			
T. Sherwood	Midfield	5	5	
G. Flitcroft	Midfield		7	
S. Perez	Midfield			
B. McKinlay	Midfield		9	
A. Reed	Midfield			
J. Wilcox	Midfield	4	5	2
D. Duff	Midfield	4		
K. Gallacher	Forward	16		
K. Davies	Forward			
P. Pedersen	Forward			
C. Sutton	Forward	18	8	1
M. Dahlin	Forward	4	2	
J. Corbett	Forward			

Transfers after 15 July 1998:

....

....

....

....

....

....

....

David Pleat: *on the manager*

ROY HODGSON

Began like a bomb when he returned from his life on the Continent, but was then forced to accept the reality of a strong competition. He has money available and the ability to lead Blackburn back to the summit. Steely, thoughtful manager, who is a big achiever on a difficult route to the top.

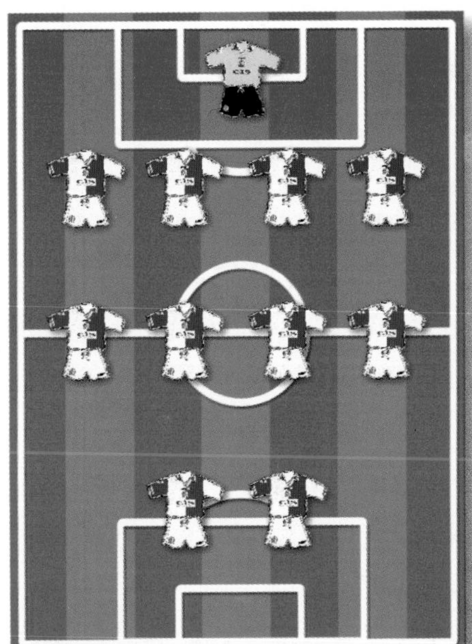

Trevor Brooking: *tactics*

Manager Roy Hodgson must have been delighted with three-quarters of last season, but the late downturn in results was a reflection on a lack of depth in their squad. Generally the back four was a reliable platform, superbly marshalled by Colin Hendry but in attack too much reliance was placed on Chris Sutton and Kevin Gallacher. The massive signing of young Kevin Davies should help resolve that problem, and exciting youngster Damian Duff should continue to improve.

Blackburn Rovers are situated a mile from Blackburn town centre in Ewood Park. Car parking can be found at Albion Road and Hollin Bridge Street.

DIRECTIONS

From The North and South:

Exit M6 at junction 31 onto A59/A677 towards Blackburn. After 1 1/2 miles the road splits. Keep to the A677. After approximately 5 miles turn right at the Esso garage onto Montague Street, cross over King Street into Byron Street, left into Canterbury Street and follow the one-way system until the T-junction with the Bolton Road A666. Turn right for Ewood Park.

From The South:

Exit M61 junction 8 onto A674. After 5 miles turn right onto the A6062 for 3 miles until the Bolton Road A666. Turn right and Ewood Park is 1/4 mile down on your left.

From The East:

Exit M65 junction 6, turn left onto the A6119 Whitebirk Road for 1/2 mile, turn right onto the A677 for 1/2 mile and then bear left onto the A679 for 1 mile, then left onto the A666 for 1 1/4 miles. Ewood Park is on the left.

Blackburn Station is well served for buses to ground.

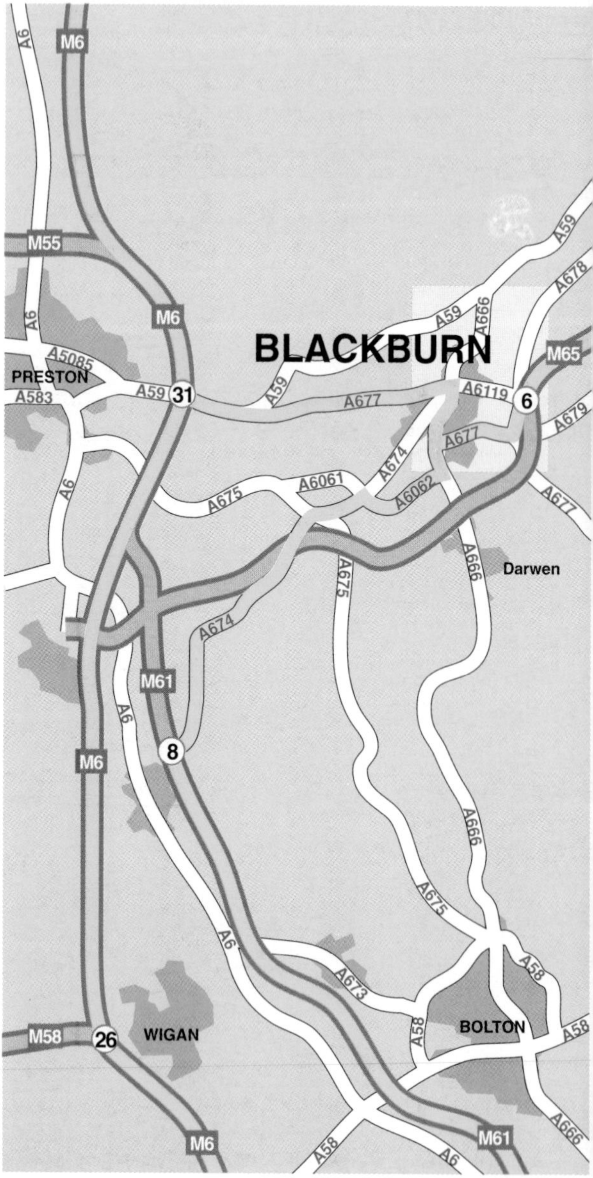

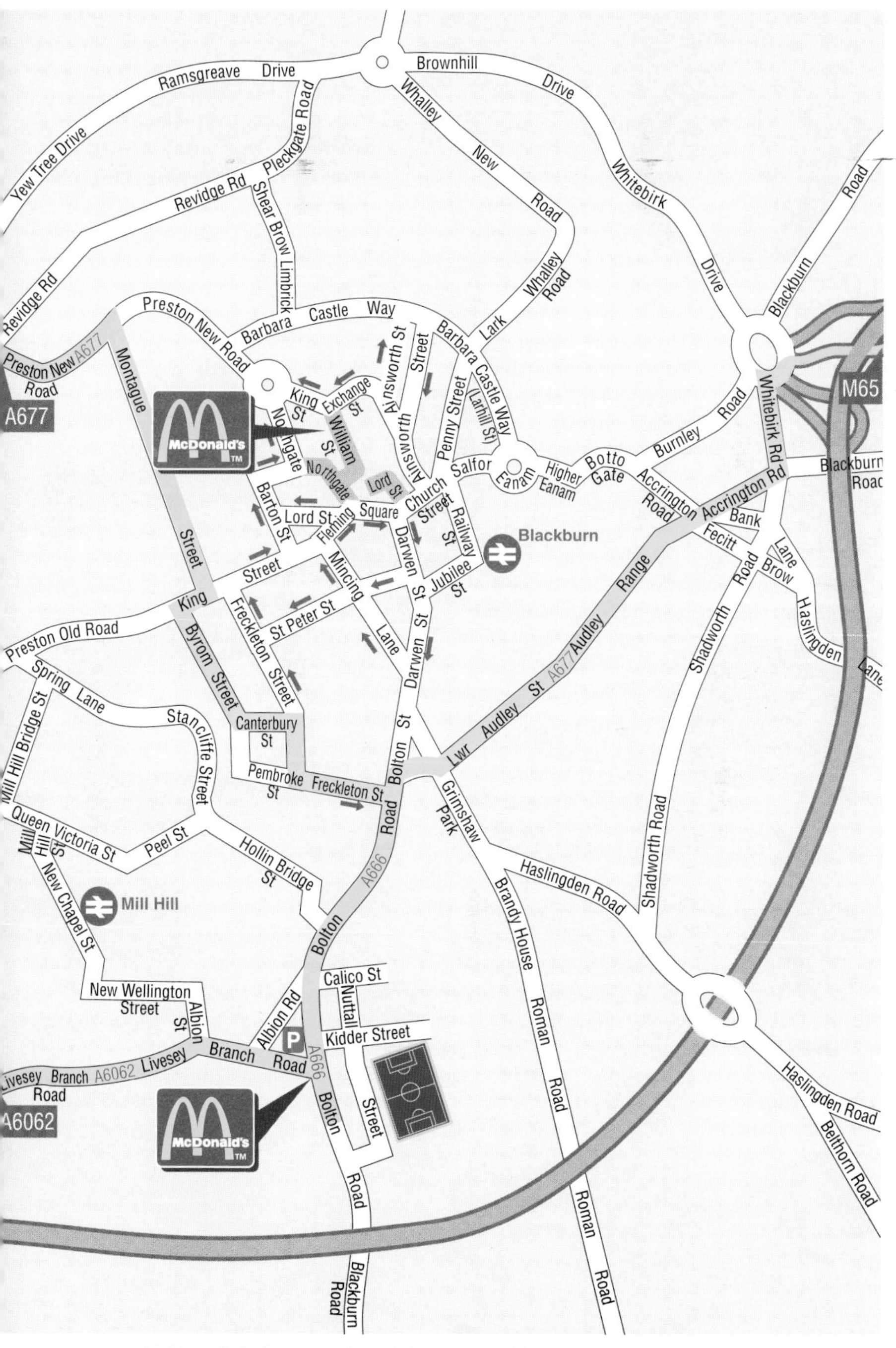

McDonald's™ Livesey Branch Road, Ewood Mill, Blackburn BB2 4LQ
McDonald's™ 21-23 King William Street, Blackburn BB1 7DJ

Charlton Athletic FC

Charlton Athletic FC
The Valley
Floyd Road
Charlton
London
SE7 8BL
Club No: 0181·333·4000
Fax No: 0181·333·4001
Tickets: 0181·333·4010
Internet: www.charlton-athletic.co.uk

AWAY

HOME

HOME

MESH computers plc

Bobby Robson: *view from abroad*

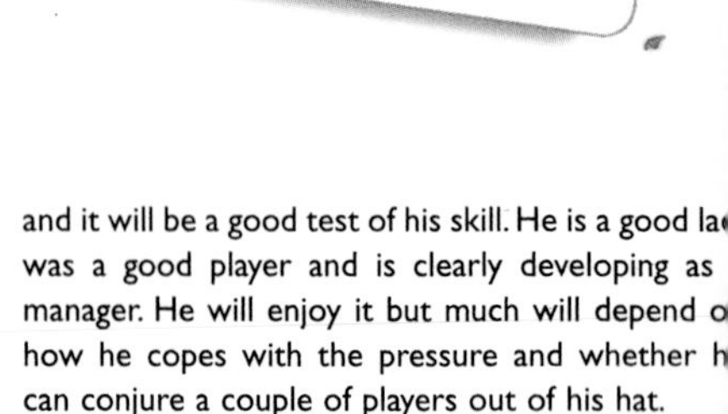

Big test for them. I loved the way they clinched their promotion against first Ipswich Town and then Sunderland. They rose to the occasion both times but now they have got to do that twenty or more times in a season against even better teams just to stay up. Alan Curbishley will have to buy well and it will be a good test of his skill. He is a good la was a good player and is clearly developing as manager. He will enjoy it but much will depend o how he copes with the pressure and whether h can conjure a couple of players out of his hat.

Bob Harris: *view in England*

They are the new romantics of the Premier League. They hardly had time to celebrate the "game of the season", winning the play off at Wembley, before the bookmakers were establishing them as odds on favourites to go straight back down. Alan Curbishley will have different ideas with players like Kinsella, Rufus and Mendonca all likely t establish themselves as Premier League players c true quality. With the character they showe throughout the season the Cinderella club of th Premiership may yet cause a few surprises.

INFORMATION HOTLINES

ClubCall: 0891·12·11·46

**Calls cost 50p per minute at all times*
Club Call, Avalon House, 57-63 Scrutton St, London, EC2A 4PJ

CLUB SHOPS

CLUB SHOPS

The Valley Floyd Road, Charlton, London, SE7 8BL

Opening Times:

Monday-Fridays: 10.00am-6.00pm
Match Saturdays: 10.00am-30 mins after full time.
Match Sundays: 10.00am-30 mins after full time.
Match Evenings: 10.00am-30 mins after full time.

Tel: 0181·333·4000

Fax: 0181·333·4021

Mail Order Service: 0181·333·4035

BOOKING INFORMATION

General Enquiries:	0181·333·4010
Credit Card Bookings:	0181·333·4010
Travel Club:	0181·265·5283
Recorded Info:	0891·12·11·46

CATERING

FOOD

Fish & Chips	£2.60
Cheese Burger	£2.10
Fries	£1.00
Hot Dogs & Fries	£2.30
Chicken Curry	£2.20
Burger	£1.95
Jumbo Dog	£1.90
Pasties	£1.70

BAR

Tea	£0.60
Coffee	£0.70
Drinking Chocolate	£0.65
Pepsi	£0.90
Soup	£0.65

MISCELLANEOUS

Due to building work, some areas of the stadium may not be open for August 1998. Visiting fans may not be admitted for first 2/3 games of the season. Please check nearer time.

RICHARD RUFUS

Born just down the road in Lewisham, Rufus joined his local club as a trainee and crowned four seasons in Charlton's first team with his first goal for the club in that dramatic 4-4 draw in the Wembley playoff against Sunderland. Now the 25 year old central defender will pits his wits and his athleticism against the likes of Alan Shearer and Dennis Bergkamp as Charlton seek Premiership survival. Capped by England at under 21 level he has the potential to meet the challenge.

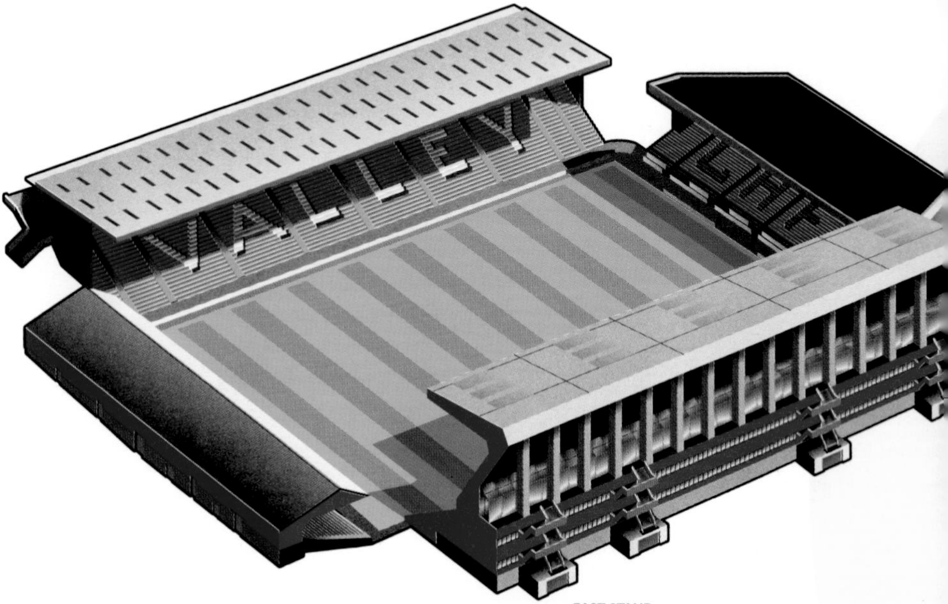

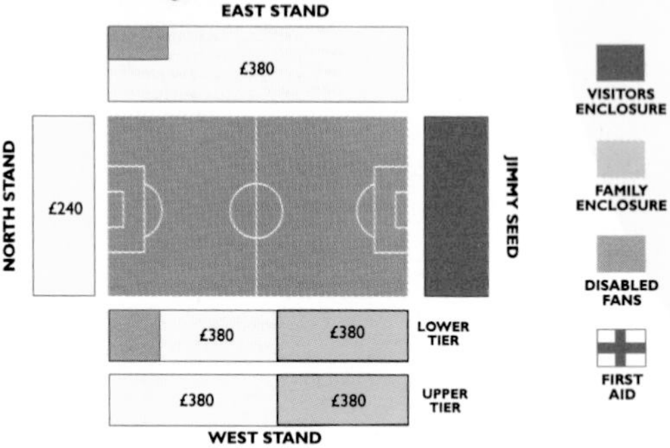

VALLEY

EAST STAND

	£380

NORTH STAND £240

JIMMY SEED

	£380	£380	LOWER TIER
	£380	£380	UPPER TIER

WEST STAND

VISITORS ENCLOSURE

FAMILY ENCLOSURE

DISABLED FANS

FIRST AID

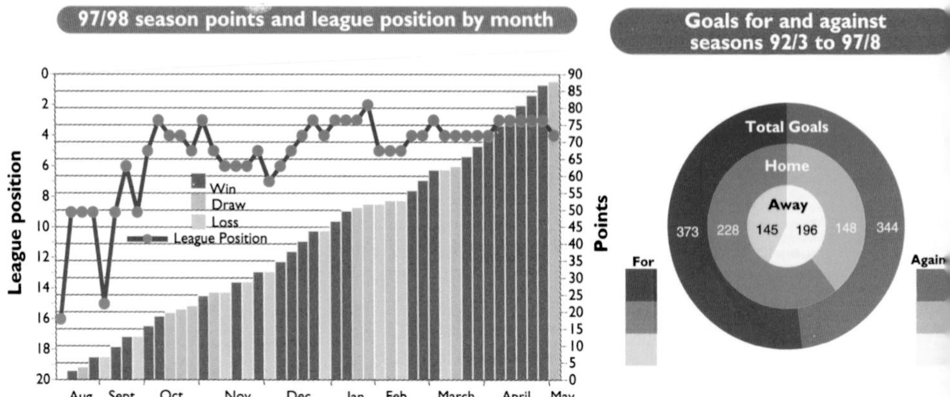

Goals scored by position by season

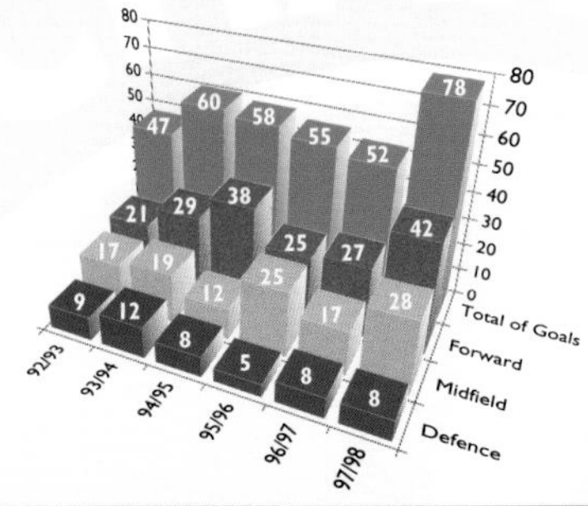

Bookings by position by season

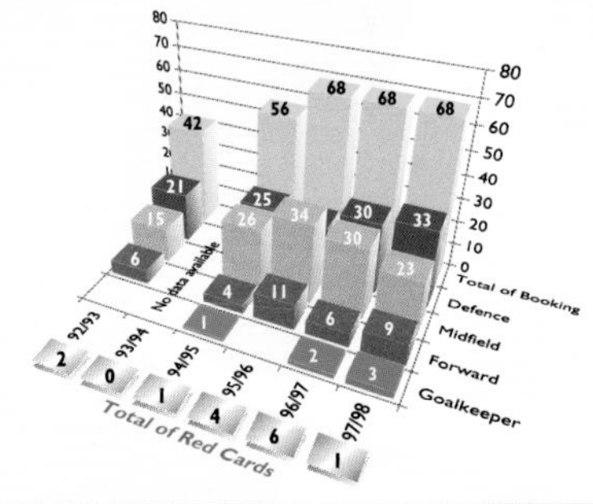

Goals scored by position by month 97/98

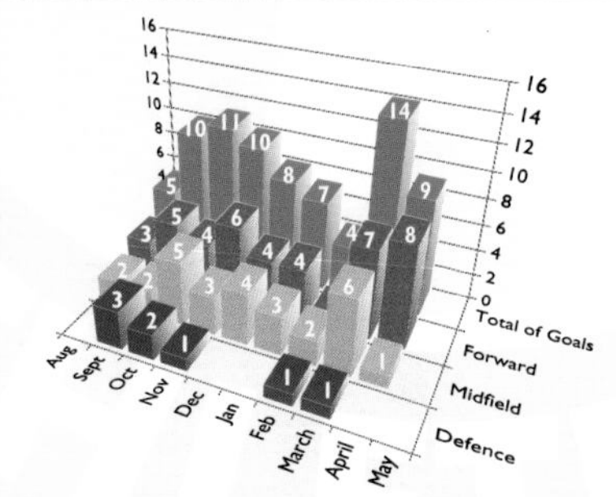

Final league position by season

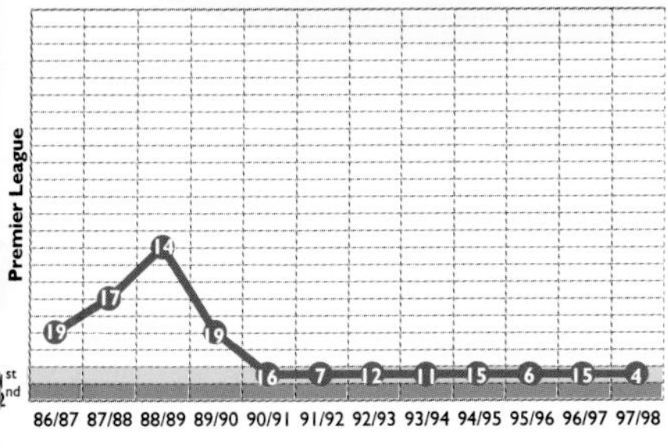

THE CARLING PREMIERSHIP FIXTURE LIST

HOME MATCH · AWAY MATCH · LAST SEASON: WIN · LAST SEASON: DRAW · LAST SEASON: LOSS

Opponent	Date	Last season
NEWCASTLE UNITED	15/8	N/A
SOUTHAMPTON	22/8	N/A
ARSENAL	29/8	N/A
MANCHESTER UNITED	9/9	N/A
DERBY COUNTY	12/9	N/A
LIVERPOOL	19/9	N/A
COVENTRY CITY	26/9	N/A
NOTTINGHAM FOREST	3/10	2-5
CHELSEA	17/10	N/A
WEST HAM UNITED	24/10	N/A
TOTTENHAM HOTSPUR	2/11	N/A
LEICESTER CITY	7/11	N/A
MIDDLESBROUGH	14/11	3-0
LEEDS UNITED	21/11	N/A
EVERTON	28/11	N/A
BLACKBURN ROVERS	5/12	N/A
SHEFFIELD WEDNESDAY	12/12	N/A
ASTON VILLA	21/12	N/A
WIMBLEDON	26/12	N/A
ARSENAL	28/12	N/A
SOUTHAMPTON	9/1	N/A
NEWCASTLE UNITED	16/1	N/A
MANCHESTER UNITED	30/1	N/A
WIMBLEDON	6/2	N/A
LIVERPOOL	13/2	N/A
DERBY COUNTY	20/2	N/A
NOTTINGHAM FOREST	27/2	4-2
COVENTRY CITY	6/3	N/A
LEICESTER CITY	13/3	N/A
TOTTENHAM HOTSPUR	20/3	N/A
CHELSEA	3/4	N/A
WEST HAM UNITED	5/4	N/A
MIDDLESBROUGH	10/4	1-2
LEEDS UNITED	17/4	N/A
EVERTON	24/4	N/A
BLACKBURN ROVERS	1/5	N/A
ASTON VILLA	8/5	N/A
SHEFFIELD WEDNESDAY	16/5	N/A

Trust us to help Football

MAJOR PROJECTS

The Trust's main task is to help League clubs to implement the Taylor Report. Since 1990, over £136m has been award towards ground improvements costing some £418m. In its 20 years the Trust h received £250 million from Littlewoods Vernons and Zetters and Littlewoods Spot the Ball..

CCTV

The introduction of CCTV throughout football has been the most important measure in the campaign against hooliganism. CCTV is an initiative pioneered by the Trust. Since 1979 near £6m has been awarded towards the installation and upgrading of equipment.

SAFETY AND IMPROVEMENTS

Initiatives to improve the safety and comf of spectators and to upgrade facilities fo families, for supporters with disabilities, for women and for community use are gr aided by the Trust from funds donated Littlewoods Pools from their Spot the Ball competition.

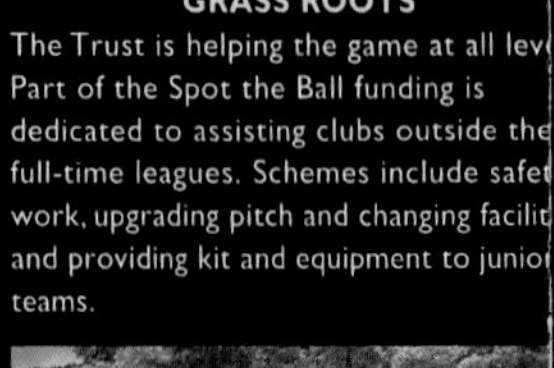

GRASS ROOTS

The Trust is helping the game at all lev Part of the Spot the Ball funding is dedicated to assisting clubs outside the full-time leagues. Schemes include safet work, upgrading pitch and changing facilit and providing kit and equipment to junio teams.

THE FOOTBALL TRUST

Helping the game

The Football Trust,
Walkden House,
10 Melton Street,
London NW1 2EJ.

THE SQUAD

Key: Goalkeeper · Defender · Midfield · Forward · No of goals · No of clean sheets · No of yellow cards · No of red cards

Player	Position	Goals / Clean sheets	Yellow cards	Red cards
A. Patterson	Goalkeeper	7	1	
M. Salmon	Goalkeeper	3	1	
S. Ilic	Goalkeeper	10	1	
S. Royce	Goalkeeper			
A. Barness	Defender	1	5	
E. Youds	Defender		3	
M. Bowen	Defender		4	
P. Konchesky	Defender			
D. Mills	Defender	1		
S. Brown	Defender	2	6	
G. Poole	Defender			
M. Lee	Defender			
R. Rufus	Defender		6	
C. Powell	Defender			
S. Balmer	Midfield		4	
M. Holmes	Midfield	1		
K. Jones	Midfield	3	5	
M. Kinsella	Midfield	6	6	
P. Mortimer	Midfield	4	1	
S. Newton	Midfield	5	2	1
K. Nicholls	Midfield		1	
S. Parker	Midfield		1	
J. Robinson	Midfield	8	5	
N. Redfearn	Midfield			
A. Hunt	Forward			
M. Bright	Forward	7	3	
B. Allen	Forward	2	1	
P. Emblen	Forward			
S. Jones	Forward	7	4	
C. Mendonca	Forward	23		

Transfers after 15 July 1998:

....

....

....

....

David Pleat: *on the manager*

ALAN CURBISHLEY

Replaced Danny Wilson as flavour of the month and will need to be at his coaching, calculating best. He has few players ready for this new standard but watch Kinsella amongst one or two others. Curbishley must take great credit for the rise of Charlton not just at first team level but at reserve and youth as well. Alert, steady, eager to learn and has clear ambitions.

Trevor Brooking: *tactics*

What an amazing 4-4 play-off match that was at Wembley, and naturally comparison with Barnsley's task last season are bound to be made. 4-4-2 is now favoured by a majority of teams in the top flight, but Alan Curbishley will be happy with any system that gives him the required defensive stability. The other query surrounds striker Clive Mendonca. Can he score as frequently when up against the better defenders in the Premiership?

Despite it's surburban location, the Valley is very easily accessible by road and rail

DIRECTIONS

By Rail:

On Connex South East (overground) Charlton station is 15 mins from London bridge and 22 mins from Charring Cross on the Dartford via Greenwich/Woolwich line

By Road: From north

Route one is M1 southbound, M25 to Dartford bridge, over bridge to J2. Take A2 London bound until road becomes A102 (M). Take Woolwich Ferry turn -off (3rd exit) towards woolwich and Thames Barrier. The Valley is Approximately one mile on right.

Route two is M1, M25, M11, Then A13 to Blackwall tunnel on to A102 (M). Then as above.

By Road: From east/west/south

All on to M25, then to Junction 2 (as above).

If travelling by car, tune into Charlton live on 106.8 fm, saturdays from 1.30pm.

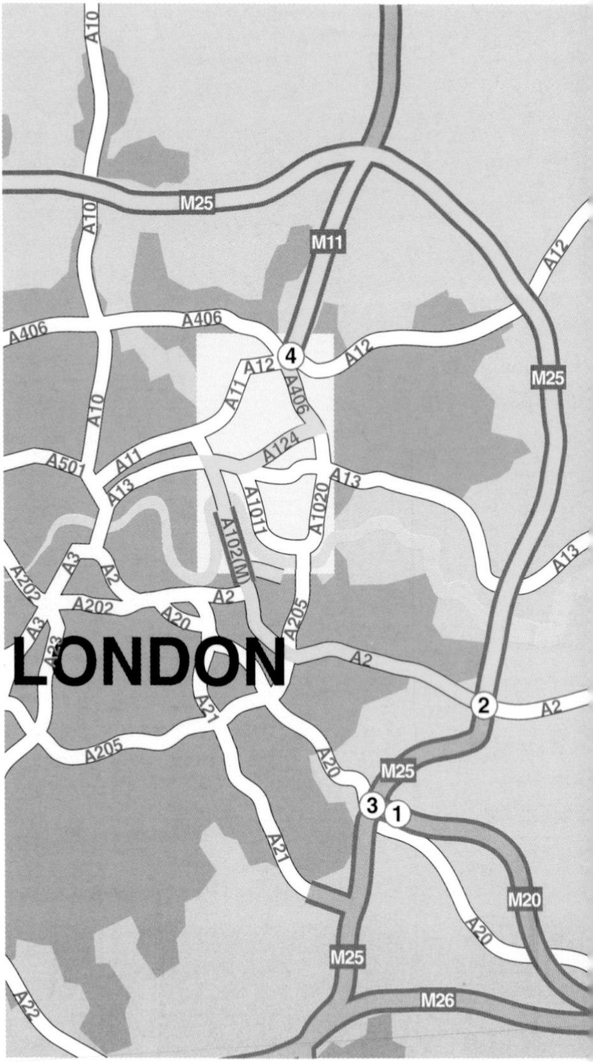

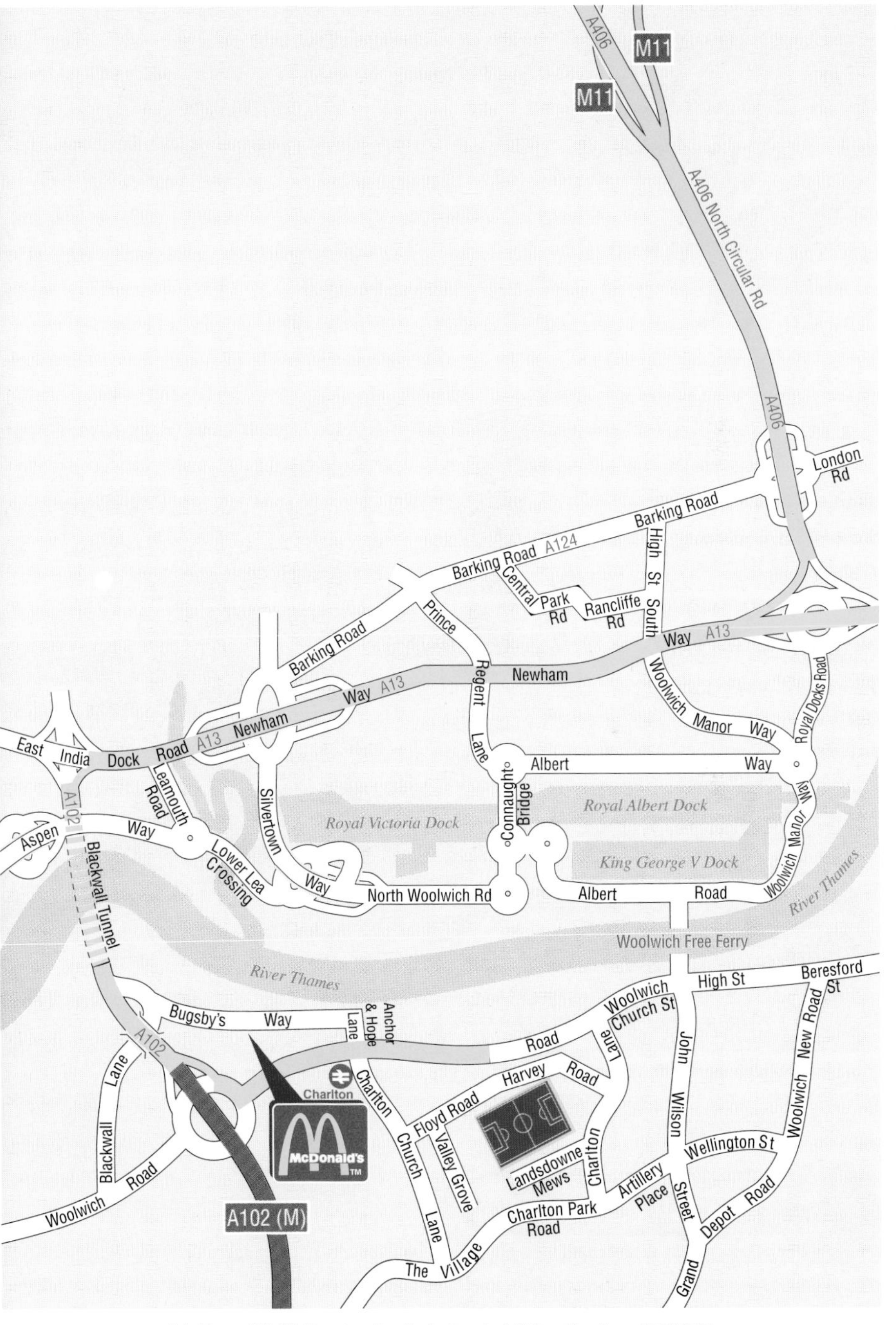

McDonald's™ Penninsular Park, Bugsby's Way, Charlton SE7 7TZ

Chelsea FC

Chelsea FC
Stamford Bridge
Fulham Road
London SW6 1HS

Club No: 0171·385·5545
Fax No: 0171·381·4831
Tickets: 0171·386·7799
Internet: www.chelseafc.co.uk

Bobby Robson: *view from abroad*

They will have enjoyed winning the two trophies last season and having had a sniff of it they will want more. But winning cups is very different from winning league titles. You cannot question their ambition with the imported players they are bringing in; Vialli knows the Italian market as well as anyone. He did a marvellous job in taking over from Gullit but if he is to move on he must improve the defence and stop the goals leaking in. They lost far too many games and they cannot do that and expect to progress. They have the class now they must add the consistency.

Bob Harris: *view in England*

Four cups in twelve months displays the remarkable quality down at the Bridge these days. Now hoping that they can follow the same path marched by Arsenal and Manchester United in achieving success in FA and the European Cup Winner' Cups and then taking the Championship. Having survived the loss of Gullit, the Blues will be looking for stability under Vialli if they are to improve on that fourth position last season.

INFORMATION HOTLINES

ClubCall:	0891·12·11·59*
Prize Line:	0891·12·10·11*

Calls cost 50p per minute at all times
Club Call, Avalon House, 57-63 Scrutton St, London, EC2A 4PJ

CLUB SHOPS

CHELSEA MEGASTORE

Stamford Bridge

Opening Times:

Monday-Saturday: 10.00am-6.00pm
Match Saturdays: 10.00am-7.00pm
Match Sundays: 11.00am-4.00pm
12.00pm-6.00pm (3pm kick off)
10.00am-4.00pm (4pm kick off)
Match Evenings: 10.00am-10.00pm

Tel: 0171·565·1490

Fax: 0171·565·1491

Mail Order Service: 0870·603·0005

BOOKING INFORMATION

General Enquiries:	0171·385·5545
Credit Card Bookings:	0171·386·7799
Travel Club (Elizabeth Duff Travel):	0345·023243
Junior Club Line:	0171·385·0710
Chelsea Village Hotel:	0171·565·1400

CATERING

FOOD

Hamburger	£2.50
Hot Dog	£2.50
Pies	£2.00
Chips	£1.00
Sandwiches	£2.00
Confectionery	£0.60
Carvery Meal	£19.50

BAR

Lager (Pint)	£2.50
Bitter (Pint)	£2.40
Soft Drinks	£1.00

MISCELLANEOUS

Stadium Tours
Contact Shaun Gore - Tel: 0171·385·0710
Fridays 11.00am - 1.00pm
Corporate Hospitality
Contact Carole Phair - Tel: 0171·385·7809
Various matchday packages (South Stand Galleria), match and matchball sponsorships available.
Conference and banqueting - Tel: 0171·385·7980
Chelsea Village Hotel 3 star.
160 en-suite bedrooms. Manager Edward Murray.
Reservations 0171 565 1400
Literature
Programme price £2.50, Onside Magazine £1.00
Pre Match & Half Time Entertainment
Channel Chelsea - transmitting matchdays in concourses with player interviews, match replays, fan interviews etc.
Radio Chelsea (0171·565·1494) on matchdays, 1494am

CHELSEA FC

BRIAN LAUDRUP

The galaxy of stars that Messrs. Hoddle, Gullit and now Vialli have attracted to Stamford Bridge from the international market now includes one of the most gifted European forwards of his generation. Where others attack the 18-yard line, Laudrup's dazzling close control enables him to attack the six-yard line, turning defenders inside out and finishing in deadly fashion. One felt he was partly wasted at Ibrox - he certainly won't be at Chelsea.

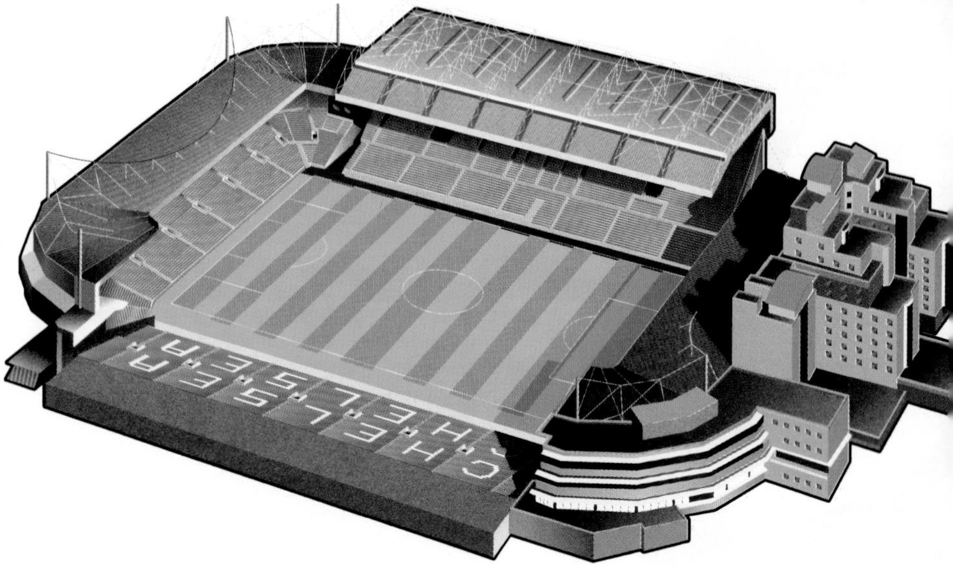

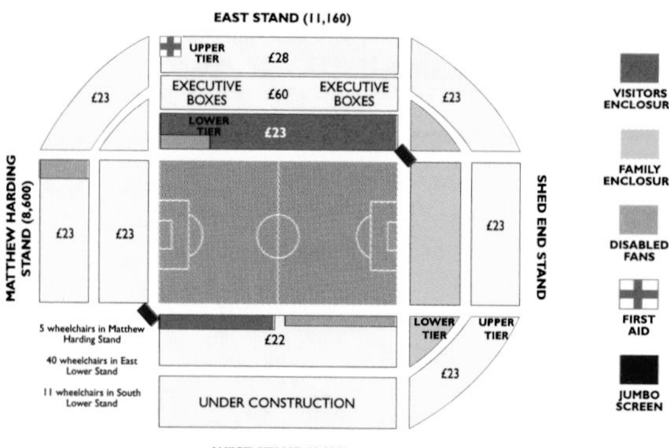

97/98 season points and league position by month

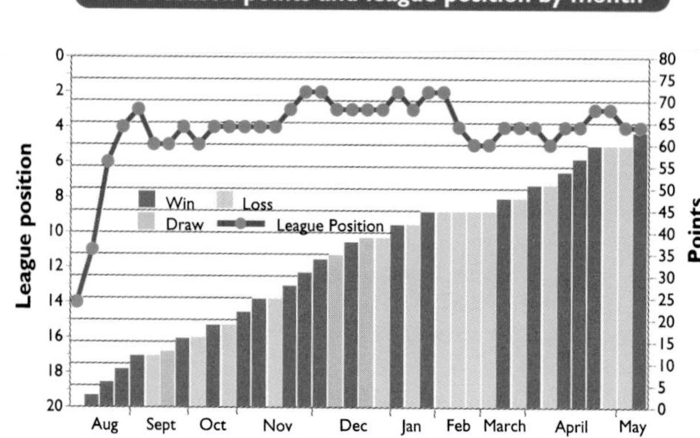

Goals for and against seasons 92/3 to 97/8

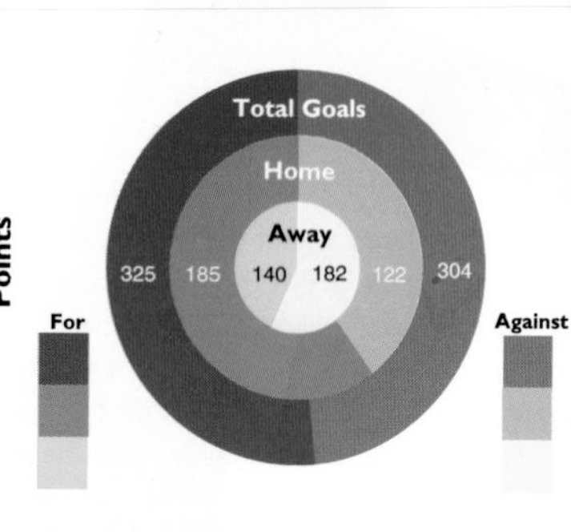

CHELSEA FC

Goals scored by position by season

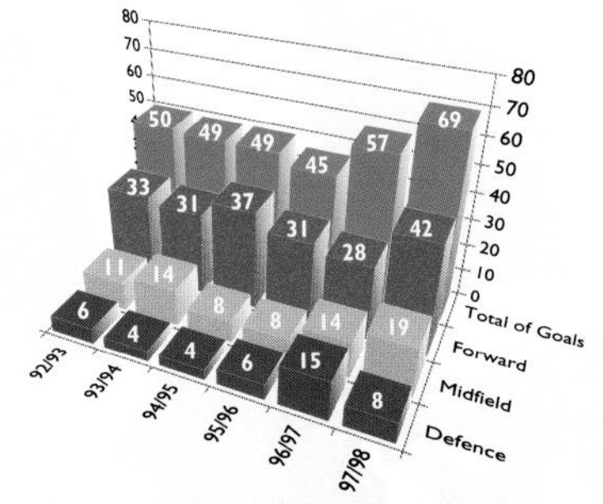

Bookings by position by season

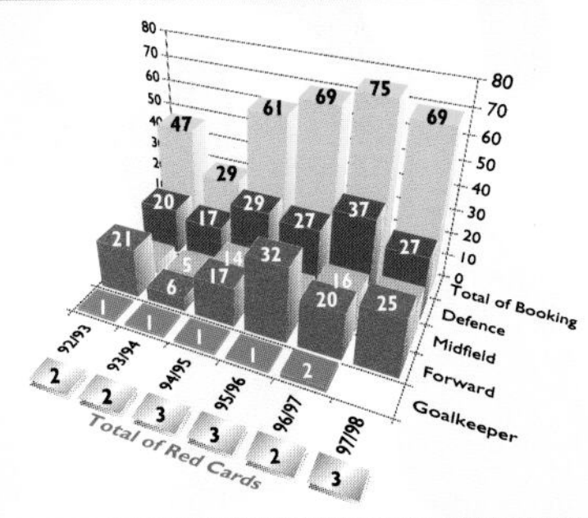

Goals scored by position by month 97/98

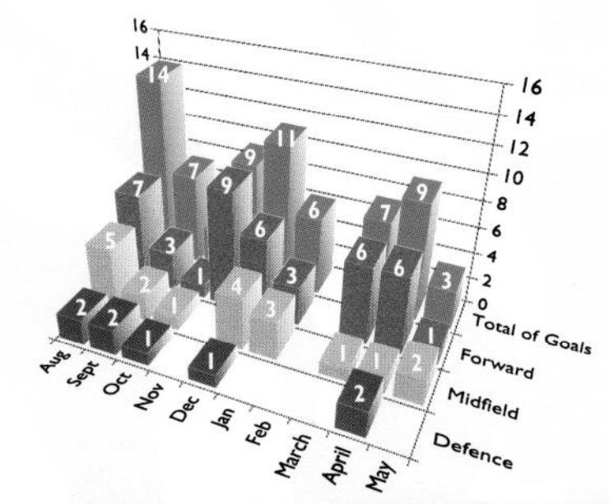

Final league position by season

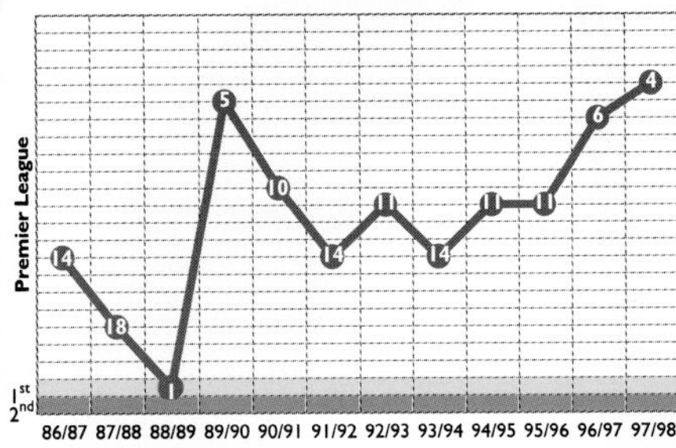

THE CARLING PREMIERSHIP FIXTURE LIST

HOME MATCH
AWAY MATCH
LAST SEASON: WIN
LAST SEASON: DRAW
LAST SEASON: LOSS

Opponent	Date	Last season
COVENTRY	15/8	2-3
NEWCASTLE	22/8	1-0
ARSENAL	9/9	2-3
NOTTM FOREST	12/9	N/A
BLACKBURN	19/9	0-1
MAN UTD	23/9	2-2
MIDDLESBROUGH	26/9	N/A
LIVERPOOL	3/10	2-4
CHARLTON	17/10	N/A
LEEDS	24/10	1-3
ASTON VILLA	31/10	0-1
WEST HAM	7/11	1-2
WIMBLEDON	14/11	1-1
LEICESTER	21/11	0-2
SHEFF WED	28/11	1-0
EVERTON	5/12	1-3
DERBY	12/12	1-0
TOTTENHAM	19/12	2-0
SOUTHAMPTON	26/12	0-1
MAN UTD	28/12	0-1
NEWCASTLE	9/1	1-3
COVENTRY	16/1	3-1
ARSENAL	30/1	0-2
SOUTHAMPTON	6/2	4-2
BLACKBURN	13/2	0-1
NOTTM FOREST	20/2	N/A
LIVERPOOL	27/2	4-1
MIDDLESBROUGH	6/3	N/A
WEST HAM	13/3	2-1
ASTON VILLA	20/3	2-0
CHARLTON	3/4	N/A
LEEDS	5/4	0-0
WIMBLEDON	10/4	2-0
LEICESTER	17/4	1-0
SHEFF WED	24/4	4-1
EVERTON	1/5	2-0
TOTTENHAM	8/5	6-1
DERBY	16/5	4-0

WE'LL MAKE SURE
YOU'LL ALWAYS
HAVE SOMETHING TO
STICK IT TO.

THE SQUAD

Key: Goalkeeper · Defender · Midfield · Forward · No of goals · No of clean sheets · No of yellow cards · No of red cards

Player	Position	Goals / Clean sheets	Yellow cards	Red cards
E. De Goey	Goalkeeper	12		
D. Kharine	Goalkeeper	2		
K. Hitchcock	Goalkeeper			
A. Ferrer	Defender			
F. Sinclair	Defender	1	2	1
M. Duberry	Defender		2	
D. Lee	Defender			
A. Myers	Defender			
F. Leboeuf	Defender	5	6	1
M. Desailly	Defender			
S. Clarke	Defender		1	2
G. Le Saux	Defender	1	2	
C. Babayaro	Defender		1	
B. Laudrup	Midfield			
D. Petrescu	Midfield	5	3	
P. Hughes	Midfield			
G. Poyet	Midfield		4	1
B. Lambourde	Midfield		1	1
N. Crittenden	Midfield			
R. DiMatteo	Midfield	4	6	
E. Newton	Midfield		2	
J. Morris	Midfield	1		
D. Wise	Midfield	3	10	
M. Nicholls	Midfield	3	1	
G. Zola	Forward	8	2	
P. Casiraghi	Forward			
T. Andre Flo	Forward	11		
P. Hughes	Forward		1	
G. Vialli	Forward	11	4	

Transfers after 15 July 1998:

GIANLUCA VIALLI

A second successive manager in disguise. Has charisma and will enjoy the role but he is essentially the coach and co-ordinator with a sound backroom staff dictated by the Wizard of the Bridge, Ken Bates. Expect Vialli to enjoy another relatively successful season. Popular with the players, Luca is intelligent and knowledgeable at the top level.

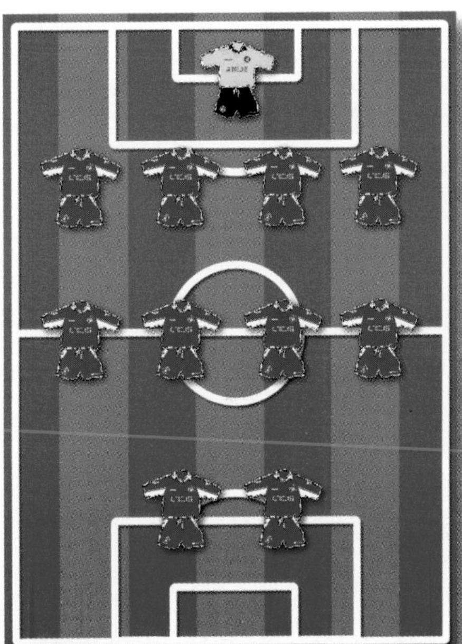

Trevor Brooking: *tactics*

They switched to a 4-4-2 last season, and promptly collected the Coca-Cola Cup and European Cup Winners' Cup. I still have doubts as to whether they can defend consistently enough to win The Premiership, but their skill level is equal to anyone, and they certainly should be one of the main challengers to Arsenal and Manchester United. A first full season in charge for Gianluca Vialli and I wonder how often he will figure as a player?

Chelsea play at Stamford Bridge in central London. Parking restrictions during the game make it advisable to park away from the ground and travel by Tube.

DIRECTIONS

From The North:
From the M1 turn off onto the A406 North Circular Road at Junction 1. Turn off onto the A40 and stay on until the junction with the M41. Turn right onto the M41 and continue for 1 mile before turning onto the A3220 Holland Road. Follow the A3220 for 2 miles before turning right onto the A304 Fulham Road. Stamford Bridge is quarter of a mile along on the right.

From The North West:
From the M40, continue into the A40 and stay on until the junction with the M41. Then as route for North.

From The West:
Get on the M4 and at Junction 1 continue along the A4 for 4 miles until it becomes the Cromwell Road. Turn right onto the A3220 Earls Court Road then as route for North.

From The South West:
From the M3 turn off onto the M25 at Junction 2. Continue for 10 miles until you reach Junction 15 at which point turn off onto the M4. Then as route for the West.

The nearest tube station is Fulham Broadway on the District Line.

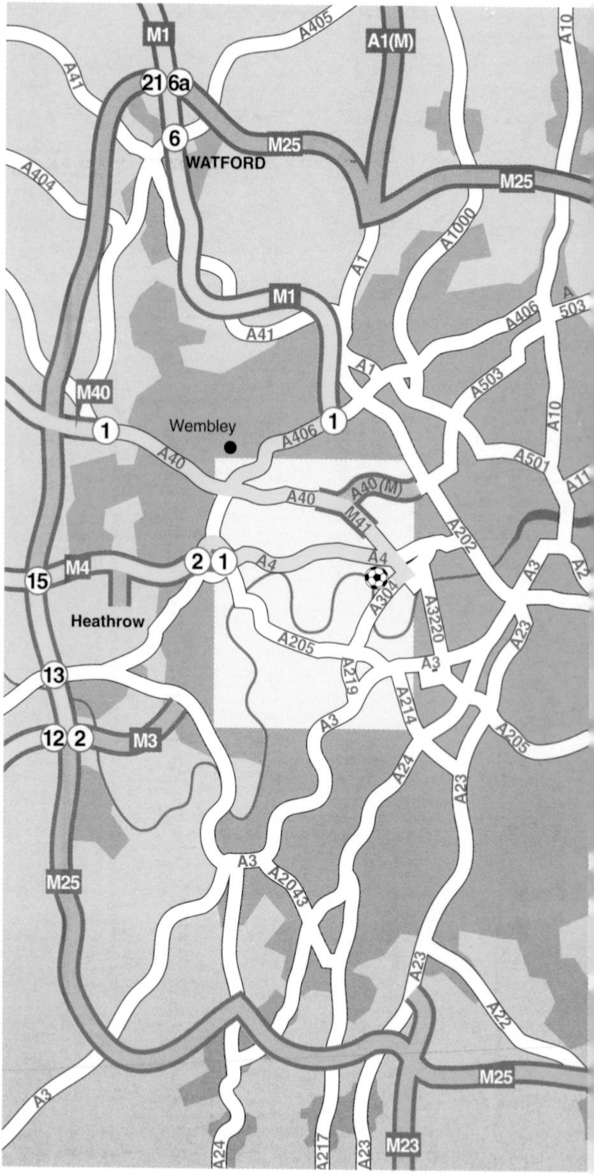

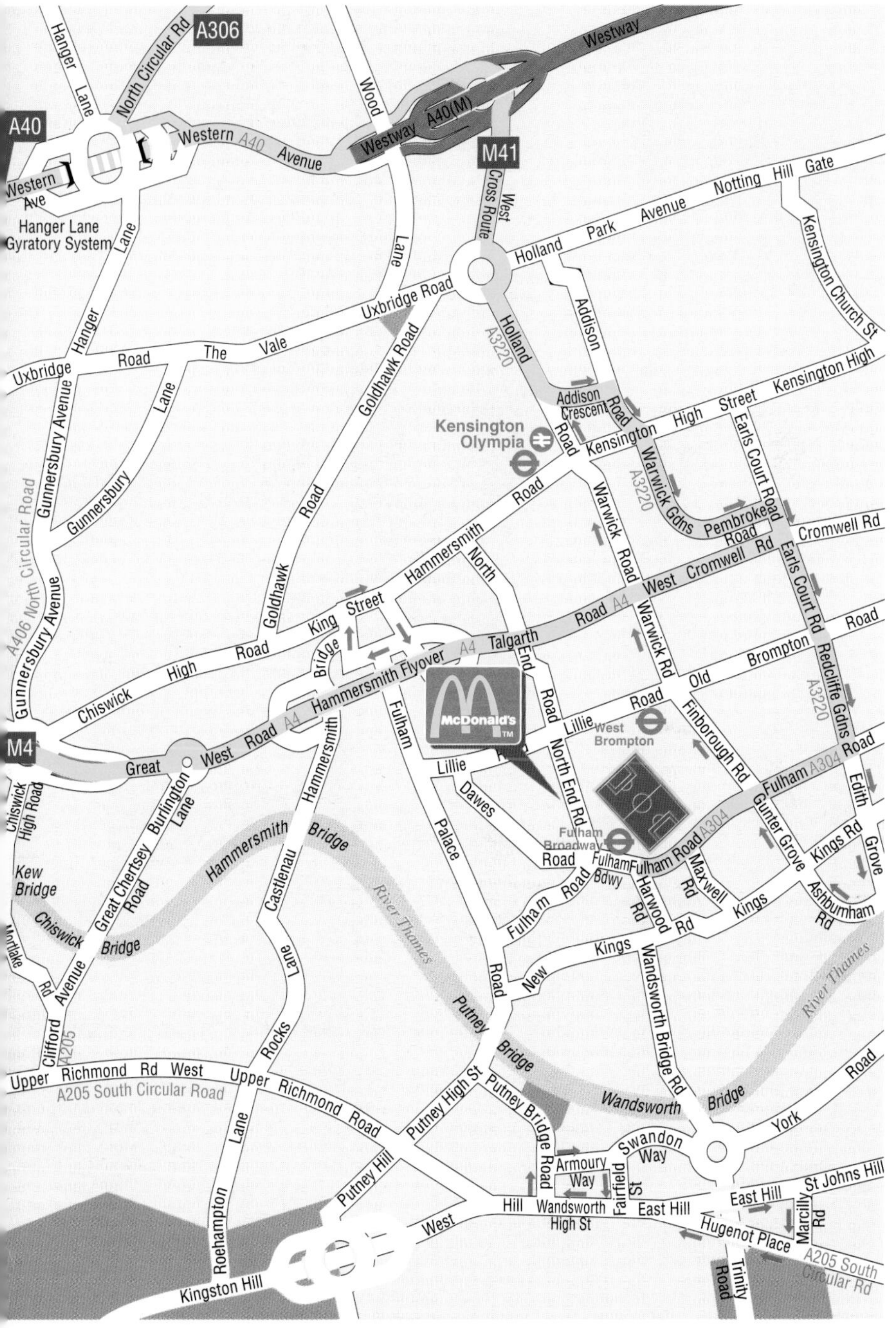

McDonald's™ 312-314 North End Road, Fulham, London SW6 1NG

Coventry City FC

Coventry City FC
Highfield Road Stadium
King Richard Street
Coventry CV2 4FW

Club No: 01203·234000
Fax No: 01203·234015
Tickets: 01203·234020
Internet: www.ccfc.co.uk

Bobby Robson: *view from abroad*

Beginning to emerge as a team who are not going to be haunted by relegation every season. Over the years they are usually one of the teams tipped to go down but under Gordon Strachan, building on what Ron Atkinson left him, they have increased their stature. They are no longer an eas knock over, they had some good away results las season and I see them continuing in that vein. The buy well and cheap and I see them looking to be saf by March and then chasing a place in Europe.

Bob Harris: *view in England*

The Highfield Road fans could be forgiven for a considerable raising of their expectancy level this season. Such has been the impact of Gordon Strachan and his shrewd dealings in the transfer market, avoiding relegation is no longer the priority from August onwards. Indeed there is a very real feeling in the City that the clu can challenge this season for one of the domesti cups and certainly a place in Europe.

INFORMATION HOTLINES

ClubCall: 0891·12·11·66*

Calls cost 50p per minute at all times

Club Call, Avalon House, 57-63 Scrutton St, London, EC2A 4PJ

CLUB SHOPS

SKY BLUE LEISURE

Highfield Road Stadium

Opening Times:

Monday-Friday: 9.00am-5.00pm
Match Saturdays: 9.00am-3.00pm, 4.45pm-5.45pm
Match Sundays: 9.00am-4.00pm, 5.45pm-6.30pm
Match Evenings: 9.00am-7.45pm, 9.30pm-10.15pm

Tel: 01203·234030

Fax: 01203·234015

Mail Order Service: 01203·234030

SKY BLUE LEISURE

Unit 6, Cathedral lane shopping centre

Opening Times:

Monday-Saturday: 9.00am-5.30pm
Match Saturdays: 9.00am-6.00pm

Tel: 01203·633619

BOOKING INFORMATION

General Enquiries:	01203·234030
Credit Card Bookings:	01203·578000
Travel Club:	01203·633127
Recorded Info:	01203·234000
Business & Conference Centre	01203·234014

CATERING

FOOD

Chips	£1.00
Pies	£1.55
Burgers/Hot Dogs	£2.10
Confectionery	£0.80

BAR

Tea/Coffee/Hot Chocolate	£1.00
Coca Cola	£1.15

MISCELLANEOUS

Business & Conference Centre
Contact: Raj Athwell 01203·234014

Corporate Hospitality
Hospitality available from £70-£200 depending on game.
Contact Julie Grimmet - Tel: 01203·234010/234080

Literature
Programme price £2

Pre Match & Half Time Entertainment
Sky Blue Crew/Sky Blue Sam

COVENTRY CITY FC

DARREN HUCKERBY

Sold by Newcastle without playing a first team game, 22-year-old Huckerby has since forced his way to the forefront of Premiership strikers. His electric pace and keen understanding with Dion Dublin was a key factor in Coventry's best season for years. If he can add a shade more composure to his final shot or pass, Huckerby could figure in Glenn Hoddle's plans for Euro 2000, besides finishing among the leading marksman this season.

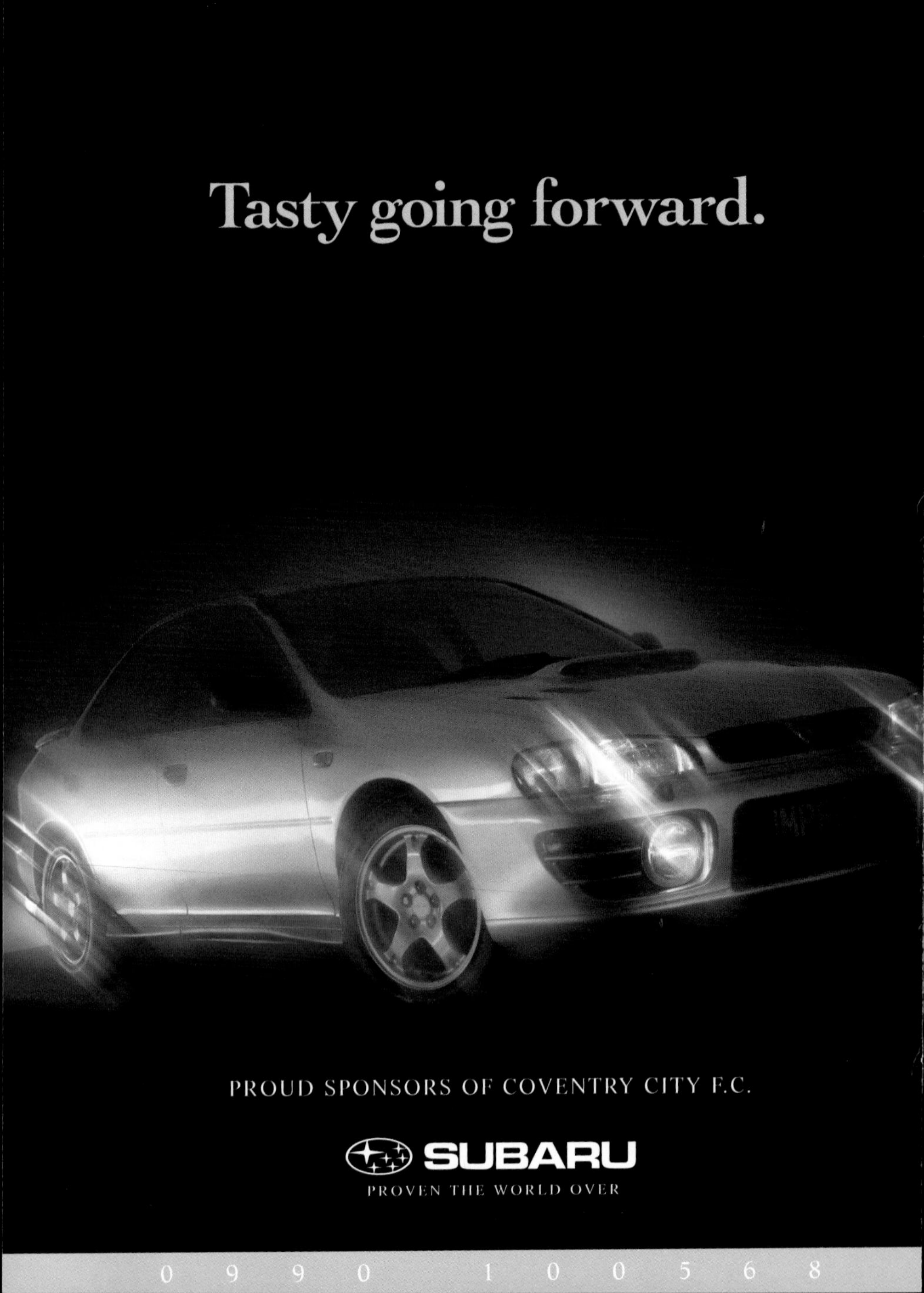
Tasty going forward.
PROUD SPONSORS OF COVENTRY CITY F.C.
SUBARU
PROVEN THE WORLD OVER
0 9 9 0 1 0 0 5 6 8

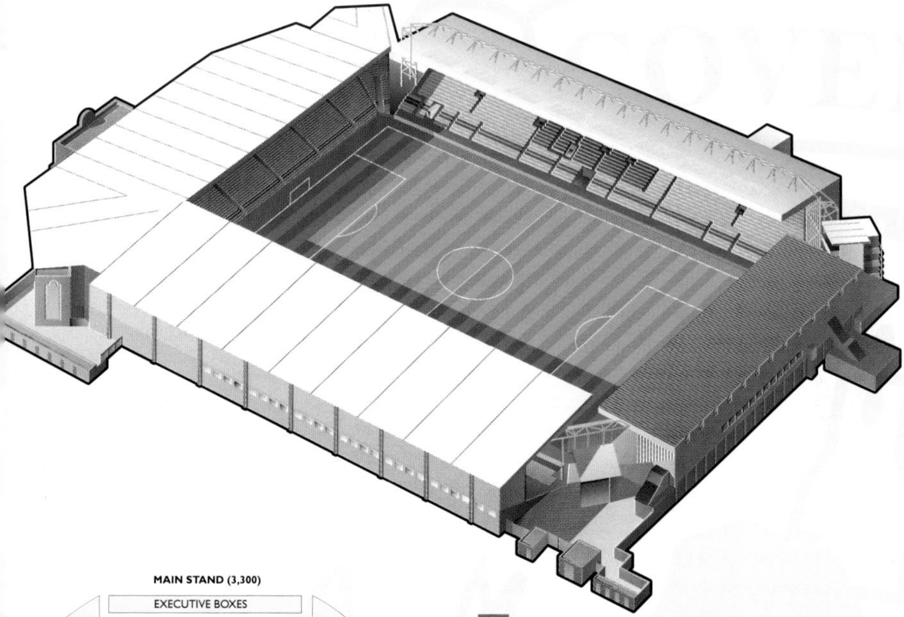

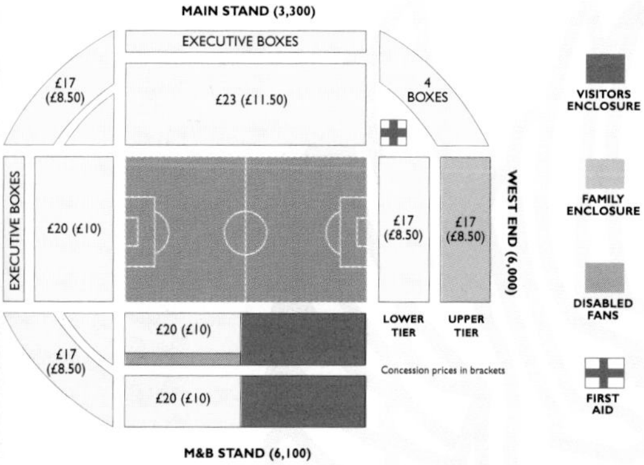

MAIN STAND (3,300)
EXECUTIVE BOXES
£17 (£8.50)
£23 (£11.50)
4 BOXES
EXECUTIVE BOXES
£20 (£10)
£17 (£8.50)
£17 (£8.50)
WEST END (6,000)
LOWER TIER
UPPER TIER
£20 (£10)
£17 (£8.50)
£20 (£10)
Concession prices in brackets
M&B STAND (6,100)
VISITORS ENCLOSURE
FAMILY ENCLOSURE
DISABLED FANS
FIRST AID

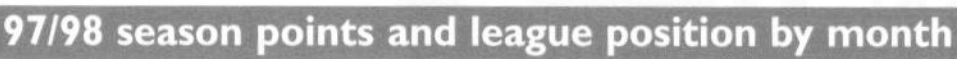

97/98 season points and league position by month

Win
Loss
Draw
League Position
Points
80
75
70
65
60
55
50
45
40
35
30
25
20
15
10
5
0
Aug
Sept
Oct
Nov
Dec
Jan
Feb
Mar
April
May

Goals for and against seasons 92/3 to 97/8

Total Goals
Home
Away
265
141
124
189
133
322
For
Against

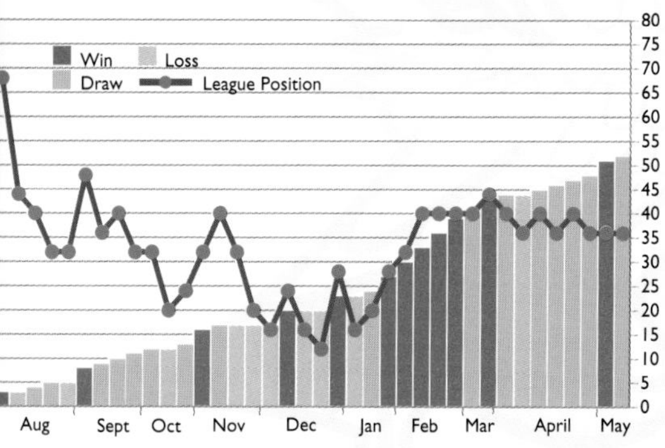

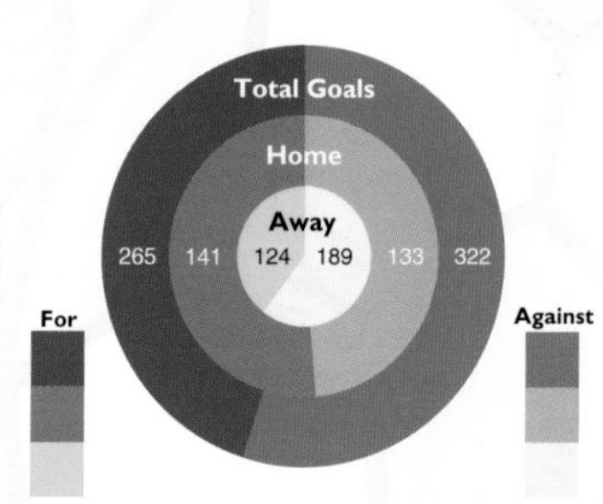

Goals scored by position by season

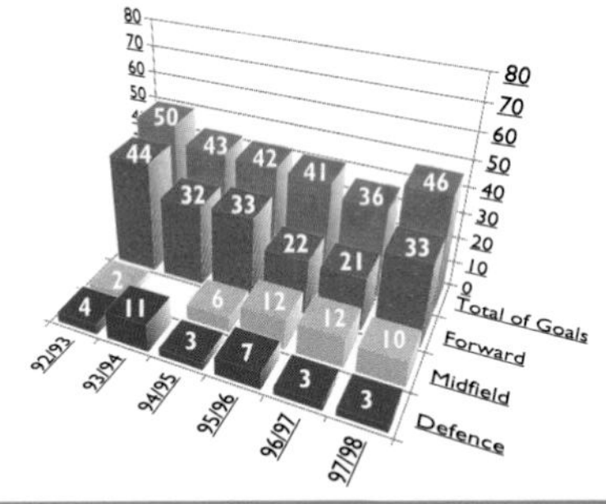

Bookings by position by season

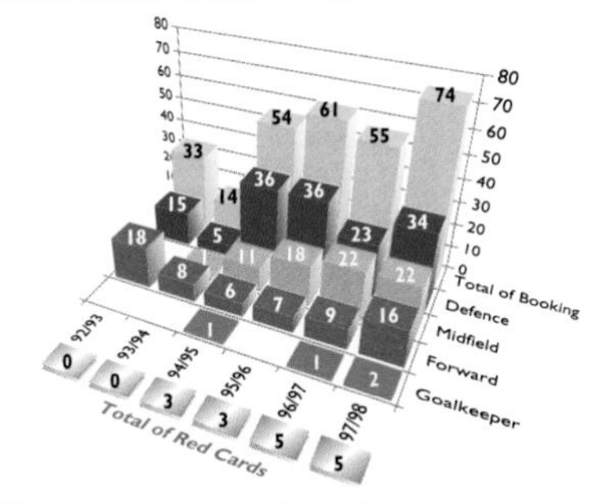

Goals scored by position by month 97/98

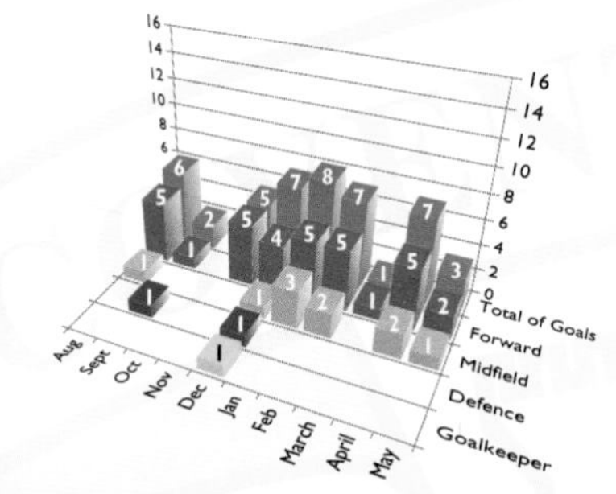

Final league position by season

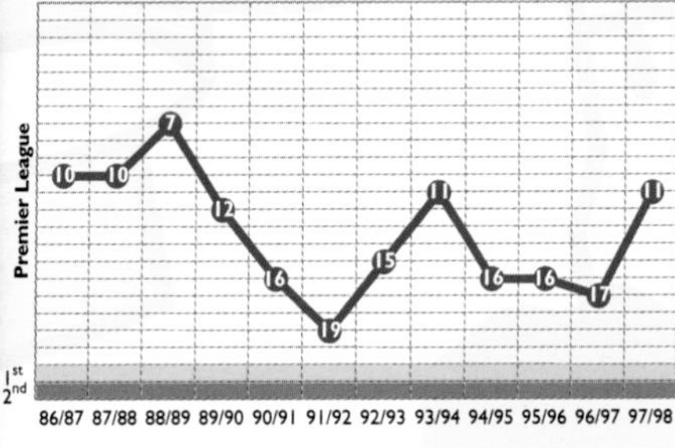

THE CARLING PREMIERSHIP FIXTURE LIST

HOME MATCH
AWAY MATCH
LAST SEASON: WIN
LAST SEASON: DRAW
LAST SEASON: LOSS

Opponent	Date	Last season
CHELSEA	15/8	3-2
NOTTM FOREST	22/8	N/A
WEST HAM	29/8	1-1
LIVERPOOL	9/9	0-1
MAN UTD	12/8	0-3
NEWCASTLE	19/9	2-2
CHARLTON	26/9	N/A
ASTON VILLA	3/10	1-2
SHEFF WED	17/10	1-0
SOUTHAMPTON	24/10	2-1
ARSENAL	31/10	2-2
BLACKBURN	7/11	0-0
EVERTON	14/11	0-0
MIDDLESBROUGH	21/11	N/A
LEICESTER	26/11	0-2
WIMBLEDON	5/12	2-1
LEEDS	12/12	3-3
DERBY	19/12	1-0
TOTTENHAM	26/12	4-0
WEST HAM	28/12	0-1
NOTTM FOREST	9/1	N/A
CHELSEA	16/1	1-3
LIVERPOOL	30/1	1-1
TOTTENHAM	6/2	1-1
NEWCASTLE	13/2	0-0
MAN UTD	20/2	3-2
ASTON VILLA	27/2	0-3
CHARLTON	6/3	N/A
BLACKBURN	13/3	2-0
ARSENAL	20/3	0-2
SHEFF WED	3/4	0-0
SOUTHAMPTON	5/4	1-0
EVERTON	10/4	1-1
MIDDLESBROUGH	17/4	N/A
LEICESTER	24/4	1-1
WIMBLEDON	1/5	0-0
DERBY	8/5	1-3
LEEDS	16/5	0-0

THE SQUAD

Key: Goalkeeper · Defender · Midfield · Forward · No of goals · No of clean sheets · No of yellow cards · No of red cards

Player	Position	Goals / Clean sheets	Yellow cards	Red cards
S. Ogrizovic	Goalkeeper	7		
M. Hedman	Goalkeeper	6		
B. Borrows	Defender			
R. Nilsson	Defender			3
G. Breen	Defender	1	1	1
J. Wallemme	Defender			
L. Daish	Defender			
P. Williams	Defender		10	2
I. Brightwell	Defender			
R. Shaw	Defender		1	
D. Burrows	Defender		8	
M. Hall	Defender	1	8	
P. Telfer	Midfield	3	8	
M. O'Neill	Midfield			
S. Shilton	Midfield			
G. Boateng	Midfield	1	4	1
T. Soltvedt	Midfield	1	1	
W. Boland	Midfield		4	
G. McAllister	Midfield		1	
N. Whelan	Midfield	6	4	
J. Salako	Midfield		1	
A. Ducros	Midfield			
G. Strachan	Midfield			
D. Dublin	Forward	18	4	1
V. Moldovan	Forward	1		
S. Haworth	Forward		1	
D. Huckerby	Forward	14	9	
M. Johansen	Forward			

Transfers after 15 July 1998:

David Pleat: *on the manager*

GORDON STRACHAN

The fiery Scot is learning quickly with a good chairman to back him. His players are maturing into an effective force. Beat the odds last season with Dublin and Huckerby a constant menace. Expect Strachan to continue to be in great demand. A determined, feisty, hard worker who realises the importance of team before self.

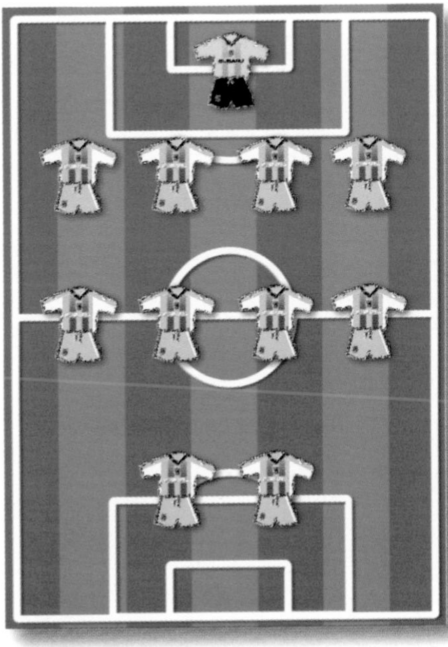

Trevor Brooking: *tactics*

Last season they provided a welcome relief for their supporters away from relegation struggles and Gordon Strachan will want to build on the progress achieved. Darren Huckerby was an exciting matchwinner in attack and Dion Dublin's outstanding season just failed to win him a trip to France with England during the summer. Changed his playing system on occasions, but seemed to favour 4-4-2 late on.

Coventry City play at the Highfield Road Stadium, less than a mile from the city centre. There is some car parking off Kingsway.

DIRECTIONS

From The North:

Take the M1 to Junction 21 and join the M69 continuing at Junction 2 onto the A4600 following signs to the centre. This road becomes the Walsgrave Road which turns right into Swan Lane. The ground is ahead on the left.

From The South:

Take M40 to Junction 15 onto A46. Continue on A46 which changes to A4114 for approx 10 miles. Then take A423 signposted city centre. After approximately 2 miles take A4600 signposted Leicester. Follow this road for half a mile and just before road bridge turn left into Swan Lane. The Ground is on the left.

From The West/East:

Approaching on the M6 in either direction, turn off onto the A4600 at Junction 2. Then as route for North.

Coventry Railway Station is situated one mile from the ground. Buses leave from Trinity Street Bus Station.

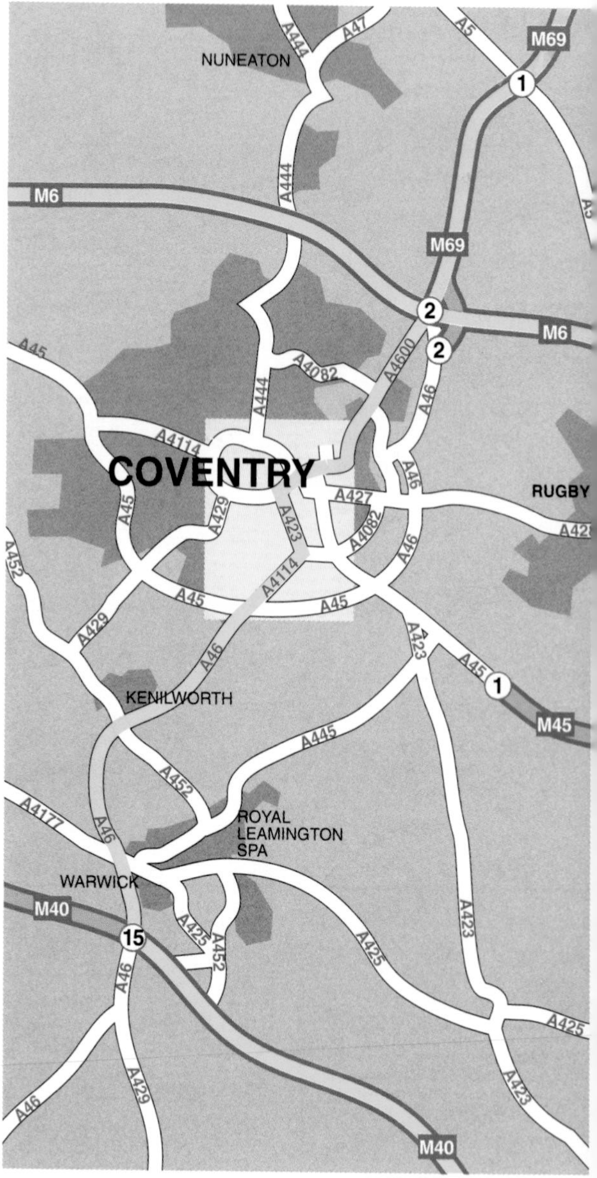

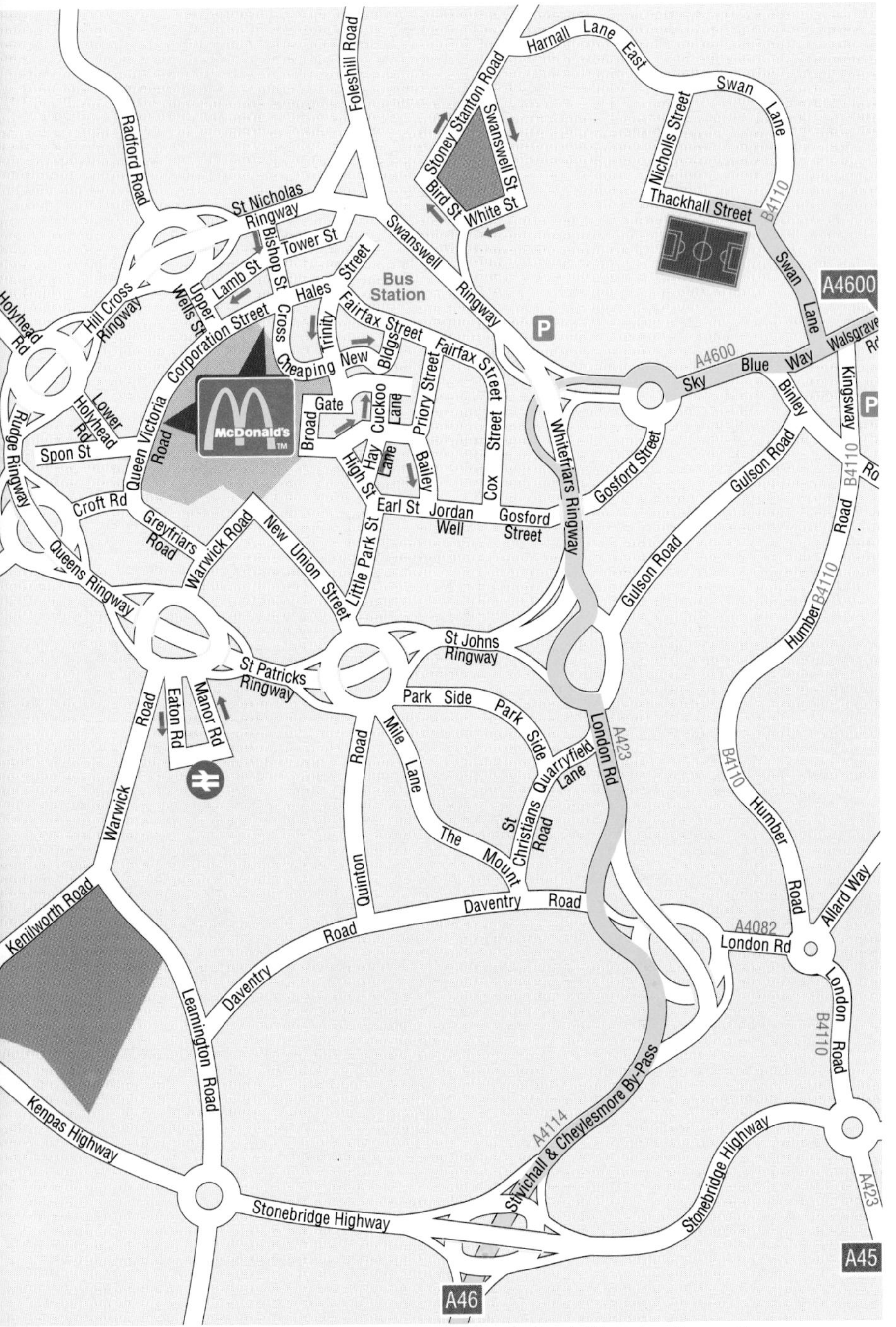

McDonald's™ Oscars Food Court, Kiosk K1, West Orchards Shopping Centre, Coventry
McDonald's™ Cross Cheaping CV1 1HF

Derby County FC
Pride Park Stadium
Derby
DE24 8XL

Club No: 01332·202202
Fax No: 01332·667540
Tickets: 01332·209209
Internet: www.dcfc.co.uk

Bobby Robson: *view from abroad*

They are a middle of the league team and these days that is no shame at all. They will remember the success under Clough and Mackay but nowadays the division is divided into three and Derby will be happy to be in that middle bunch, steering clear of the relegation zone and seeking out one of the places in Europe. Jim Smith is a clever manager whose cunning in the transfer market will keep the club in a respectable position.

Bob Harris: *view in England*

Jim Smith is not a man to stand still. He was happy with a place in the top ten last season but is keen to move on. This may mean changes at Pride Park but Jim will do it quietly and efficiently, buying at the right time and the right price. Fostering the club's romance with attractive, attacking football while trying to board up a defence which, on occasions last season, can be an embarrassment. A few more away goals and points and Derby could be booking that return to Europe at the end of this season.

INFORMATION HOTLINES

ClubCall: 0891·12·11·87*
Prize Line: 0891·33·22·13*

Calls cost 50p per minute at all times
Club Call, Avalon House, 57-63 Scrutton St, London, EC2A 4PJ

CLUB SHOPS

RAMS SUPERSTORE

Located in North East Corner

Opening Times:

Monday-Friday: 9.00am-6.00pm
Match Saturdays: 9.00am-Kick Off plus 1 hour after match
Normal Saturday: 9.00am-5.30pm
Match Sundays: 10.00am-Kick Off plus 1 hour after match
Normal Sundays: 10.00am-4.00pm
Match Evenings 9.00am-Kick Off plus 1 hour after match

Tel: 01332·209000
Fax: 01332·667540
Mail Order Tel: 01332·209999

BOOKING INFORMATION

General Enquiries:	01332·202202
Credit Card Bookings	01332·209999
Travel Club	01332·209999

CATERING

FOOD

Cheese & Onion Pastie	£1.55
Pizza Slice (available in southwest corner only)	£1.80
Fries	£1.00
Burger	£2.10
Cheeseburger	£2.25
Hot Dog	£2.10
Chickenburger	£2.40
Steak & Kidney Pie	£1.55
Meat & Potato Pie	£1.55
Cornish Pastey	£1.55

BAR

Lager (Pint)/Bitter (Pint)	£2.00
Pure Orange Juice	£0.70
Lucozade Sports Pack	£1.30
Coca-Cola/Diet/Fanta 14oz	£1.15
Tea, Coffee, Soup, Bovril & Hot Chocolate	£1.00

MISCELLANEOUS

Stadium Tours
Graham Proudler Tel: 01332·667578
Corporate Hospitality
For Corporate hospitality and sponsorship contact Simon Moore/Andy Dawson tel: 01332·667575 or 01332·667538
Restaurant facilities call Dominque Alexander tel: 01332·667589
Literature
Programme - The Ram £2 and bi-monthly magazine 'Rampage'
Pre Match & Half Time Entertainment
Pre-match and half-time DJ playing selection of chart and popular music.
Premium Club Prize Draw (Members only)
Gold Rush Prize Draw - Matchday

RORY DELAP

Having paid Carlisle an initial £500,000 for Delap three months before the end of last season, Jim Smith will be expecting to see the best of the 22-year-old Republic of Ireland International, which could lift the fee to around £1million. Delap showed his versatility as a wing back in the closing games, but may be able to express himself better in a more orthodox midfield role.

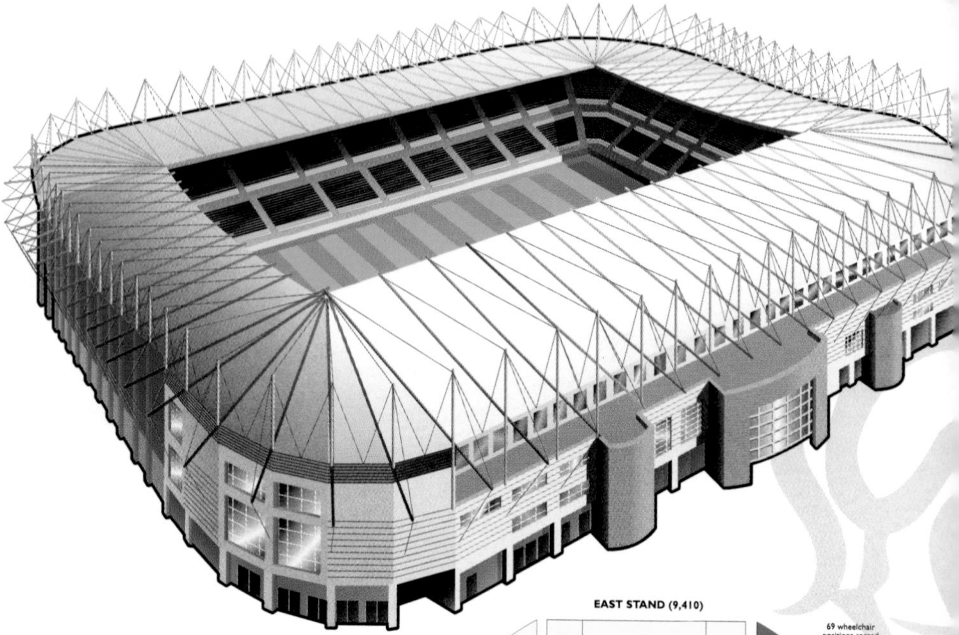

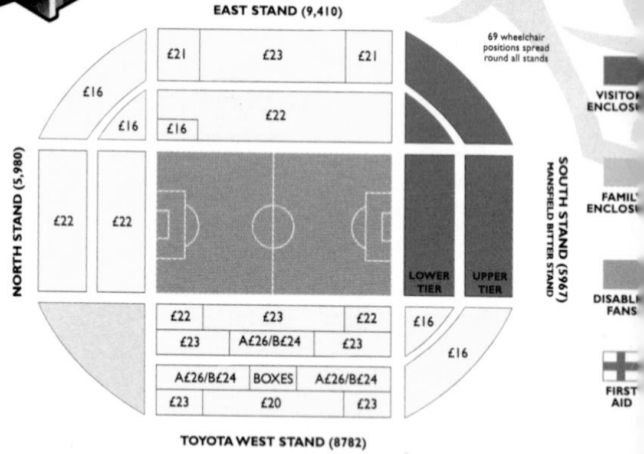

EAST STAND (9,410)
69 wheelchair positions spread round all stands
£21
£23
£21
£16
£22
£16
£16
NORTH STAND (5,980)
£22
£22
LOWER TIER
UPPER TIER
SOUTH STAND (5967) MANSFIELD BITTER STAND
£22
£23
£22
£23
A£26/B£24
£23
£16
£16
A£26/B£24
BOXES
A£26/B£24
£23
£20
£23
TOYOTA WEST STAND (8782)
VISITOR ENCLOSURE
FAMILY ENCLOSURE
DISABLED FANS
FIRST AID

97/98 season points and league position by month

Win
Loss
Draw
League Position
League position
Points
0
2
4
6
8
10
12
14
16
18
20
80
75
70
65
60
55
50
45
40
35
30
25
20
15
10
5
0
Aug
Sept
Oct
Nov
Dec
Jan
Feb
March
April
May

Goals for and against seasons 92/3 to 97/8

Total Goals
Home
Away
382
234
148
197
143
340
For
Against

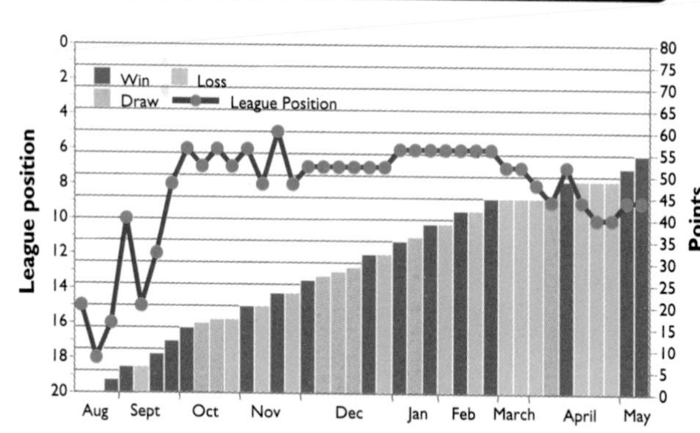

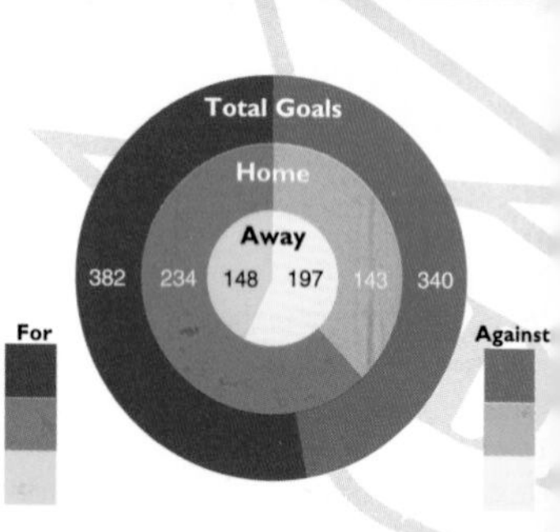

DERBY COUNTY FC

Goals scored by position by season

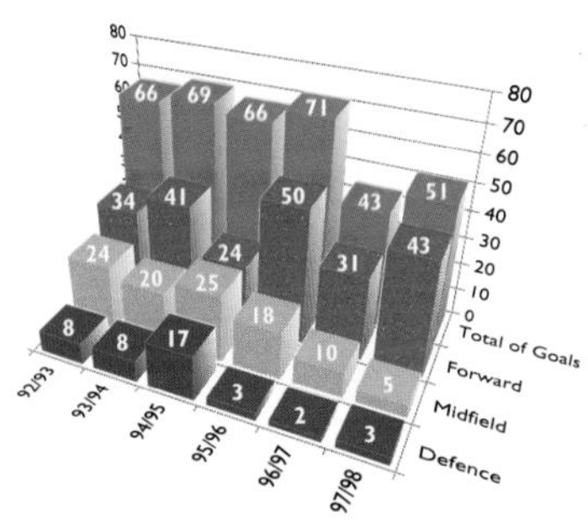

Bookings by position by season

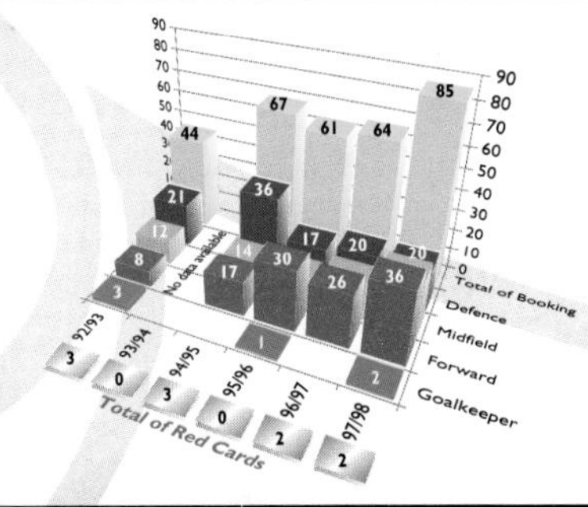

Goals scored by position by month 97/98

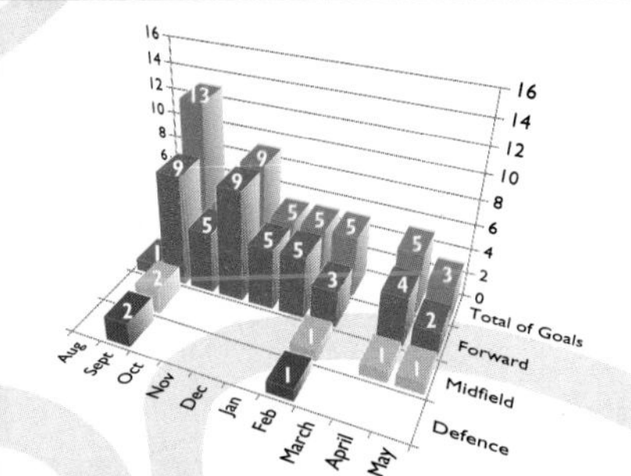

Final league position by season

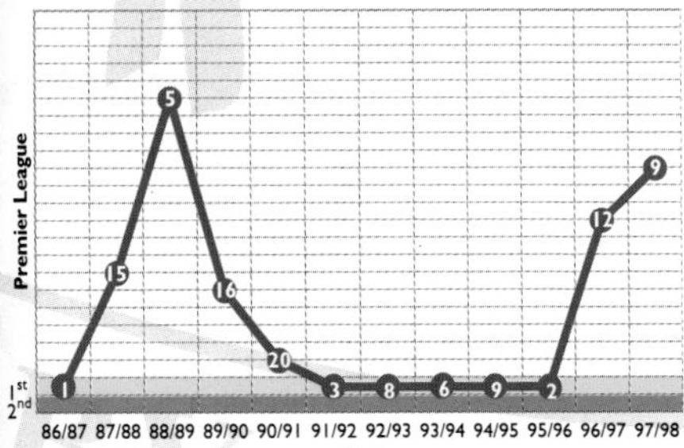

THE CARLING PREMIERSHIP FIXTURE LIST

HOME MATCH
AWAY MATCH
LAST SEASON: WIN
LAST SEASON: DRAW
LAST SEASON: LOSS

Opponent	Date	Last season
BLACKBURN	15/8	0-1
WIMBLEDON	22/8	1-1
MIDDLESBROUGH	29/8	N/A
SHEFF WED	9/9	3-0
CHARLTON	12/9	N/A
LEICESTER	19/9	0-4
ASTON VILLA	26/9	1-2
TOTTENHAM	3/10	2-1
NEWCASTLE	17/10	0-0
MAN UTD	24/10	2-2
LEEDS	31/10	0-5
LIVERPOOL	7/11	0-4
NOTTM FOREST	16/11	N/A
WEST HAM	22/11	2-0
SOUTHAMPTON	28/11	2-0
ARSENAL	5/12	3-3
CHELSEA	12/12	0-1
COVENTRY	19/12	0-1
EVERTON	26/12	2-1
MIDDLESBROUGH	28/12	N/A
WIMBLEDON	9/1	0-0
BLACKBURN	16/1	3-1
SHEFF WED	30/1	5-2
EVERTON	6/2	3-1
LEICESTER	13/2	2-1
CHARLTON	20/2	N/A
TOTTENHAM	27/2	0-1
ASTON VILLA	6/3	0-1
LIVERPOOL	13/3	1-0
LEEDS	20/3	3-4
NEWCASTLE	3/4	1-0
MAN UTD	5/4	0-2
NOTTM FOREST	10/4	N/A
WEST HAM	17/4	0-0
SOUTHAMPTON	24/4	4-0
ARSENAL	1/5	1-0
COVENTRY	8/5	3-1
CHELSEA	16/5	0-4

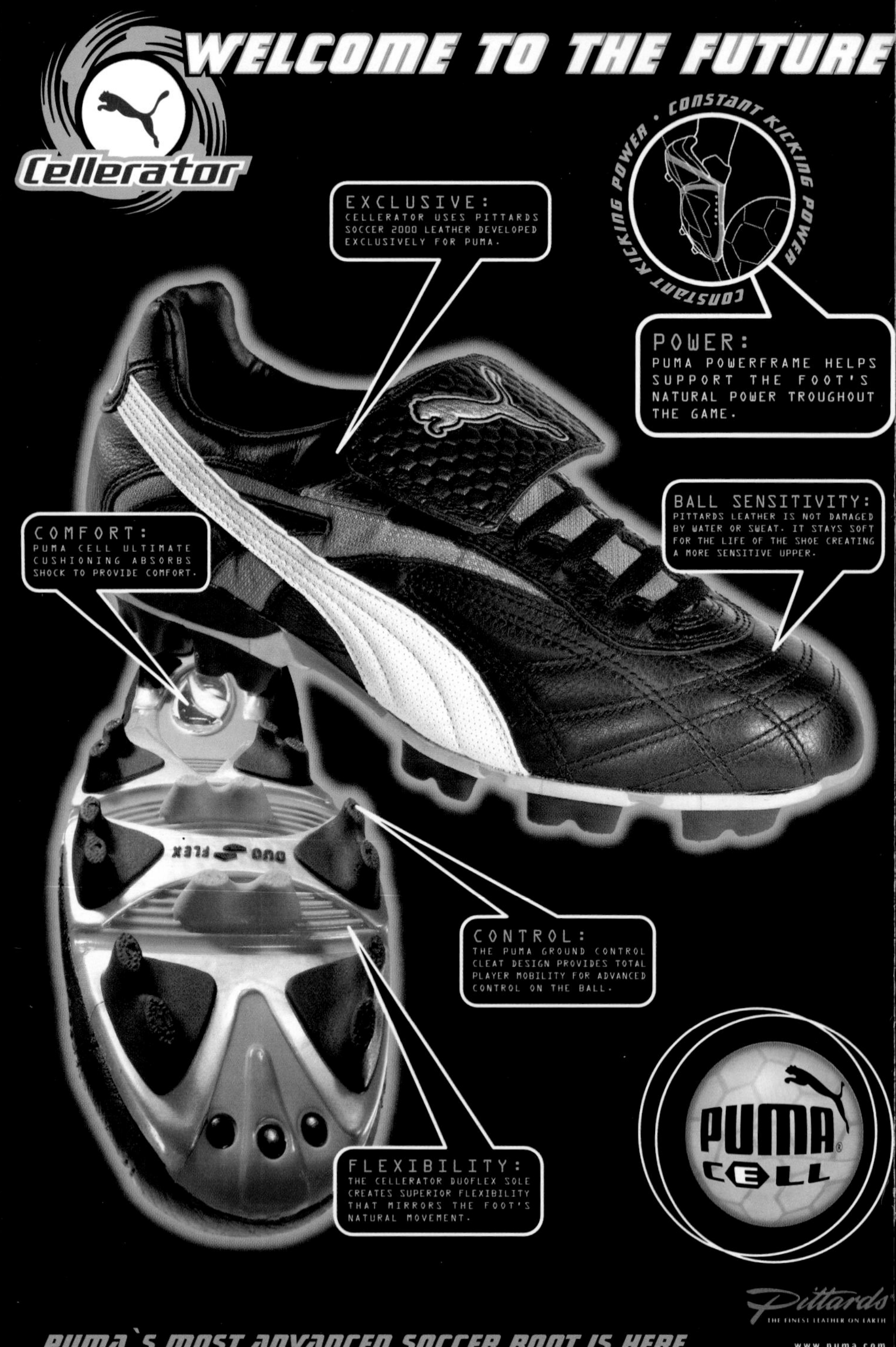
WELCOME TO THE FUTURE
Cellerator
CONSTANT KICKING POWER • CONSTANT KICKING POWER
EXCLUSIVE:
CELLERATOR USES PITTARDS SOCCER 2000 LEATHER DEVELOPED EXCLUSIVELY FOR PUMA.
POWER:
PUMA POWERFRAME HELPS SUPPORT THE FOOT'S NATURAL POWER TROUGHOUT THE GAME.
BALL SENSITIVITY:
PITTARDS LEATHER IS NOT DAMAGED BY WATER OR SWEAT. IT STAYS SOFT FOR THE LIFE OF THE SHOE CREATING A MORE SENSITIVE UPPER.
COMFORT:
PUMA CELL ULTIMATE CUSHIONING ABSORBS SHOCK TO PROVIDE COMFORT.
DUO FLEX
CONTROL:
THE PUMA GROUND CONTROL CLEAT DESIGN PROVIDES TOTAL PLAYER MOBILITY FOR ADVANCED CONTROL ON THE BALL.
FLEXIBILITY:
THE CELLERATOR DUOFLEX SOLE CREATES SUPERIOR FLEXIBILITY THAT MIRRORS THE FOOT'S NATURAL MOVEMENT.
PUMA® CELL
Pittards
THE FINEST LEATHER ON EARTH
PUMA`S MOST ADVANCED SOCCER BOOT IS HERE
www.puma.com
www.foxsports.com

THE SQUAD

Key: Goalkeeper · Defender · Midfield · Forward · No of goals · No of clean sheets · No of yellow cards · No of red cards

Player	Position	Goals / Clean sheets	Yellow cards	Red cards
M. Poom	Goalkeeper	13 (clean sheets)	2	
R. Hoult	Goalkeeper			
S. Eranio	Defender	5	9	2
R. Kozluk	Defender		1	
H. Carbonari	Defender			
I. Stimac	Defender	1	6	
G. Rowett	Defender	1	4	
J. Laursen	Defender	1	5	
S. Elliott	Defender			
S. Schnoor	Defender			
C. Dailly	Defender	1	7	
R. Delap	Midfield		2	
L. Bohinen	Midfield	1	1	
R.Van Der Laan	Midfield		2	
J. Hunt	Midfield	1	3	
L. Carsley	Midfield	1	10	
R.Willems	Forward			
D. Burton	Forward	3		
D. Sturridge	Forward	9	9	
F. Baiano	Forward	12	2	
D. Powell	Forward		5	
P.Wanchope	Forward	13	8	

Transfers after 15 July 1998:

JIM SMITH

Genial Jim, everyone's friend, will be hard pressed to match last season's second attempt at this level. With humour, hard work and dedication, Jim has encountered the roller coaster of management and has come up smiling more often than not. Currently the longest server with a good young coach in Steve McClaren. Must hope for half way.

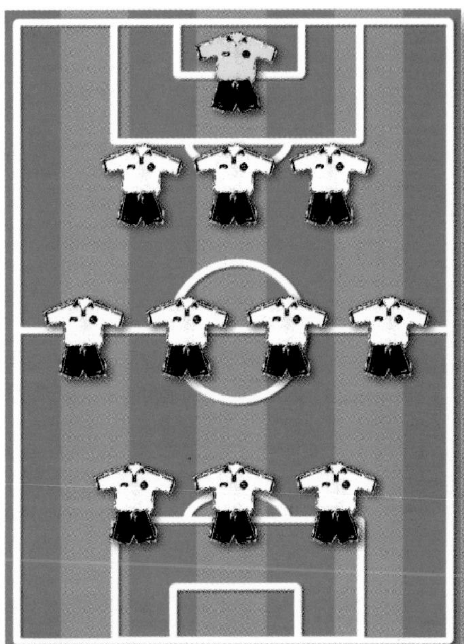

Trevor Brooking: *tactics*

Another side who made significant strides last season, when they made good use of the three central defenders, by also playing three attackers. Dean Sturridge, Paulo Wanchope and Francesco Baiano caused all sorts of problems for the opposition. The pace of Sturridge and the individual skills of Wanchope were perfectly exploited by the incisive passing and movement of the experienced Italian. Derby conceded far too many goals in the closing weeks of the season, so manager Jim Smith has made some useful defensive signings during the summer to resolve this weakness.

Derby County play at Pride Park Stadium in the vicinity of Derby Station

DIRECTIONS

From The North:

Approaching on the M1 take the exit at Junction 25 onto the A52. After approximately 5 miles and after passing under the bridge, take the left exit to the new Pride Park Stadium.

From The South:

Approaching on the M1 take the exit at Junction 24 and get onto the A6. After approximately 6 miles cross the A5111 and at the next roundabout take the right exit for the new Pride Park Stadium.

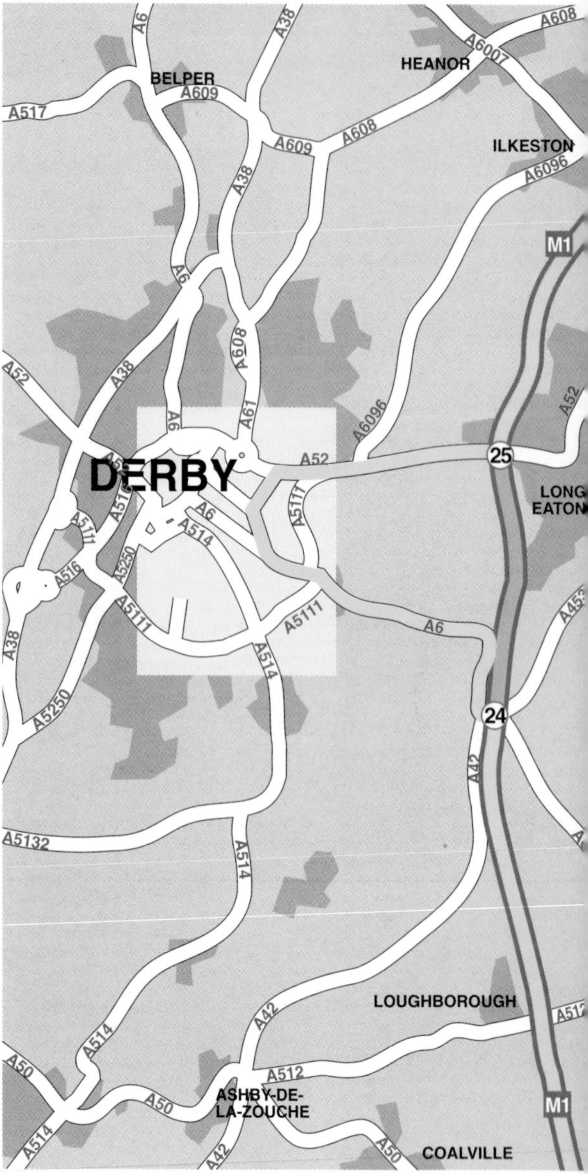

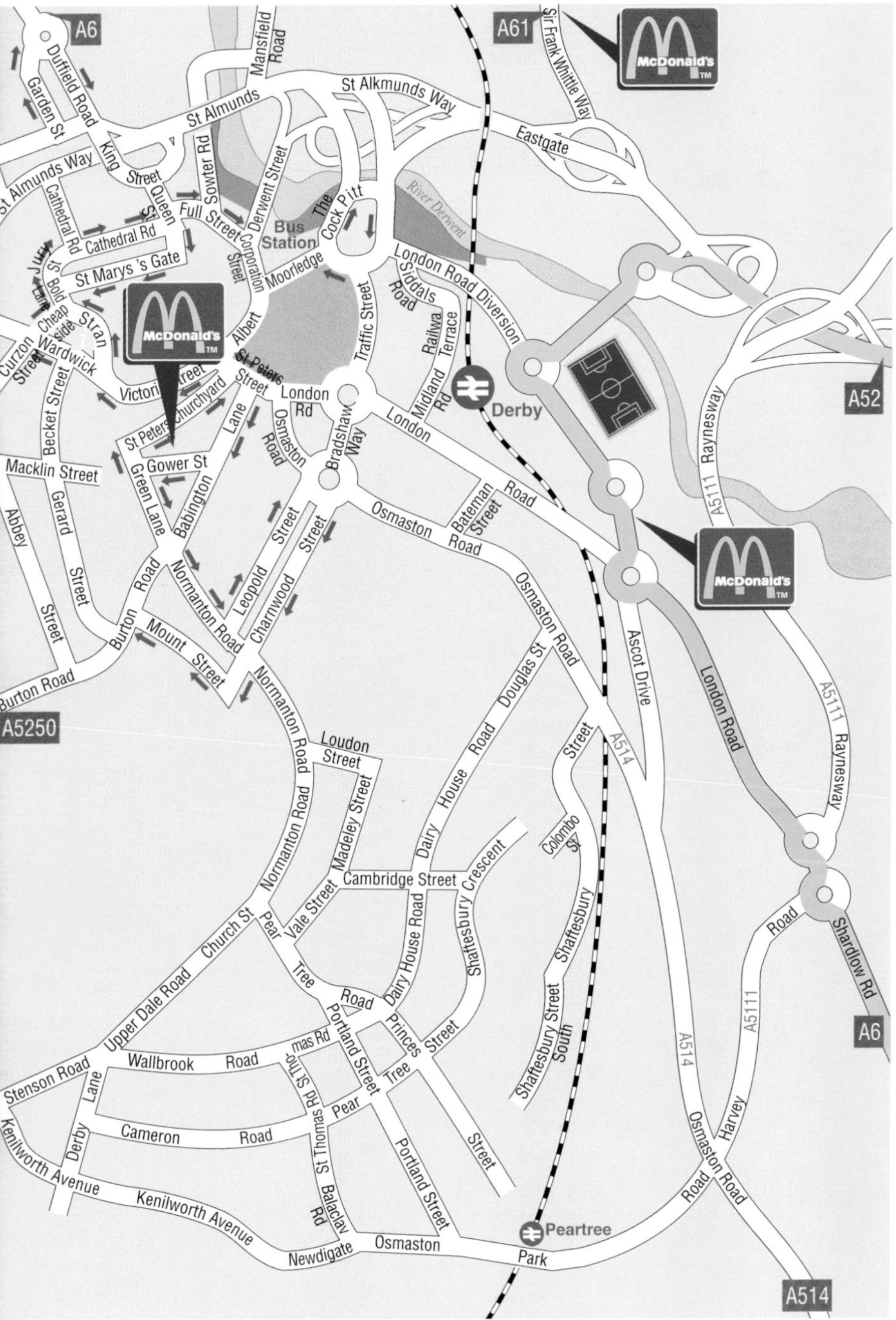

McDonald's™ Wyvern Retail Park, Chaddesden, Derby DE2 6NZ
McDonald's™ 34-44 St Peter Street, Derby
McDonald's™ Unit C, Meteor Centre, Sir Frank Whittle Road, Neadsall DE21 4SY

Everton FC

Everton FC
Goodison Park
Goodison Road
Liverpool L4 4EL

Club No: 0151·330·2200
Fax No: 0151·286·9112
Tickets: 0151·330·2300

Bobby Robson: *view from abroad*

Without doubt one of the biggest and most attractive clubs in England. A major club who are on the slide and they will want to turn that around this season and be up there with the Leeds Uniteds and Aston Villas challenging for a place in Europe. They have challenging with their famous support as they are one of the big names of our League and I find it sad that they came so close to relegation again last season. They have to somehow find quality players instead of ordinary ones that fail to excite. They have a brilliant crop of youngsters but they can't wait and good money needs to be spent to reward their patient supporters.

Bob Harris: *view in England*

The club knows only too well that their long suffering fans will not put up with the "Great Escape : Part three" this season. Everton are too big a club to languish near the foot of the table and the memory of how close they were to going down - with the same points as Bolton - will have frightened many. The new manager, Walter Smith, is a charming man with sturdy ethos. May find choppy waters at first but sure to settle and do a sound job, given a stable backroom and boardroom. He is determined, enjoys coaching and will be single minded for success.

INFORMATION HOTLINES

ClubCall: 0891·12·11·99*

**Calls cost 50p per minute at all times*

Club Call, Avalon House, 57-63 Scrutton St, London, EC2A 4PJ

CLUB SHOPS

EVERTON FC MEGASTORE

Goodison Park, Liverpool

Opening Times:

Monday-Friday: 9.00am-5.00pm
Match Saturdays: 9.30am-3.00pm, 4.45pm-5.30pm
Match Sundays: 10.00am-4.00pm, 5.45pm-6.30pm
Match Evenings: usual hours until kick off, then 1 hour after match.
Non match Saturdays: 10.00am-4.00pm

Tel: 0151·330·2030
Fax: 0151·286·0100
Mail Order Service: 0151·330·2333

SATELLITE SHOP

Corner of Bullens Road, Goodison Park, L4 4EL

Opening Times:

Match Saturdays: 9.30am-3.00pm, 4.45pm-5.30pm
Match Sundays: 10.00am-4.00pm, 5.45pm-6.30pm
Match Evenings: usual hours until kick off, then 1 hour after match.

BOOKING INFORMATION

General Enquiries:	0151·330·2200
Credit Card Bookings:	0151·471·8000
Travel Club:	0151·330·2277
Entertainment Complex:	0151·330·2499
Commercial Department:	0151·330·2224
The Official Supporters Club Line:	0151·330·2208
Box Office	0151·330·2300
Conference & Banqueting	0151·330·2499
Sponsorship & Hospitality	0151·330·2400
Commercial Department	0151·330·2224
Community Department	0151·330·2307

CATERING

FOOD

Pies	£1.40
Pot Noodle	£1.50
Sausage Roll	£1.20
Bacon Bap	£1.50
Jumbo Pasties	£1.75
Eccles Cake	£0.70
Sandwiches	from £1.50
Large Hot Dog	£1.80
Pizza	from £1.00

BAR

Lager (Pint)	£1.80
Bitter (Pint)	£1.80
Pepsi, Diet Pepsi, Tango	£1.20
Tea, Coffee, Bovril, Soup	£1.00
White Wine (glass)	£1.60

MISCELLANEOUS

Stadium Tours

Tel: 0151·330·2266, Morning 11.00am, afternoon 2.00pm. Tours take place Monday, Wednesday, Friday and Sunday, £4 Adults, £3 Children, £3 OAP's.

Lounge Membership Available 1998/99

Tel: 0151·330·2400

Hospitality packages encompass Captains Table and Joe Mercer Suite, Alex Young Lounge and Legends Sports Bar. Various Sponsorship and Matchball sponsorship options.

Literature

Programme price £2.00 Evertonian magazine £1 monthly.

Miscellaneous Entertainment

Family fun nights around some reserve fixtures including pre-match and half time entertainment, competitions and give-aways.

Radio Everton broadcasts on matchdays on 1602am.

TV Everton available at Goodison Park on matchdays.

RICHARD DUNNE

Still young enough at 18 to be part of the F.A. Youth Cup winning team that lightened the end of Everton's dark season, the massively built Dunne will surely figure in more first team games this time round. The Dublin-born YTS product has all the physical attributes, as well as the presence and temperament, to develop into a dominating defender.

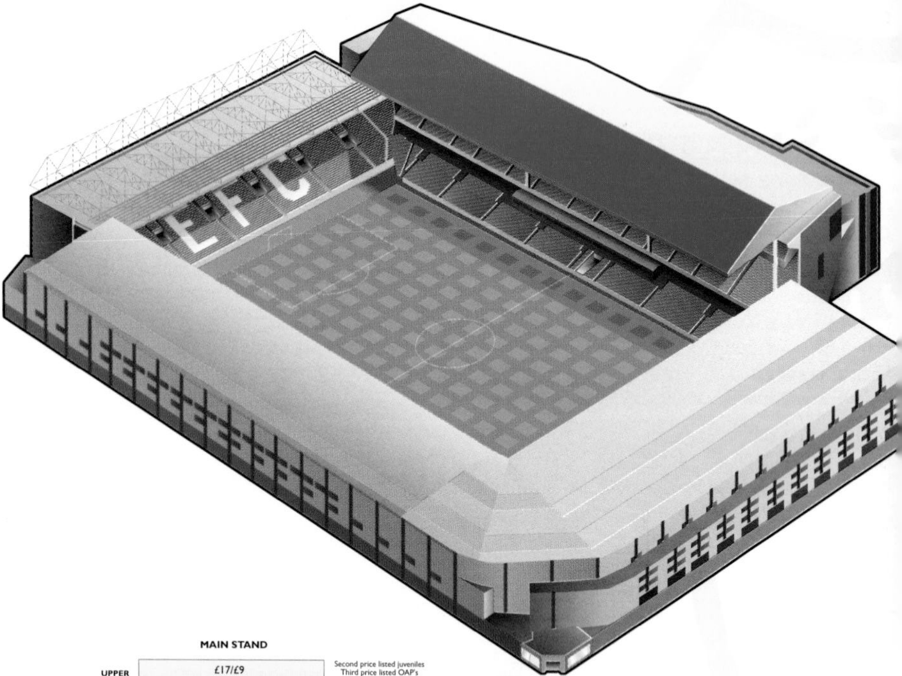

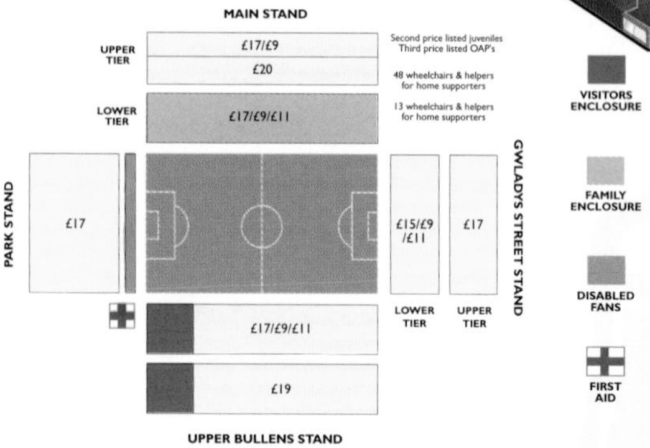

MAIN STAND
UPPER TIER
£17/£9
£20
Second price listed juveniles
Third price listed OAP's
48 wheelchairs & helpers for home supporters
LOWER TIER
£17/£9/£11
13 wheelchairs & helpers for home supporters
PARK STAND
£17
£15/£9/£11
£17
LOWER TIER
UPPER TIER
GWLADYS STREET STAND
£17/£9/£11
£19
UPPER BULLENS STAND
VISITORS ENCLOSURE
FAMILY ENCLOSURE
DISABLED FANS
FIRST AID

97/98 season points and league position by month

Win
Loss
Draw
League Position
League position
Points
Aug
Sept
Oct
Nov
Dec
Jan
Feb
March
April
May

Goals for and against seasons 92/3 to 97/8

Total Goals
Home
Away
288
167
121
178
148
326
For
Against

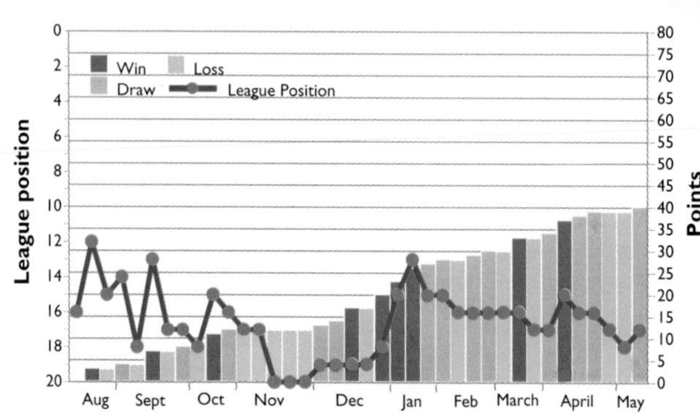

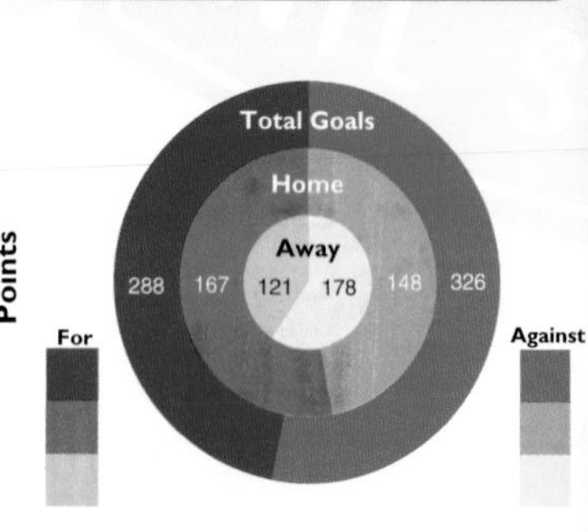

Goals scored by position by season

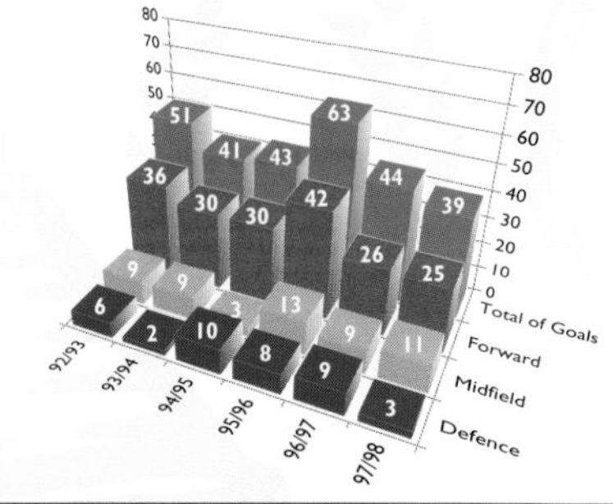

Bookings by position by season

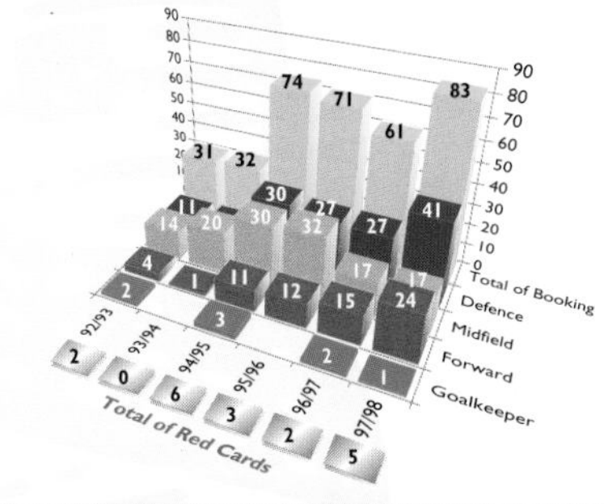

Goals scored by position by month 97/98

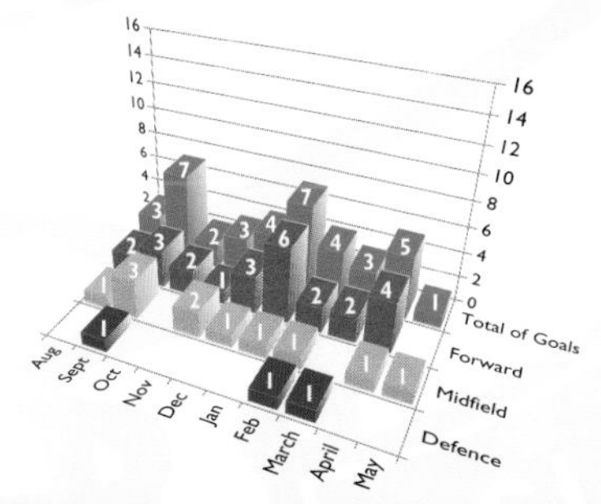

Final league position by season

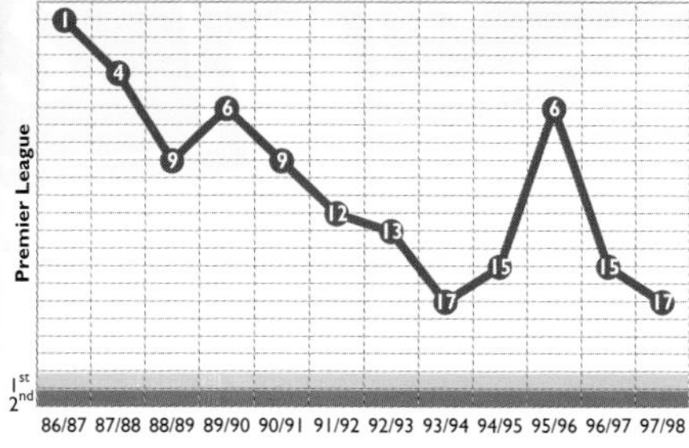

THE CARLING PREMIERSHIP FIXTURE LIST

HOME MATCH
AWAY MATCH
LAST SEASON: WIN
LAST SEASON: DRAW
LAST SEASON: LOSS

Opponent	Date	Last season
ASTON VILLA	15/8	1-4
LEICESTER	22/8	1-0
TOTTENHAM	29/8	0-2
NOTTM FOREST	9/9	N/A
LEEDS	12/9	2-0
MIDDLESBROUGH	19/9	N/A
BLACKBURN	26/9	1-0
WIMBLEDON	3/10	0-0
LIVERPOOL	17/10	2-0
SHEFF WED	24/10	1-3
MAN UTD	31/10	0-2
ARSENAL	7/11	0-4
COVENTRY	15/11	0-0
NEWCASTLE	23/11	0-0
CHARLTON	28/11	N/A
CHELSEA	5/12	3-1
SOUTHAMPTON	12/12	0-2
WEST HAM	19/12	2-2
DERBY	26/12	1-2
TOTTENHAM	28/12	1-1
LEICESTER	9/1	1-1
ASTON VILLA	16/1	1-2
NOTTM FOREST	30/1	N/A
DERBY	6/2	1-3
MIDDLESBROUGH	13/2	N/A
LEEDS	20/2	0-0
WIMBLEDON	27/2	0-0
BLACKBURN	6/3	2-3
ARSENAL	13/3	2-2
MAN UTD	20/3	0-2
LIVERPOOL	3/4	1-1
SHEFF WED	5/4	1-3
COVENTRY	10/4	1-1
NEWCASTLE	17/4	0-1
CHARLTON	24/4	N/A
CHELSEA	1/5	0-2
WEST HAM	8/5	2-1
SOUTHAMPTON	16/5	1-2

THE SQUAD

Goalkeeper · Defender · Midfield · Forward · No of goals · No of clean sheets · No of yellow cards · No of red cards

Player	Position	Goals / Clean sheets	Yellow cards	Red cards
T. Myhre	Goalkeeper	7 (clean sheets)		
P. Gerrard	Goalkeeper		1	
T. Thomas	Defender		1	
D. Watson	Defender		2	
C. Short	Defender		4	
R. Dunne	Defender			
S. Bilic	Defender		7	3
C. Tiler	Defender	1	5	
J. O'Kane	Defender		5	
T. Phelan	Defender		2	
M. Ball	Defender	1	3	
T. Grant	Midfield	1		
G. Allen	Midfield		1	
D. Williamson	Midfield		2	
G. Farrelly	Midfield	1	5	
G. McCann	Midfield		2	
N. Barmby	Midfield	2	7	
J. Parkinson	Midfield			
M. Ward	Midfield			
D. Hutchison	Midfield	1	2	
J. Oster	Midfield	1	2	
D. Cadamarteri	Midfield	4	4	
D. Ferguson	Forward	11	6	1
J. Spencer	Forward			
M. Madar	Forward	6	3	
M. Branch	Forward			

Transfers after 15 July 1998:

David Pleat: *on the manager*

WALTER SMITH

New Manager Walter Smith will add steel to the side, increase the work rate and build from the back without becoming boring as he is keen on attacking football. Used to success and will bring in players from home and abroad to ensure he and Everton move onwards and upwards.

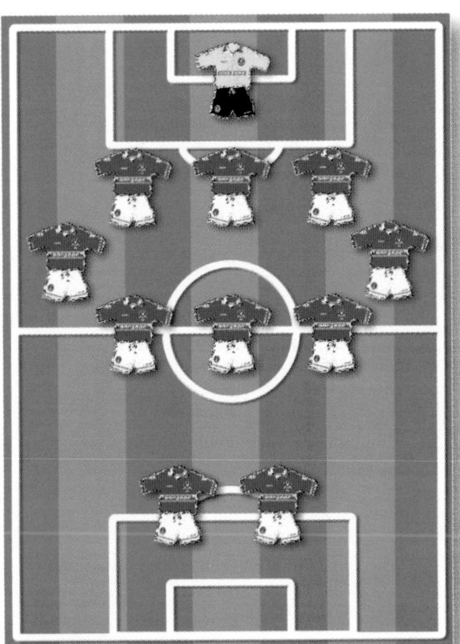

Trevor Brooking: *tactics*

Usually relied on three central defenders at the back but a lack of pace here was always an obvious shortcoming. Michael Ball looks an exciting prospect down the left, but the squad still needs strengthening if their relegation struggles are not to be repeated yet again. The aerial outlet to Duncan Ferguson also becomes far too predictable when they are lacking confidence.

Everton's Goodison Park is situated two miles north of Liverpool City Centre, opposite Stanley Park. Car parking is available in Anfield Road.

DIRECTIONS

From the North:

Approaching on the M6, exit at Junction 26 onto the M58 and continue until the end. At Junction 7 turn left onto the A59 Ormskirk Road. Continue on this road as it becomes Rice Lane, and cross over the roundabout into County Road. After 1/4 mile turn left into Everton Valley and then Walton Lane. Goodison Road and the ground are on the left.

From the South:

Approaching on the M6, exit at Junction 21a onto the M62. Exit the M62 at Junction 4 and get onto the A5080. At the junction with the A5058 turn right and continue along this road as it becomes Queens Drive. Continue to the junction with Walton Hall Avenue and turn left onto the A580 Walton Lane. Goodison Road and the ground are on the right.

From the East:

Approaching on the M62 exit at Junction 4 and get onto the A5058. Then as route for the South.

Lime Street Railway Station is in the town centre, 2 miles from Goodison Park. Kirkdale Railway Station is a 10 minute walk from the ground.

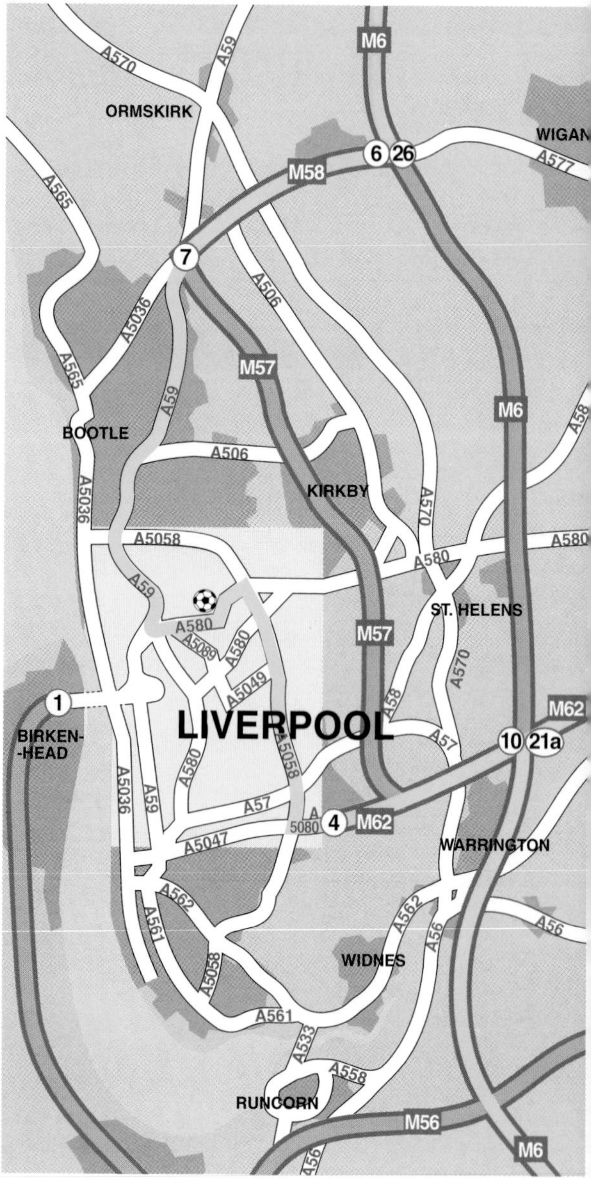

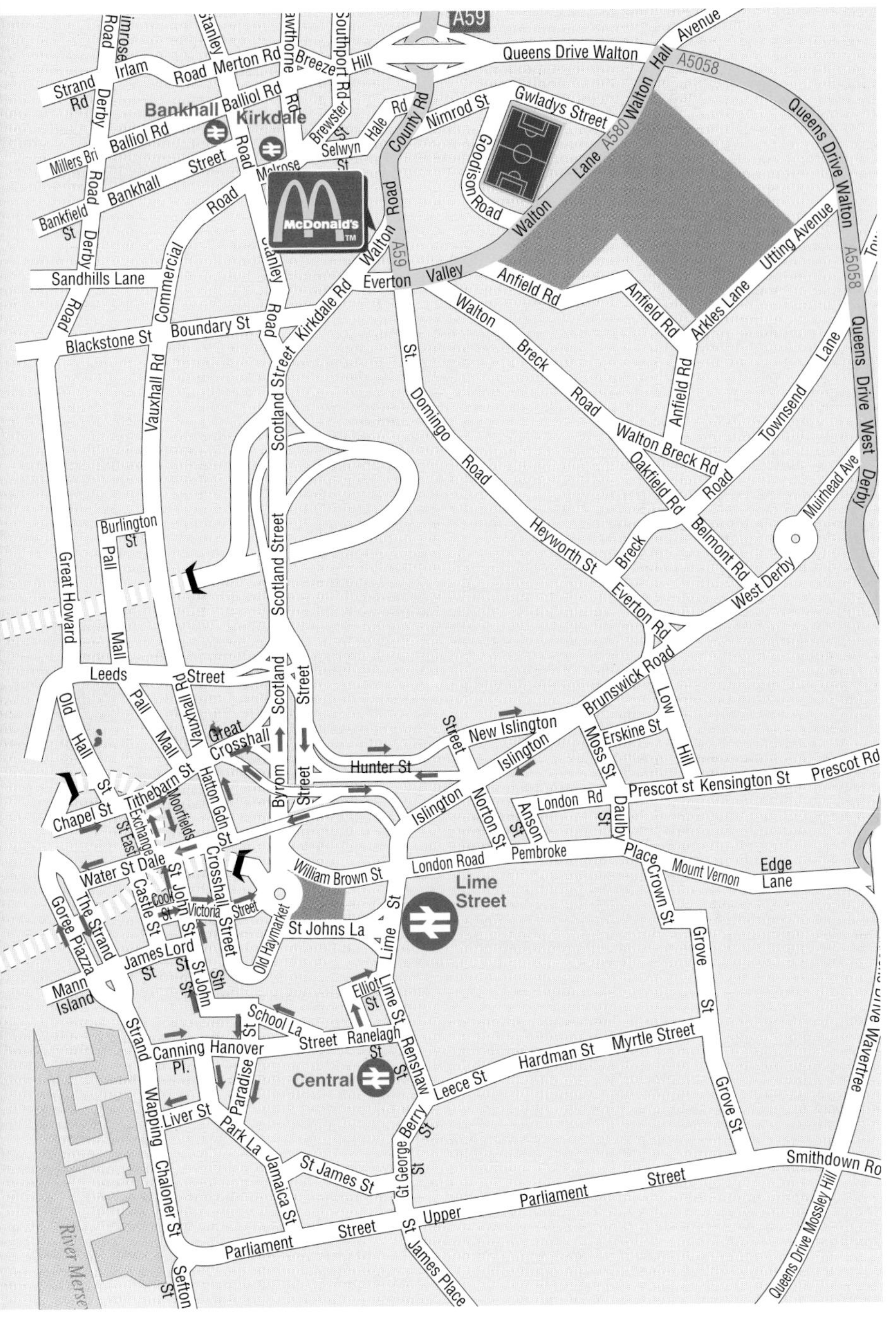

McDonald's™ 202-218 Walton Road, Kirkdale, Liverpool L4 4BD

Leeds United FC

Leeds United AFC
Elland Road
Leeds
West Yorkshire
LS11 0ES

Club No: 0113·226·6000
Fax No: 0113·226·6050
Tickets: 0113·292·0011
Internet: www.lufc.co.uk

Bobby Robson: *view from abroad*

George Graham has taken a little time to do a very good job, taking Leeds into the hierarchy of the League where you expect them to be. I believe that he will continue to improve their position and will become one of the great Leeds managers to go alongside the name of Don Revie. The club have confidence in him and he seems to be enjoying the Northern lights and his heart is in the club. He spends his money well and will always have a say about who wins the Championship.

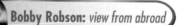

Bob Harris: *view in England*

Usually whatever George Graham wants, George Graham gets. Fifth place and a spot in the UEFA Cup looks pretty healthy to those looking up from below but for George it is not a satisfactory season if he doesn't have at least one pot to put in the Boardroom cabinet. Having weeded out the players he didn't want, the rebuilding process continues. He will demand more goals at Elland Road from his forwards and a better set of results to present to the home fans who took more enjoyment from being on the road last season. Expect Graham and his Leeds team to be at the forefront in the challenge for the minor honours this season. The Carling Premiership will have to wait a while longer.

INFORMATION HOTLINES

ClubCall:	0891·12·11·80*
Recorded Information:	0891·12·16·80*

Calls cost 50p per minute at all times
Club Call, Avalon House, 57-63 Scrutton St, London, EC2A 4PJ

CLUB SHOPS

LEEDS UNITED SOUVENIRS STORE

Elland Road

Opening Times:

Monday-Saturday: 9.00am-5.00pm
Match Saturdays: 9.00am-5.00pm
Match Evenings: all day up to game and then half an hour after full time.
Tel: 0113·226·6000
Fax: 0113·226·6083
Mail Order Service: 0113·225·1100

LEEDS UNITED SOUVENIRS STORE

10/11 Burton Arcade, Leeds

Opening Times:

Monday-Friday: 9.30am-5.15pm
Match Saturdays: 9.00am-5.15pm

Tel: 0113·247·0098
Fax: 0113·244·1940
Mail Order Service: 0113·225·1100

There are also retail outlets at the White Rose Shopping Centre, The Ridings Centre, Leeds Bradford Airport

BOOKING INFORMATION

General Enquiries:	0113·226·1000
Recorded Information:	0891 12 16 80
Travel Club:	0500·225·151
Leeds United Lottery	0113 226 1234
Leeds United Membership	0113 2266177

CATERING

FOOD

Quarter Pound Burger	£2.00
Hot Dog	£2.00
Pies	£1.50
Chips	£1.00
Crisps	£0.50
Mars/Snickers/Twix	£0.65

BAR

Lager	£2.00
Bitter	£1.80
Coffee/Soup/Bovril/Hot Chocolate/Tea	£1.00
Coke/Fanta	£1.10
Diet Coke	£1.10
Lucozade	£1.20

MISCELLANEOUS

Stadium Tours
Contact John McLelland (pre-book) - Tel: 0113·226·6237
Corporate Hospitality
Contact Amanda Johnson - Tel: 0113·226·6217
Matchday hospitality packages from£99
Sponsorship from £4000
Match ball sponsorship from £1750
Banqueting Department (pre-book) - Tel: 0113·226·1166
Literature
Programme price £2.00.
New Leeds United Magazine to be launched Sept'98
Pre Match and Half Time Entertainment
Local Bands Penalty Shoot-out Competition
Various guest appearances Sky diving

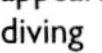

HARRY KEWELL

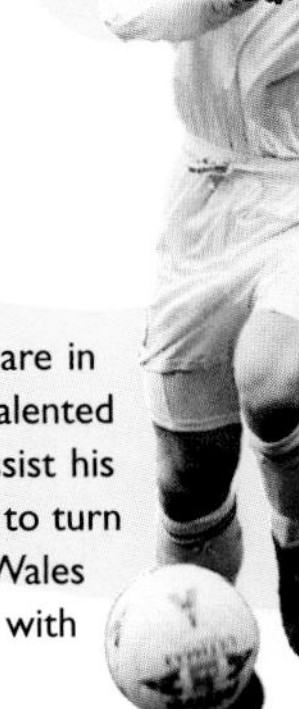

If Leeds involvement in the UEFA Cup means George Graham's team are in for a busy season, that will come as nothing new to Harry Kewell. The talented left-sided attacker spent a lot of time travelling across the world to assist his native Australia's World Cup bid under Terry Venables, but still managed to turn in some vivid performances for his club. A product of the New South Wales Soccer Academy, Kewell will not be 20 until September and is stamped with star quality.

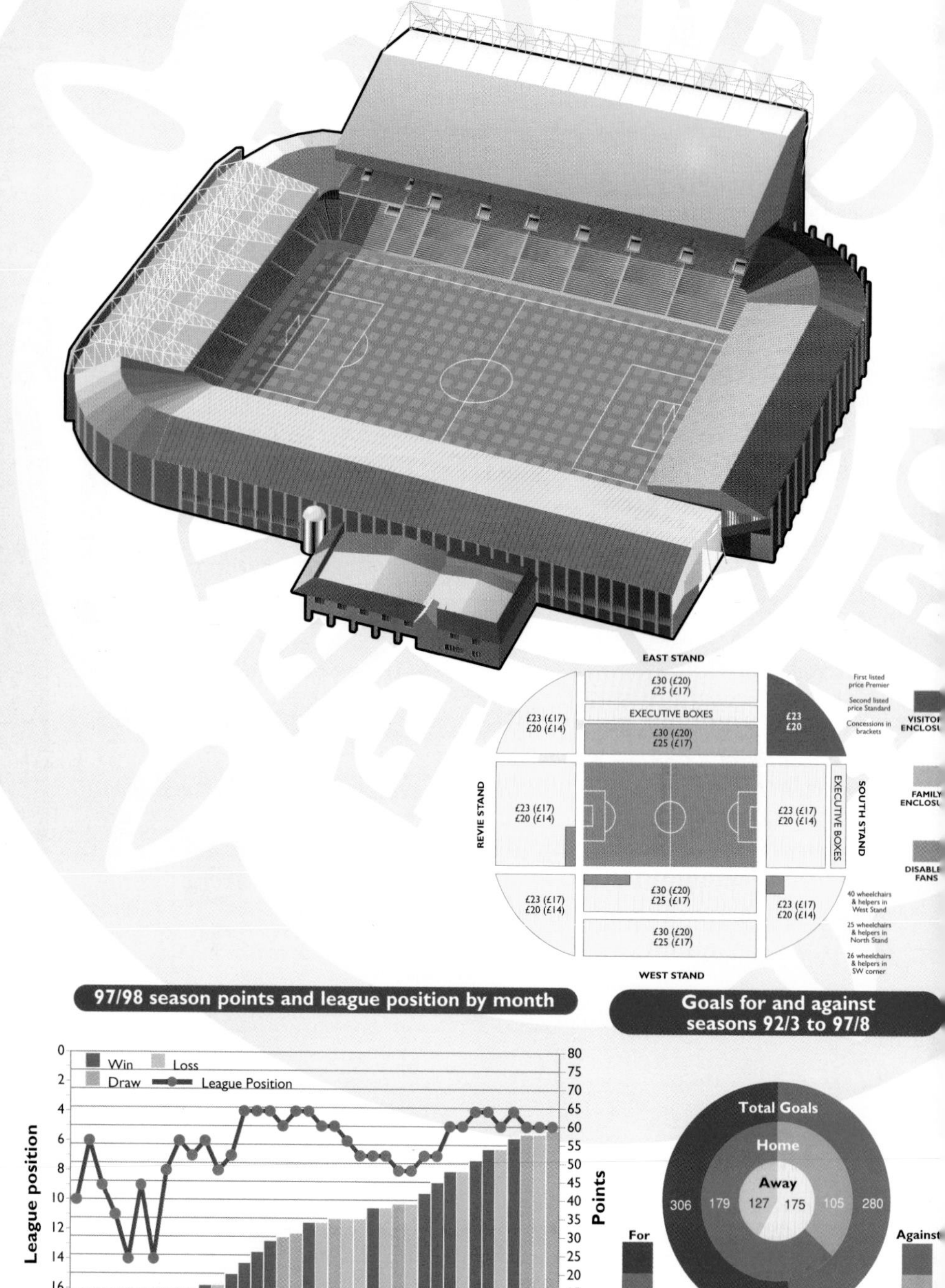
EAST STAND
£30 (£20)
£25 (£17)
EXECUTIVE BOXES
£30 (£20)
£25 (£17)
£23 (£17)
£20 (£14)
£23
£20
First listed price Premier
Second listed price Standard
Concessions in brackets
REVIE STAND
£23 (£17)
£20 (£14)
£23 (£17)
£20 (£14)
EXECUTIVE BOXES
SOUTH STAND
£23 (£17)
£20 (£14)
£30 (£20)
£25 (£17)
£23 (£17)
£20 (£14)
£30 (£20)
£25 (£17)
40 wheelchairs & helpers in West Stand
25 wheelchairs & helpers in North Stand
26 wheelchairs & helpers in SW corner
WEST STAND
97/98 season points and league position by month
Win
Loss
Draw
League Position
League position
Points
Aug
Sept
Oct
Nov
Dec
Jan
Feb
March
April
May
Goals for and against seasons 92/3 to 97/8
Total Goals
Home
Away
306
179
127
175
105
280
For
Against

Goals scored by position by season

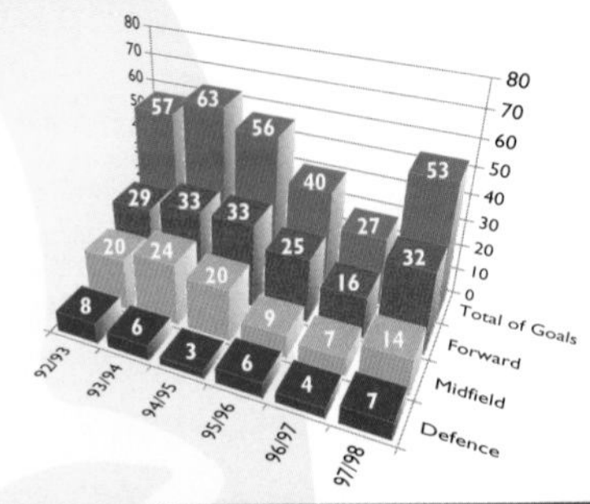

Bookings by position by season

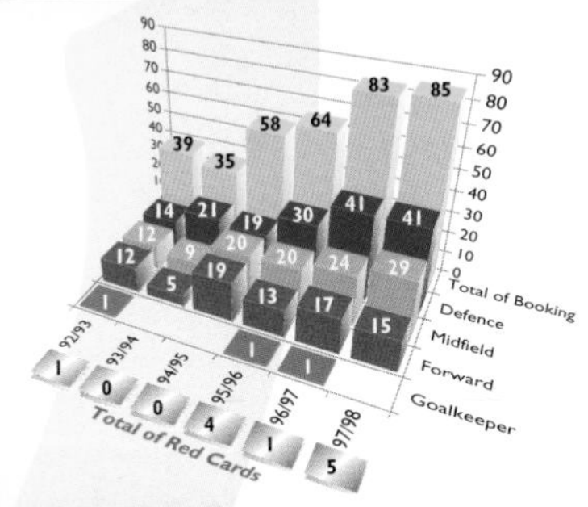

Goals scored by position by month 97/98

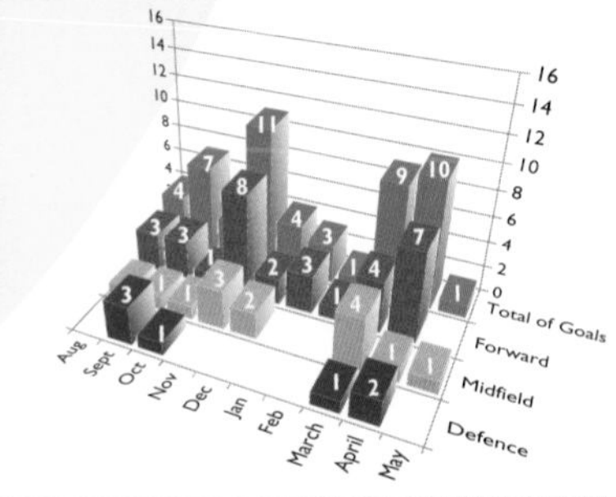

Final league position by season

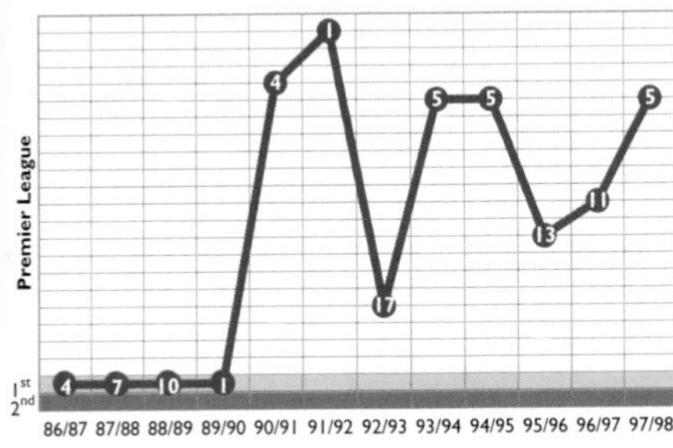

LEEDS UNITED FC

THE CARLING PREMIERSHIP FIXTURE LIST

HOME MATCH
AWAY MATCH
LAST SEASON: WIN
LAST SEASON: DRAW
LAST SEASON: LOSS

Opponent	Date	Last season
MIDDLESBROUGH	15/8	N/A
BLACKBURN	22/8	4-0
WIMBLEDON	29/8	0-1
SOUTHAMPTON	8/9	0-1
EVERTON	12/9	0-2
ASTON VILLA	19/9	1-1
TOTTENHAM	26/9	1-0
LEICESTER	3/10	0-1
NOTTM FOREST	17/10	N/A
CHELSEA	24/10	3-1
DERBY	31/10	5-0
SHEFF WED	7/11	1-2
LIVERPOOL	14/11	1-3
CHARLTON	21/11	N/A
MAN UTD	28/11	0-3
WEST HAM	5/12	3-1
COVENTRY	12/12	3-3
ARSENAL	19/12	1-2
NEWCASTLE	26/12	1-1
WIMBLEDON	28/12	1-1
BLACKBURN	9/1	4-3
MIDDLESBROUGH	16/1	N/A
SOUTHAMPTON	30/1	2-0
NEWCASTLE	6/2	4-1
ASTON VILLA	13/2	0-1
EVERTON	20/2	0-0
LEICESTER	27/2	0-1
TOTTENHAM	6/3	1-0
SHEFF WED	13/3	3-1
DERBY	20/3	4-3
NOTTM FOREST	3/4	N/A
CHELSEA	5/4	0-0
LIVERPOOL	10/4	0-2
CHARLTON	17/4	N/A
MAN UTD	24/4	1-0
WEST HAM	1/5	0-3
ARSENAL	8/5	1-1
COVENTRY	16/5	0-0

HOM®
Sports

THE SQUAD

Goalkeeper · Defender · Midfield · Forward · No of goals · No of clean sheets · No of yellow cards · No of red cards

Player	Position	Goals / Clean sheets	Yellow cards	Red cards
N. Martyn	Goalkeeper	11		
M. Beeney	Goalkeeper			
G. Kelly	Defender		7	1
A. Maybury	Defender		3	
R. Molenaar	Defender	2	4	
G. Halle	Defender	2	5	1
I. Harte	Defender			
D. Wetherall	Defender	3	7	
L. Radebe	Defender		10	1
M. Jackson	Defender			
D. Robertson	Defender		6	
D. Granville	Defender			
J. Blunt	Midfield			
L. Matthews	Midfield			
A. Haaland	Midfield	7	7	1
D. Hopkin	Midfield	1	5	
L. Bowyer	Midfield	3	5	
M. Hiden	Midfield		2	
A. Gray	Midfield			
L. Sharpe	Midfield			
B. Ribeiro	Midfield	3	5	
C. Wijnhard	Forward			
R. Wallace	Forward	10	6	
D. Lilley	Forward	1		
J. Hasselbaink	Forward	16	5	0
H. Kewell	Forward	5	3	1

Transfers after 15 July 1998:

David Pleat: *on the manager*

GEORGE GRAHAM

Gorgeous George has recovered from his enforced absence from the game and has built a thorough group to revive Elland Road hopes of Revie-type glories. A sensible wage structure may preclude him from gaining some of the best talent. His stance on players like Yeboah, Brolin and Palmer can only be admired. A tough, successful, single minded manager who is used to success.

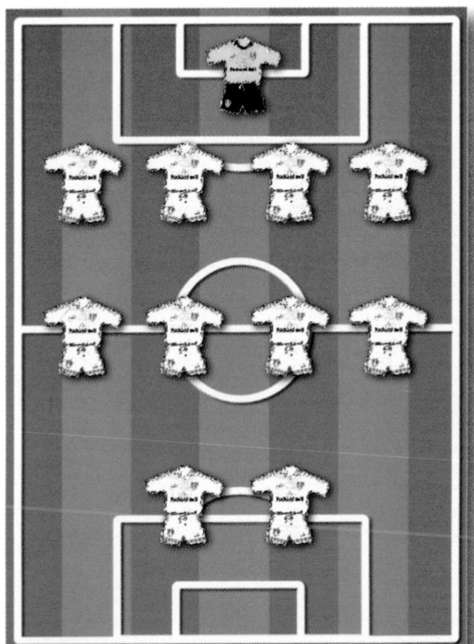

Trevor Brooking: *tactics*

An excellent season which was rewarded by winning a lucrative European place in the UEFA Cup. The foundation of the success was a typically well-organised defensive unit that relied on an effective counter-attacking style. This worked very well on their travels where striker Jimmy Floyd Hasselbaink led the line superbly. He will need more support, especially at home where Leeds are more vulnerable. Harry Kewell should continue to confirm his undoubted promise.

Elland Road is situated two miles south-west of the city centre. There are two car parks adjacent to the ground and some parking is to be found in the Heath Grove vicinity.

DIRECTIONS

From The North:

Approaching on the A1, turn off onto the A58 and continue for 13 miles. Take the A58(M) for a further half mile, turning left onto the A643. Continue across the M621, turning right into Elland Road. The ground is on the right.

From The South:

Approaching from the south on the M1, continue on the M621 until Junction 2, turning left onto the A643. Then as route for the North.

From The West/East:

Approaching on the M621, turn onto the A643 at Junction 2. Then as route for North.

Leeds Railway Station is located in the city centre approximately 2 miles away. Buses operate from Sovereign Street to the ground.

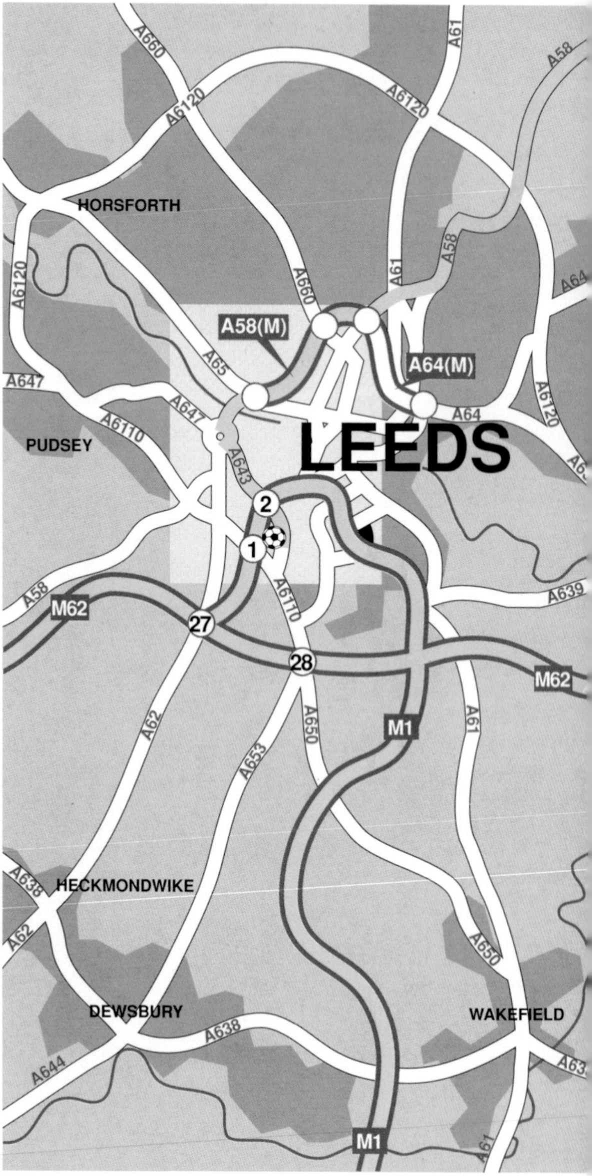

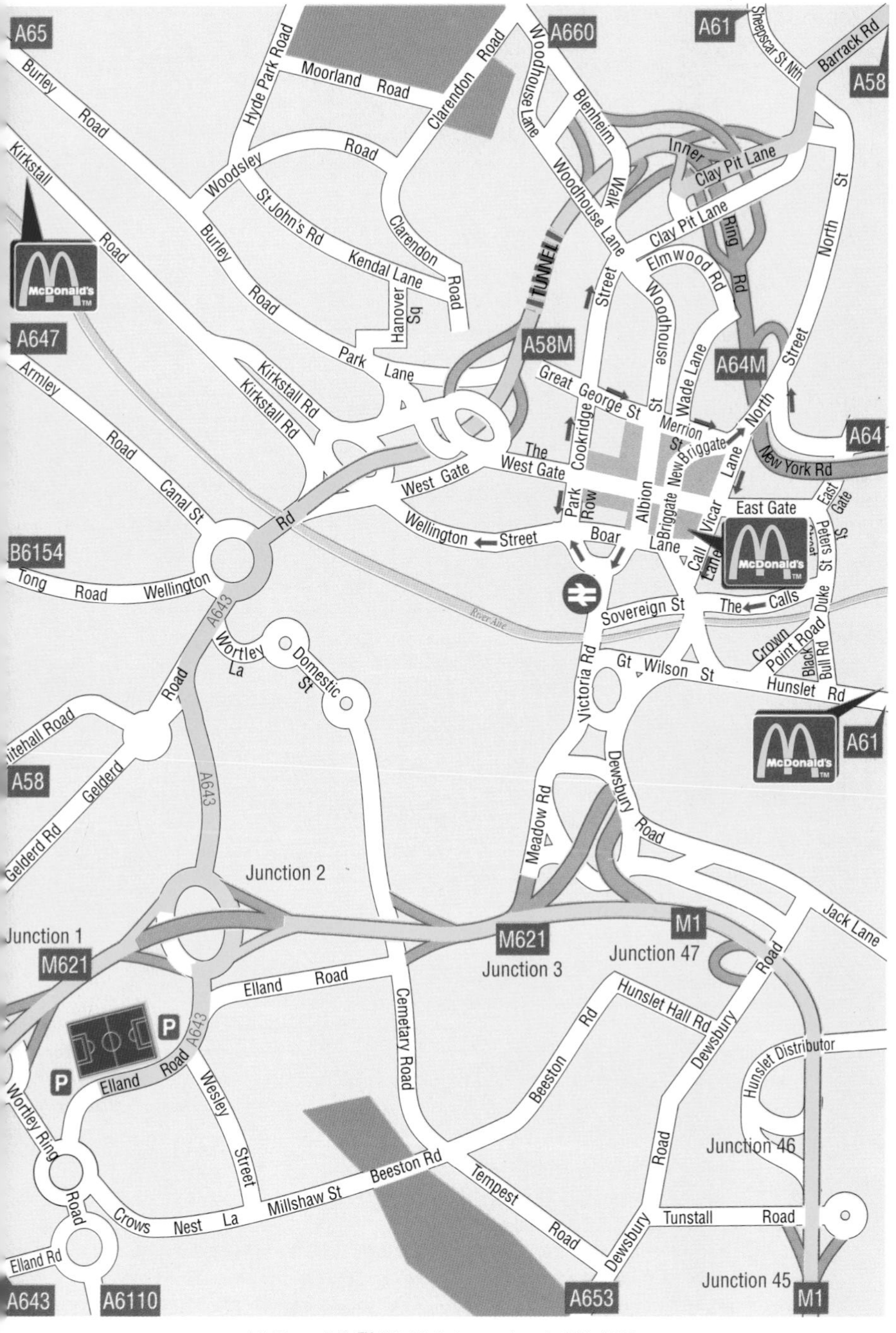

McDonald's™ 33-35 Briggate, Leeds LS1 6HD
McDonald's™ 7 Low Road, Hunslet LS10 1QR
McDonald's™ 1 Cardigan Fields Road, Kirstall

Leicester City FC

Leicester City FC
City Stadium
Filbert Street
Leicester
LE2 7FL

Club No: 0116·291·5000
Fax No: 0116·247·0585
Tickets: 0116·291·5232
Internet: www.lcfc.co.uk

Bobby Robson: *view from abroad*

Defied the odds and gave people a lot of pleasure in their European exploits before falling foul of some indifferent Continental officiating. Martin O'Neill has built a solid base to work from and providing he is backed by the board there is no reason why the Midlands club canno consolidate their position in the top grade. They los only three games at Filbert Street and conceded jus 15 goals and if they could translate that record to their away fixtures who knows where they might go

Bob Harris: *view in England*

Similar to Derby and Nottingham Forest, these three Midland clubs are all in the same bracket, they don't have the vast money coming in from the gates but get by with what they have with sensible buying, selling and wage structures. Martin O'Neill has built a solid base and his decision to stay will give the club, its players and supporters a big lift. They should now consolidate their position in the top league. But the board need to finance O'Neill's transfer wishes.

INFORMATION HOTLINES

ClubCall: 0891·12·11·85*

Calls cost 50p per minute at all times

Club Call, Avalon House, 57-63 Scrutton St, London, EC2A 4PJ

CLUB SHOPS

FOX LEISURE

City Stadium, Filbert Street

Opening Times:

Monday-Friday: 9.00am-5.30pm
Match Saturdays: 9.00am-3.00pm, 4.45pm-6.00pm
Match Sundays: 9.00am-3.00pm, 4.45pm-5.30pm
Match Evenings: 9.00am-7.45pm, 9.30pm-10.00pm

Tel: 0116·291·5253
Fax: 0116·247·0585
Mail Order Tel: 0116·291·5226

FOX LEISURE

28 Churchgate, Leicester LE1 4AJ

Opening Times:

Monday-Fridays: 9.00am-5.30pm
Match Saturdays: 9.00am-5.30pm
Open bank holidays

Tel: 0116·291·5210
Fax: 0116·291·5256
Mail Order Service: 0116·291·5226

BOOKING INFORMATION

General Enquiries:	0116·291·5296
Credit Card Bookings:	0116·291·5232
Travel Club:	0116·291·5007
Tickets (Telesales)	0116·291·5232
Ticketline	0891·12·10·28

CATERING

FOOD

Hot Dogs	£1.95
Burgers	£1.95
Pies	£1.70
Crisps	£0.50
Confectionery	£0.60

BAR

Hot Drinks	£0.90
Cold Drinks	£1.10

MISCELLANEOUS

Stadium Tours
Contact Rhian Bingham - Tel: 0116·291·5131

Corporate Hospitality
Contact Adrian Danes - Tel: 0116·291·5231
Corporate hospitality available from 4-50 people from £90. Sponsorship available from individual players to Stands. Matchball sponsorship for your company, for 8 or more people, starting at £130 per head.

Conference and Banqueting
Contact Amanda Williamson - Tel: 0116·291·5132
Full A La Carte menu available 7 days a week at the Fosse Restaurant, Filbert Street.
Contact Sarah Moire - Tel: 0116·291·5050

Literature
Programme price £2, Bi-monthly Foxes mag £2.50, Reserve team programme 50p

Pre Match & Half Time Entertainment
Leicester City Mascots Filbert Fox, Vicki Vixen & Cousin Dennis. Routines from Leicester City's Cheerleaders F.X.L. Face Painting, Mascot Tours. Half time presentation with Alan Birchenall. Hole in one competitions.

EMILE HESKEY

The 1998 World Cup came round a bit too soon for the 20-year-old Heskey, but his performance for England Under-21s in the Toulon tournament in May suggested he is capable of stepping up to full international level in the next year or two. Heskey's powerful physique and direct style will be a fundamental factor in Leicester's attempt to finish in a respectable position for the third year running. If he can add consistency to his game, personal progress will follow.

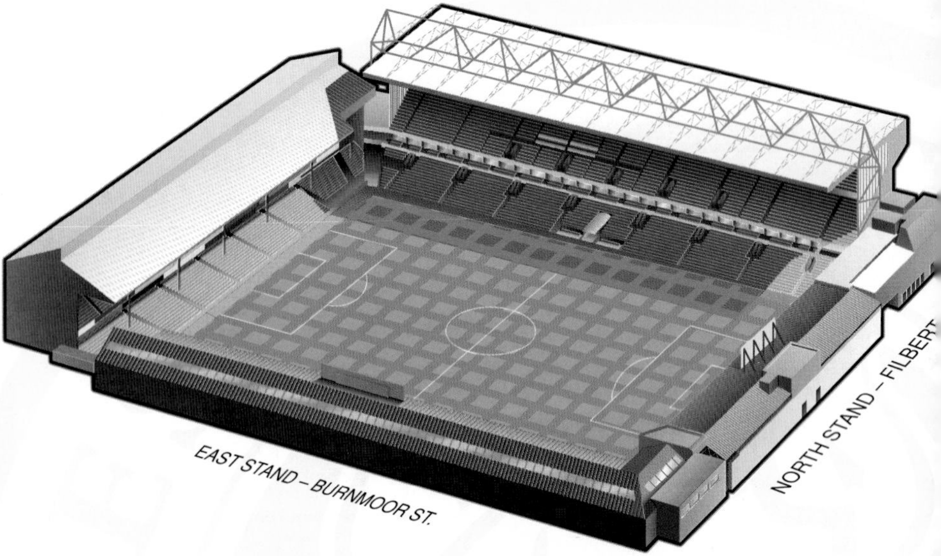

EAST STAND – BURNMOOR ST.

NORTH STAND – FILBERT

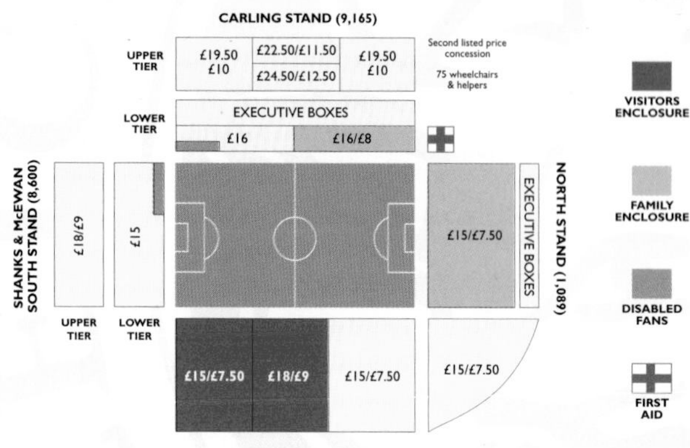

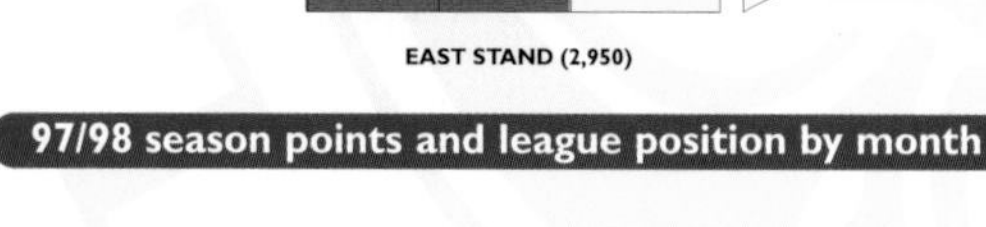

97/98 season points and league position by month

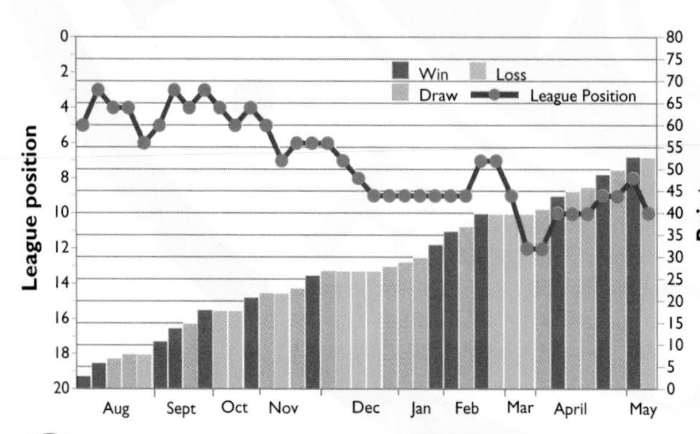

Goals for and against seasons 92/3 to 97/8

Goals scored by position by season

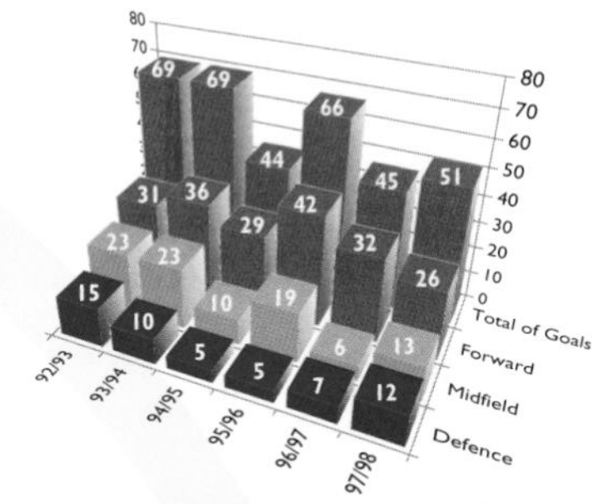

Bookings by position by season

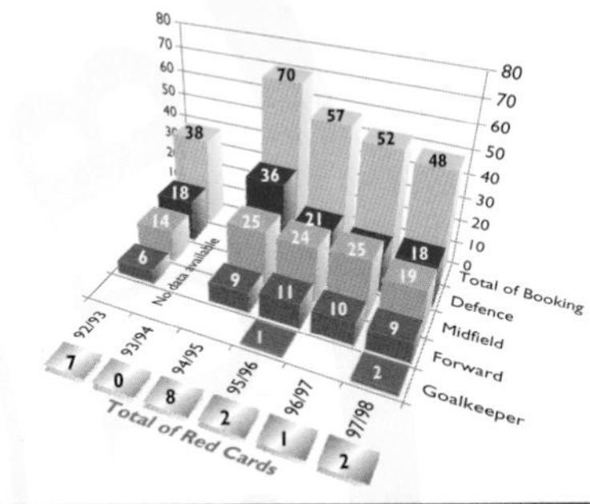

Goals scored by position by month 97/98

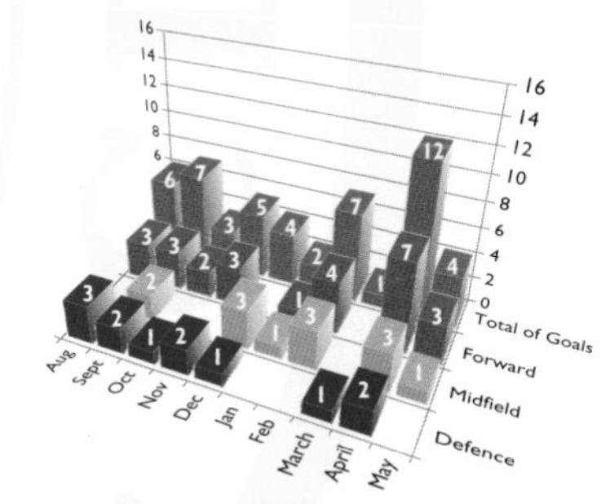

Final league position by season

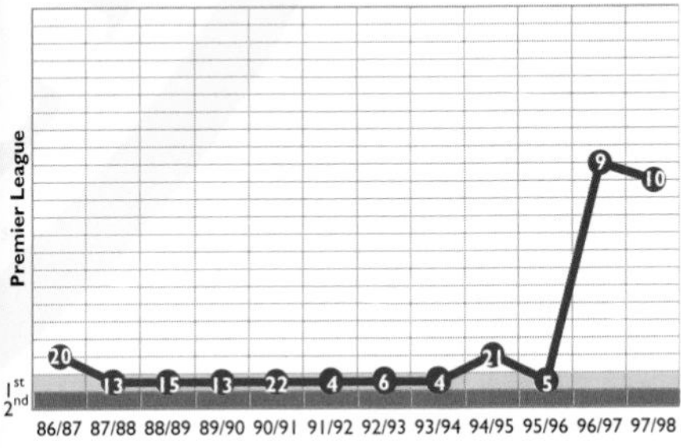

THE CARLING PREMIERSHIP FIXTURE LIST

HOME MATCH
AWAY MATCH
LAST SEASON: WIN
LAST SEASON: DRAW
LAST SEASON: LOSS

Opponent	Date	Last season
MAN UTD	15/8	1-0
EVERTON	22/8	0-1
BLACKBURN	29/8	3-5
MIDDLESBROUGH	9/9	N/A
ARSENAL	12/9	3-3
DERBY	19/9	4-0
WIMBLEDON	27/9	0-1
LEEDS	3/10	1-0
TOTTENHAM	19/10	3-0
ASTON VILLA	24/10	1-1
LIVERPOOL	31/10	0-0
CHARLTON	7/11	N/A
WEST HAM	14/11	3-4
CHELSEA	21/11	2-0
COVENTRY	28/11	2-0
SOUTHAMPTON	5/12	3-3
NOTTM FOREST	12/12	N/A
NEWCASTLE	19/12	3-3
SHEFF WED	26/12	0-1
BLACKBURN	28/12	1-1
EVERTON	9/1	1-1
MAN UTD	16/1	0-0
MIDDLESBROUGH	30/1	N/A
SHEFF WED	6/2	1-1
DERBY	13/2	1-2
ARSENAL	20/2	1-2
LEEDS	27/2	1-0
WIMBLEDON	6/3	1-2
CHARLTON	13/3	N/A
LIVERPOOL	20/3	2-1
TOTTENHAM	3/4	1-1
ASTON VILLA	6/4	1-0
WEST HAM	10/4	2-1
CHELSEA	17/4	0-1
COVENTRY	24/4	1-1
SOUTHAMPTON	1/5	1-2
NEWCASTLE	8/5	0-0
NOTTM FOREST	16/5	N/A

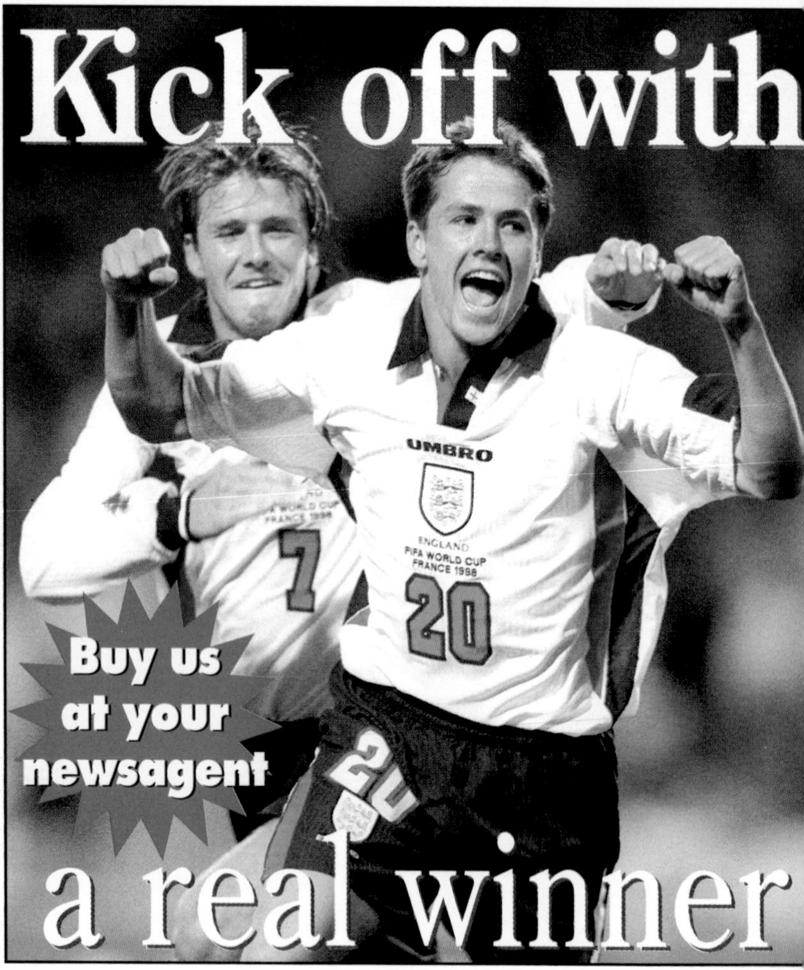

THE SQUAD

Key: Goalkeeper (GK), Defender (D), Midfield (M), Forward (F); No of goals; No of clean sheets; No of yellow cards; No of red cards

Player	Position	Goals / Clean sheets	Yellow cards	Red cards
K. Keller	Goalkeeper	14 (clean sheets)	2	
P. Arphaxed	Goalkeeper	1 (clean sheets)		
P. Kaamark	Defender		2	
S. Campbell	Defender		1	
M. Elliott	Defender	7	7	
S. Walsh	Defender	3	4	
T. Zagorakis	Defender	1	1	
R. Ullathorne	Defender	1		1
S. Prior	Defender		1	
R. Savage	Midfield	2	4	
S. McMahon	Midfield			
S. Wilson	Midfield	2		
M. Izzet	Midfield	4	5	
S. Taylor	Midfield			
N. Lennon	Midfield	2	6	
G. Parker	Midfield	3	1	
S. Guppy	Midfield	2	4	
E. Heskey	Forward	10	5	1
G. Fenton	Forward	3	1	
I. Marshall	Forward	7	2	
T. Cottee	Forward	4		

Transfers after 15 July 1998:

MARTIN O'NEILL

He has a lyrical bounce in all his work and is the number one passion player amongst the managers on the touchline. He has a wealth of experience and has undertaken the proper apprenticeship to progress quickly up the ladder and now looks to be on an unstoppable ride to manage one of the biggest clubs in the land. Bright and almost too brainy! He has shown that he can cope with conflict.

Trevor Brooking: *tactics*

They have an excellent defensive unit that seems to excel with the three central defenders where Matthew Elliot is a tower of strength. Goals were hard to come by though, and too much responsibility was placed on Emile Heskey to conjure up the required quota, without the necessary support. Their transfer budget appears lower than most other Premiership clubs.

Leicester City play at Filbert Street, south of Leicester City Centre. There is some street parking and a car park off Upperton Road as well as city centre car parks.

DIRECTIONS

From The North:

Exit M1 at Junction 22 heading for Leicester on the A50. Follow Leicester and city centre signs over five roundabouts for 6 miles until junction with Fosse Road North A5125. Turn right onto the A5125 for 1 mile then left onto the A47 King Richards Road. After half a mile turn right into Narborough Road North A46. After half a mile turn left onto Upperton Road, crossing the river and taking the first right for Filbert Street.

From The South:

Exit M1 at Junction 21 and head for Leicester on the A46. After half a mile take the second exit at the roundabout staying on the A46 Narborough Road. After approximately 3 miles, turn right into Upperton Road, crossing the river and taking the first right for Filbert Street.

From The West:

Approaching on the M69, at Junction 21 with the M1, get onto the A46. Then as route for the South.

The main railway station is about one mile from the ground. No buses run directly to the ground so it is about a 20 minute walk.

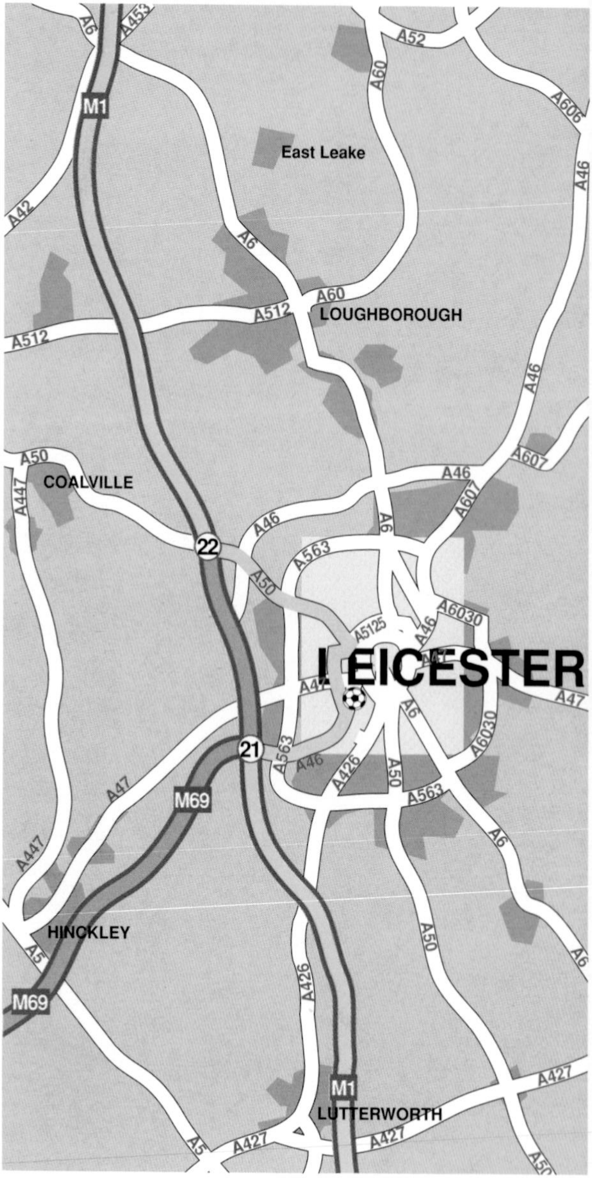

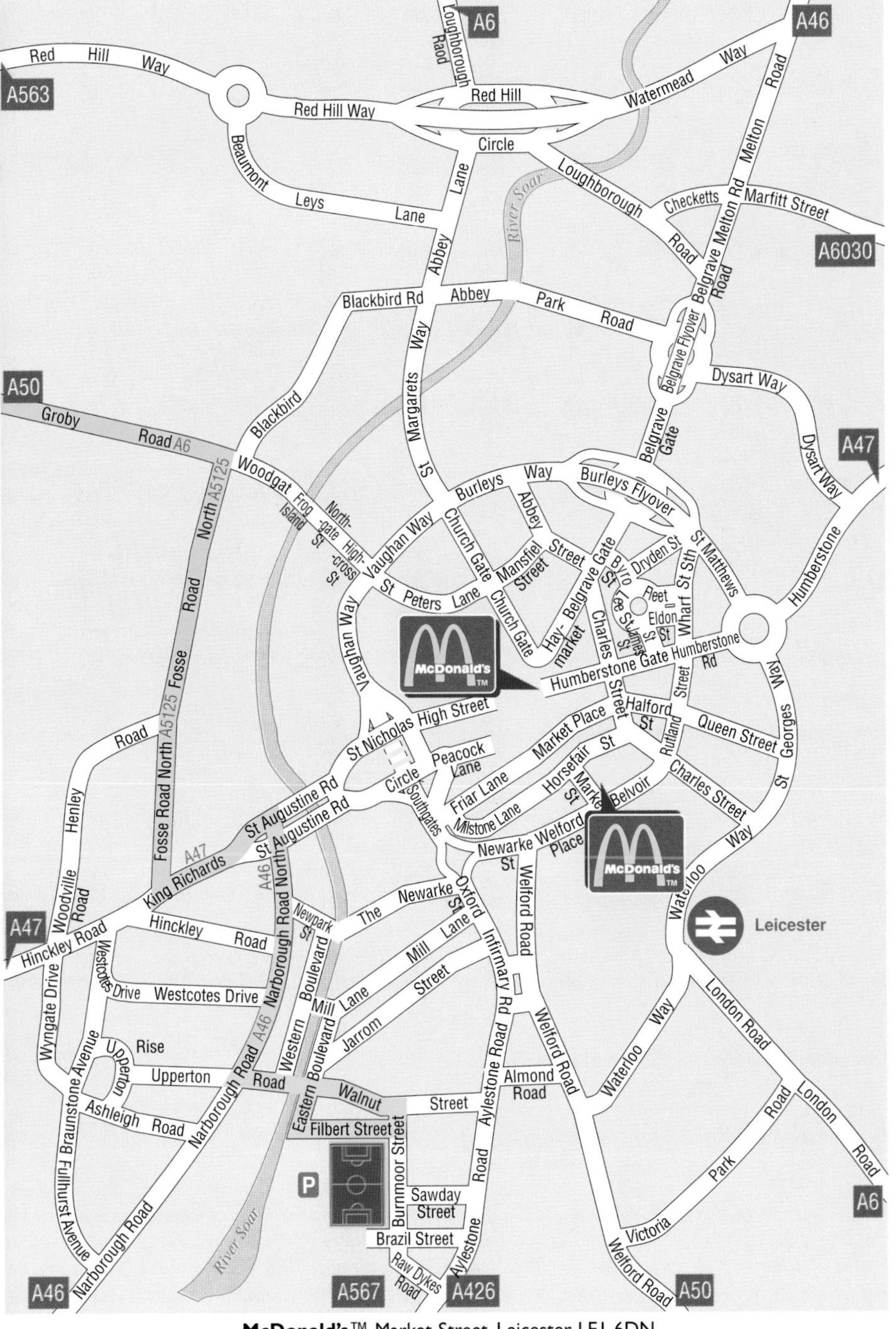

McDonald's™ Market Street, Leicester LE1 6DN
McDonald's™ 6-10 Eastgates, Leicester LE1 4FB

Liverpool FC

Liverpool FC
Anfield Road
Liverpool
L4 0TH

Club No: 0151·263·2361
Fax No: 0151·260·8813
Tickets: 0151·260·8680 (office hours only)

AWAY

HOME

HOME

Bobby Robson: *view from abroad*

One of the greatest clubs in the world and time they were challenging for honours again at home and abroad. They need their usual stability and continuity and long may it remain as one of the most stable clubs in European football. They will be looking for more consistency. On any given day they can beat anybody but on another day anybody can beat them. They will want to remove that tag this season. They have represented England so well over the years in Europe and I hope, with Fowler fit again, they will be challenging the best.

Bob Harris: *view in England*

Third in the table would satisfy most clubs, but not Liverpool, and rightly so. This is not just one of England's big clubs, they are a team feared and respected throughout Europe. That reputation is in danger of being devalued as the wait for a trophy goes on. The quality abounds, the supporters remain enchanted by the club and all it needs is for the side to find a consistency level which has deserted them in recent seasons. They finished 13 points adrift of Champions Arsenal and their priority will be to close that gap. Winning one of the three cups, particularly the UEFA Cup, will be the icing on the cake and with a fit again Fowler, the outstanding Owen plus McManaman and Redknapp who would argue against them?

INFORMATION HOTLINES

ClubCall: 0891·12·11·84*

Calls cost 50p per minute at all times

Club Call, Avalon House, 57-63 Scrutton St, London, EC2A 4PJ

CLUB SHOPS

LIVERPOOL SUPERSTORE

Kop Grandstand

Opening Times:

Monday-Friday: 9.00am-5.00pm
Saturday: 9.00am-4.30pm
Sunday: 10am-4pm
Match Saturdays: 9.00am-45 mins after game
Match Sundays: 9.00am-45 mins after game
Match Evenings: 9.00am-45 mins after game

Tel: 0151·263·1760

Mail Order Service: 0990·532·532

BOOKING INFORMATION

General Enquiries:	0151·260·8680
Credit Card Bookings:	0151·263·5727
Recorded Info:	0151·260·9999
Travel Club	0151·260·8680

CATERING

FOOD

Pies	£1.30
Pasties	£1.30
Ham Batch	£1.30
Hot Dogs	£2.00
Cheese & Onion Batch	£1.30
Sausage Rolls	£1.10
Crisps	£0.50
Chocolate	£0.40
Eccles Cake	£0.80

BAR

Lager	£1.80
Bitter	£1.80
Soft Drinks	£1.30
Tea, Coffee	£1.00

MISCELLANEOUS

International Supporters Club
0151·261·1444
Museum & Stadium Tours
Call 0151·260·6677 for details
Corporate Hospitality
Contact Jim Kennefick - Tel: 0151·263·9199
A range of hospitality packages are available.
Sales Conferences and Banqueting:
Contact Philip Crowther - Tel: 0151·263·7744
Literature
Programme price £2.00, Official Magazine £2.50
Pre Match & Half Time Entertainment
DJ's playing the latest chart music over the Tannoys

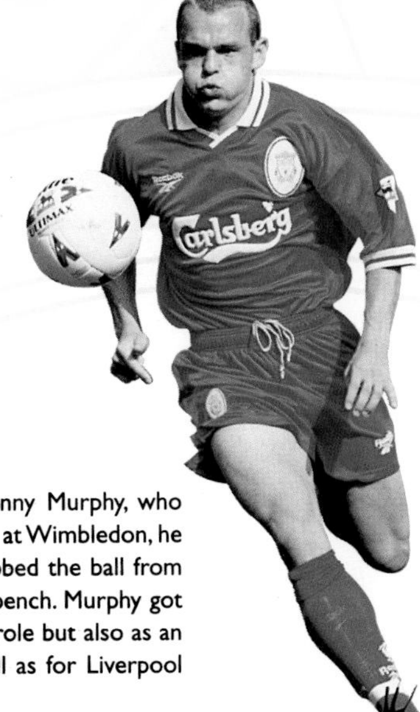

DANNY MURPHY

It was a frustrating first season at Anfield for 21-year-old Danny Murphy, who arrived last summer from Crewe. On the first day of the season at Wimbledon, he was about to volunteer for a penalty when Michael Owen grabbed the ball from him, and what followed was a regular place on the substitutes bench. Murphy got his chance late in the season, not only in his preferred midfield role but also as an emergency striker. This will be a critical season for him, as well as for Liverpool themselves.

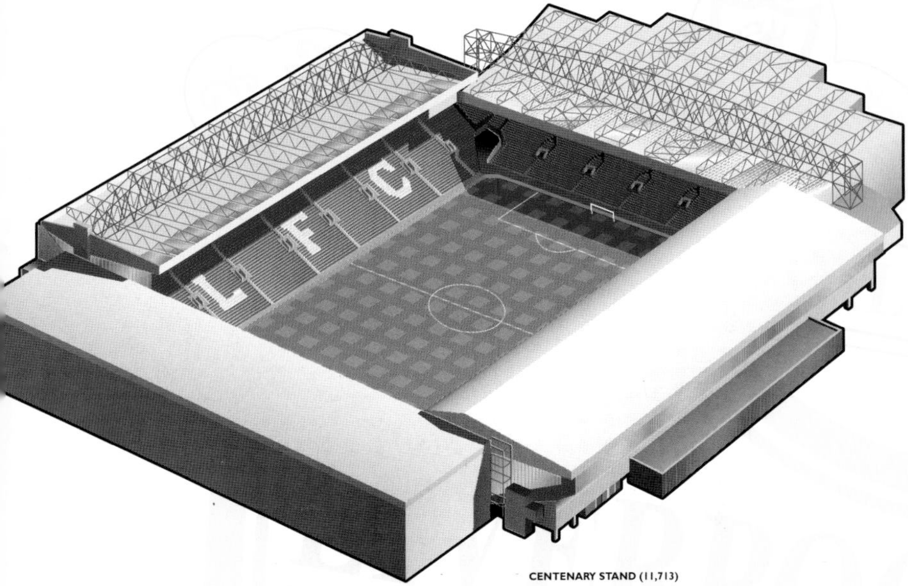

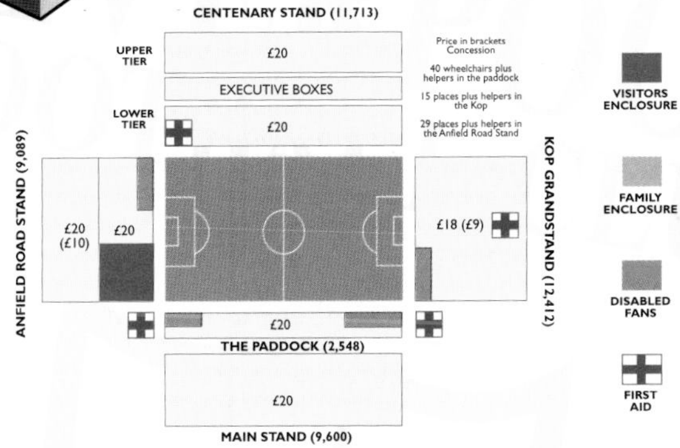

CENTENARY STAND (11,713)
UPPER TIER
£20
EXECUTIVE BOXES
LOWER TIER
£20
Price in brackets Concession
40 wheelchairs plus helpers in the paddock
15 places plus helpers in the Kop
29 places plus helpers in the Anfield Road Stand
ANFIELD ROAD STAND (9,089)
£20 (£10)
£20
KOP GRANDSTAND (12,412)
£18 (£9)
£20
THE PADDOCK (2,548)
£20
MAIN STAND (9,600)
VISITORS ENCLOSURE
FAMILY ENCLOSURE
DISABLED FANS
FIRST AID

97/98 season points and league position by month

Win
Loss
Draw
League Position
Points
80
75
70
65
60
55
50
45
40
35
30
25
20
15
10
5
0
Aug
Sept
Oct
Nov
Dec
Jan
Feb
March
April
May

Goals for and against seasons 92/3 to 97/8

Total Goals
Home
Away
386
238
148
158
102
260
For
Against

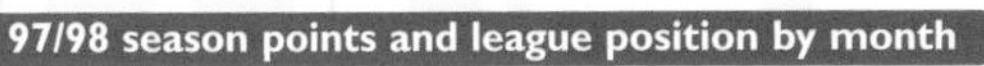

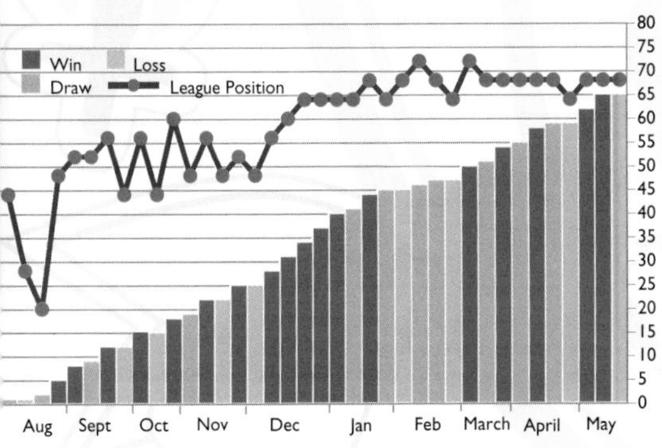

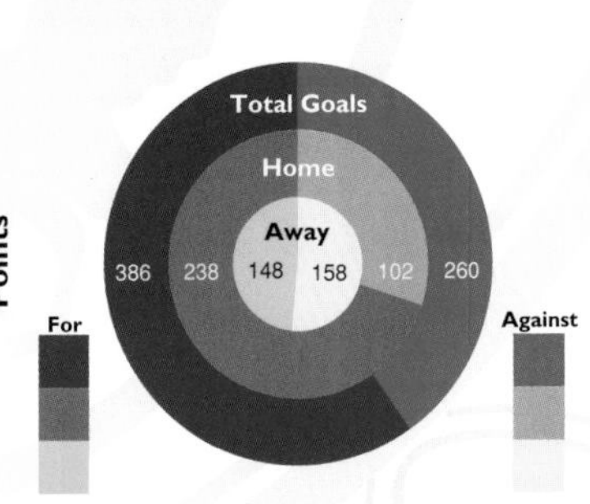

Goals scored by position by season

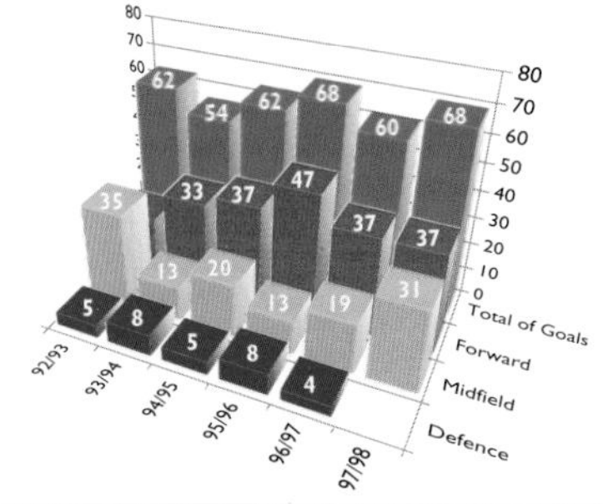

Bookings by position by season

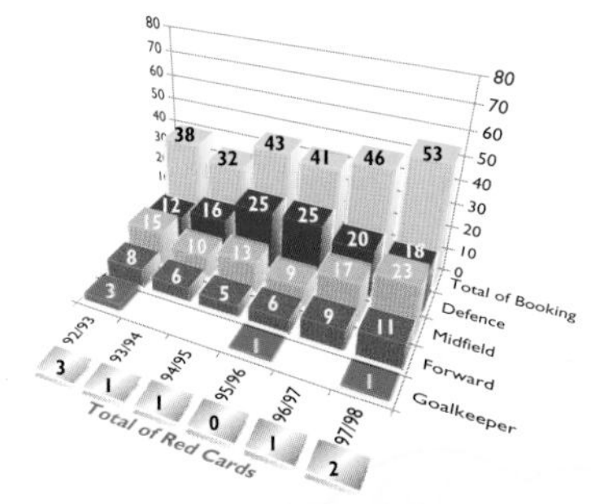

Goals scored by position by month 97/98

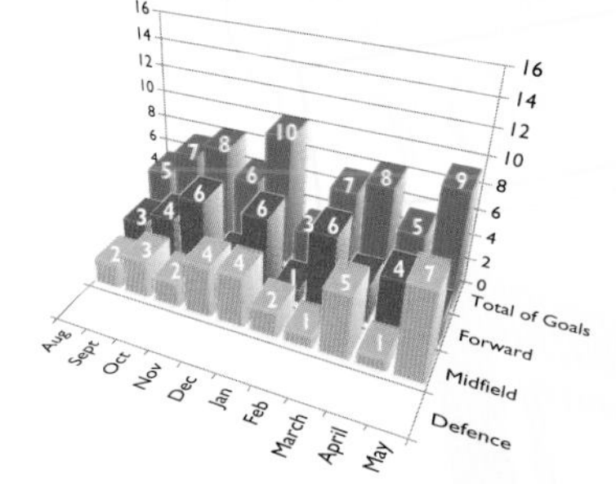

Final league position by season

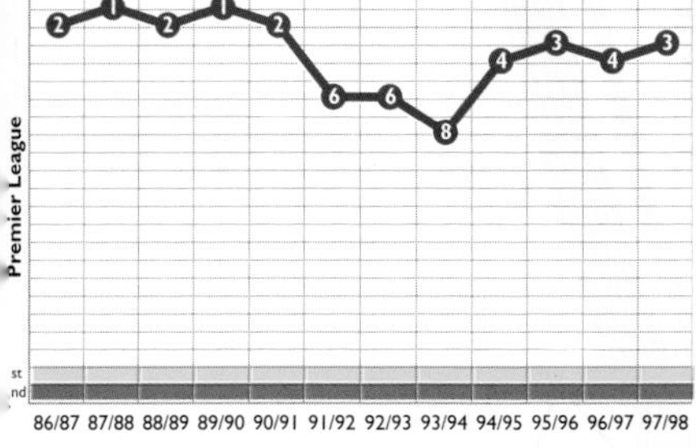

THE CARLING PREMIERSHIP FIXTURE LIST

HOME MATCH
AWAY MATCH
LAST SEASON: WIN
LAST SEASON: DRAW
LAST SEASON: LOSS

Opponent	Date	Last season
SOUTHAMPTON	16/8	1-1
ARSENAL	22/8	4-0
NEWCASTLE	30/8	2-1
COVENTRY	9/9	1-0
WEST HAM	12/9	1-2
CHARLTON	19/9	N/A
MAN UTD	26/9	1-1
CHELSEA	4/10	4-2
EVERTON	17/10	0-2
NOTTM FOREST	24/10	N/A
LEICESTER	31/10	0-0
DERBY	7/11	4-0
LEEDS	14/11	3-1
ASTON VILLA	21/11	1-2
BLACKBURN	29/11	0-0
TOTTENHAM	5/12	3-3
WIMBLEDON	13/12	1-1
SHEFF WED	19/12	2-1
MIDDLESBROUGH	26/12	N/A
NEWCASTLE	28/12	1-0
ARSENAL	9/1	1-0
SOUTHAMPTON	16/1	2-3
COVENTRY	30/1	1-1
MIDDLESBROUGH	6/2	N/A
CHARLTON	13/2	N/A
WEST HAM	20/2	5-0
CHELSEA	27/2	1-4
MAN UTD	6/3	1-3
DERBY	13/3	0-1
LEICESTER	20/3	1-2
EVERTON	3/4	1-1
NOTTM FOREST	5/4	N/A
LEEDS	10/4	2-0
ASTON VILLA	17/4	3-0
BLACKBURN	24/4	1-1
TOTTENHAM	1/5	4-0
SHEFF WED	8/5	3-3
WIMBLEDON	16/5	2-0

IF YOU EVER WANTED TO KNOW THE RESULT?

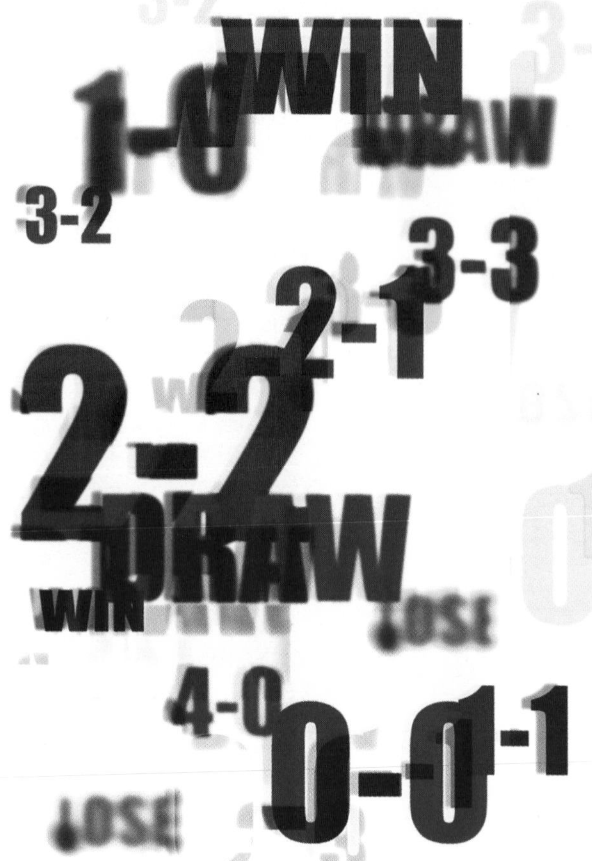

THE SQUAD

Goalkeeper · Defender · Midfield · Forward · No of goals · No of clean sheets · No of yellow cards · No of red cards

Player	Position	Goals / Clean sheets	Yellow cards	Red cards
D. James	Goalkeeper	11 (clean sheets)	1	
B. Friedel	Goalkeeper	1 (clean sheets)		
T. Warner	Goalkeeper			
R. Jones	Defender		1	
. McAteer	Defender	2	3	
M. Wright	Defender			
N. Ruddock	Defender			
D. Matteo	Defender		3	
P. Babb	Defender		4	
. Carragher	Defender		3	
B. Kvarme	Defender		4	
S. Bjornebye	Defender		2	
S. Harkness	Defender		4	
D. Staunton	Defender			
S. McManaman	Midfield	11	1	
. Cassidy	Midfield			
. Redknapp	Midfield	3	3	
M. Thomas	Midfield	1	3	
P. Ince	Midfield	8	8	
D. Murphy	Midfield		1	
O. Leonhardsen	Midfield	6	2	
D. Thompson	Midfield	1	1	
P. Berger	Midfield	3		
M. Owen	Forward	18	2	1
K. Riedle	Forward	6	1	
S. Dundee	Forward			
R. Fowler	Forward	9	2	1

Transfers after 15 July 1998:

David Pleat: *on the manager*

ROY EVANS

A genuine, likeable, solid and steady man but he knows better than anyone else does the need to start winning trophies again at Anfield. The pressure will rarely be absent. He will be looking for that all important good start, not just for the team but for himself. It would make the season a whole lot easier for everyone.

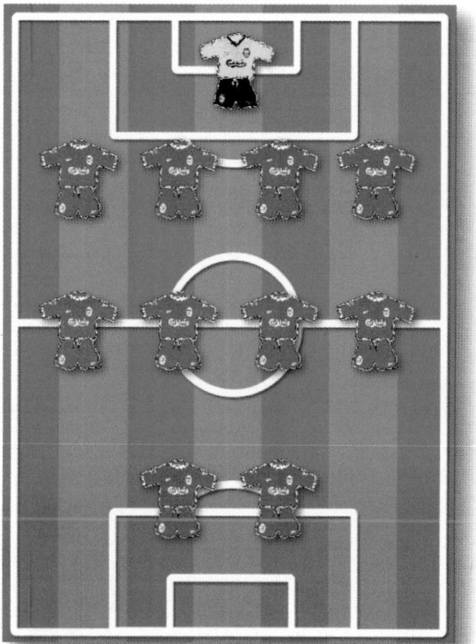

Trevor Brooking: *tactics*

When will they sustain a Premiership challenge? Not until they can defend far more consistently, and improve their obvious weakness on crosses. Switched from three central defenders to a flat back four halfway through last season, but still gave too many soft goals away. Michael Owen will certainly build on a quite superb first season, but the midfield department needs to improve their goal tally.

Liverpool's Anfield Road ground is situated two miles north of Liverpool City Centre, close to Stanley Park. There is a sizeable car park by the Sports Centre in the park.

DIRECTIONS

From the North:

Approaching on the M6, exit at Junction 26 onto the M58 and continue until the end. At Junction 7 turn left onto the A59 Ormskirk Road. Continue on this road as it becomes Rice Lane, and cross over the roundabout into County Road. After 1/4 mile turn left into Everton Valley and then right into Anfield Road. The ground is on the right.

From the South:

Approaching on the M6, exit at Junction 21a onto the M62. Exit the M62 at Junction 4 and get onto the A5080. At the junction with the A5058 turn right and continue along this road as it becomes Queens Drive. Continue to the junction with Walton Hall Avenue and turn left onto the A580 Walton Lane. Turn left into Anfield Road and the ground is on the right.

From the East:

Approaching on the M62 exit at Junction 4 and get onto the A5058. Then as route for the South.

Lime Street Railway Station is in the town centre, 2 miles from Anfield. Kirkdale Railway Station is 30 minutes walk from the ground.

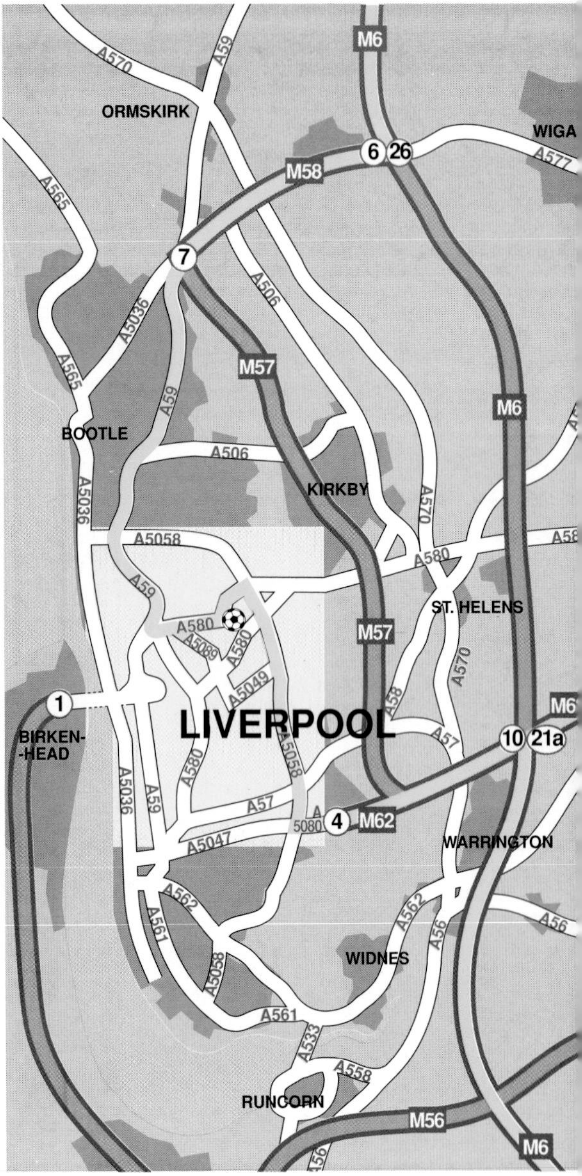

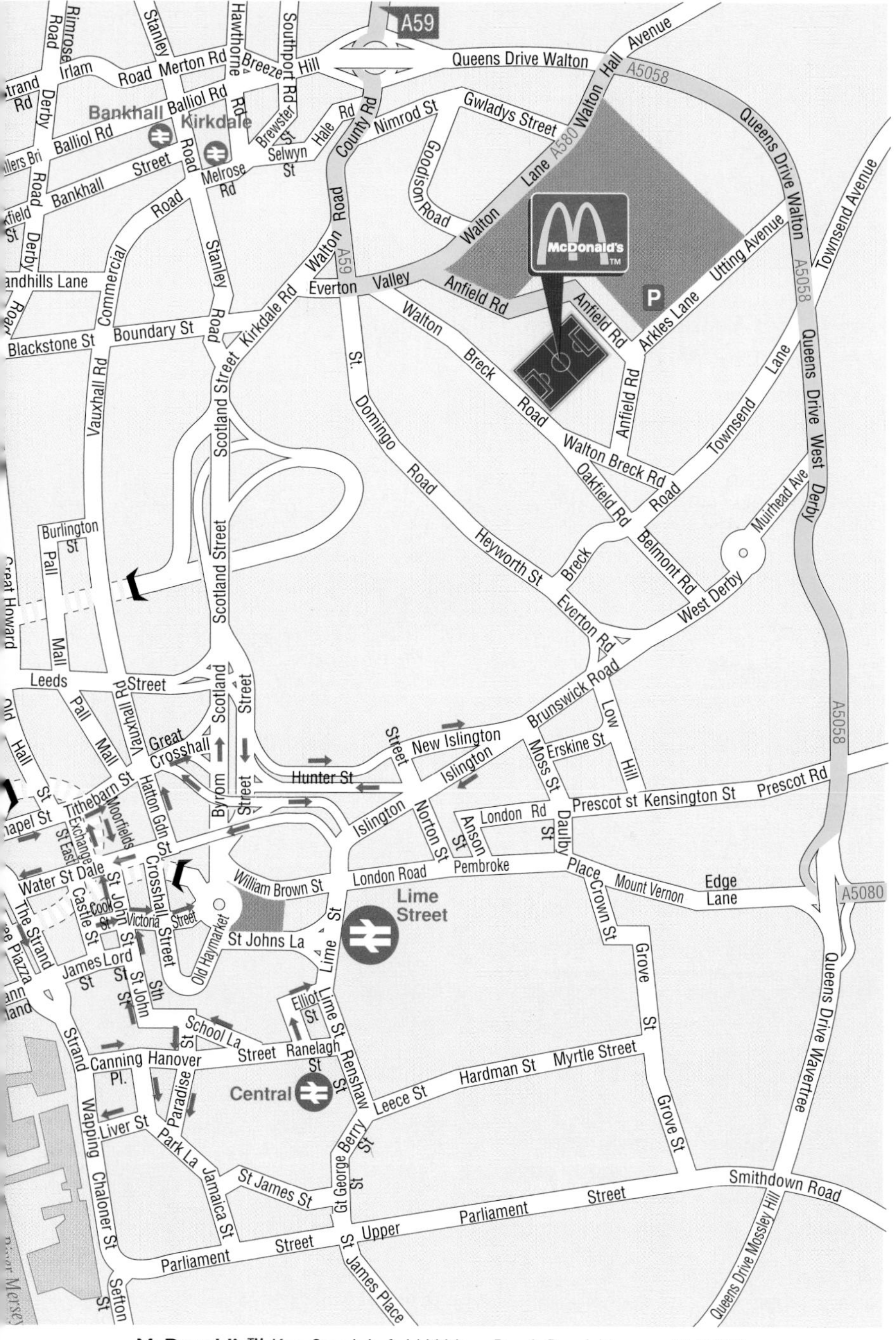

McDonald's™ Kop Stand, Anfield, Walton Breck Road, Liverpool L4 0UP

Manchester United FC

Manchester United FC
Sir Matt Busby Way
Old Trafford
Manchester M16 0RA

Club Number: 0161·872·1661
Fax Number: 0161·876·5502
Internet: www.manutd.com

Bobby Robson: *view from abroad*

My favourites to win it again because they will be angry, bitter and sick at the way they won nothing last season after promising so much. Alex Ferguson can afford to replace any weak links, following up the purchase of Jaap Stam. They will be looking to take the Premiership and to make a rea impact on the Champions League at the expense o the two cups. They need to look at themselves i Europe after their failure to puncture Monaco' defence.

Bob Harris: *view in England*

The odds were long for Alex Ferguson and his team to finish without a trophy. They will be even longer this season. For once they are the hunters and not the hunted. You can be certain that they will not, this time, take their eye off the Premiership while seeking European glory in the Champions League. The two went hand in hand at the start of the season and collapsed at the same time. They will take heart from the fact that they scored more goals and conceded fewer than Arsenal. Nothing less will satisfy Stam and company this season than reclaiming the crown from Premiership champions Arsenal.

INFORMATION HOTLINES

ClubCall: 0891·12·11·61*

**Calls cost 50p per minute at all times*
Club Call, Avalon House, 57-63 Scrutton St, London, EC2A 4PJ

BOOKING INFORMATION

General Enquiries:	0161·872·1661
Club General Enquiries:	0161·930·1968
Travel Club:	0161·872·5208
Recorded Info:	0161·872·0199

CLUB SHOPS

MEGASTORE

21-26 United Road, Old Trafford

Opening Times:

Monday-Saturday: 10.00am-6.00pm
Match Saturdays: 9.00am-6.00pm
Sundays: 10.00am-4.00pm
Match Evenings: 9.00am-10.30pm

Tel: 0161·848·8181
Fax: 0161·877·1066
Mail Order Service: 0161·877·9777

SUPERSTORE

Sir Matt Busby Way

Opening Times:

Monday-Saturday: 9.00am-5.00pm
Match Saturdays: 9.00am-6.00pm
Match Sundays: 10.00am-7.00pm
Match Evenings: 9.00am-10.30pm

Tel: 0161·848·8181
Mail Order Service: 0161·877·9777

CATERING

FOOD

Pies	£1.30
Pasties	£1.30
Cheeseburger	£1.80
M&M's (Large)	£1.80
Chocolate Bar	£0.60

BAR

Lager	£2.10
Bitter	£2.10
Soft Drinks	£1.60
Juice	£0.50
Coffee/Tea/Bovril	£1.00

MISCELLANEOUS

Stadium Tours
Museum & Tour Centre - Tel: 0161·877·4002
Corporate Hospitality
Contact Commercial Department - Tel: 0161·872·3488
Conference/Banqueting - Tel: 0161·872·3331/7722
Club Restaurants
Manchester United Catering
Tel: 0161·872·3331. Fax: 0161·876·0166
Red Cafe - Manchester United themed video restaurant. In North Stand. Opening Times Mon-Sun 9am-10pm Match Saturdays: After match. Match Evenings: Until 10.00pm
Tel: 0161·930·2930. Fax: 0161·876·0166
Literature
Programme price £1.80
Pre Match & Half Time Entertainment
Manchester United's own radio station broadcasts direct from Old Trafford every match-day. Programmes include full match commentary, team interviews, music etc. 1413am.

JAAP STAM

All eyes will be focused on Alex Ferguson's £10.75 million capture from PSV Eindhoven - a deal completed before Stam went to the World Cup with Holland. He will underpin a United defence which has lacked a certain authority since the departure of Steve Bruce. But Stam is far more than an inspirational stopper. He has the flair to bring the ball across the halfway line and stimulate the attack, to make goals as well as score them. His influence will help determine whether United regain their championship crown.

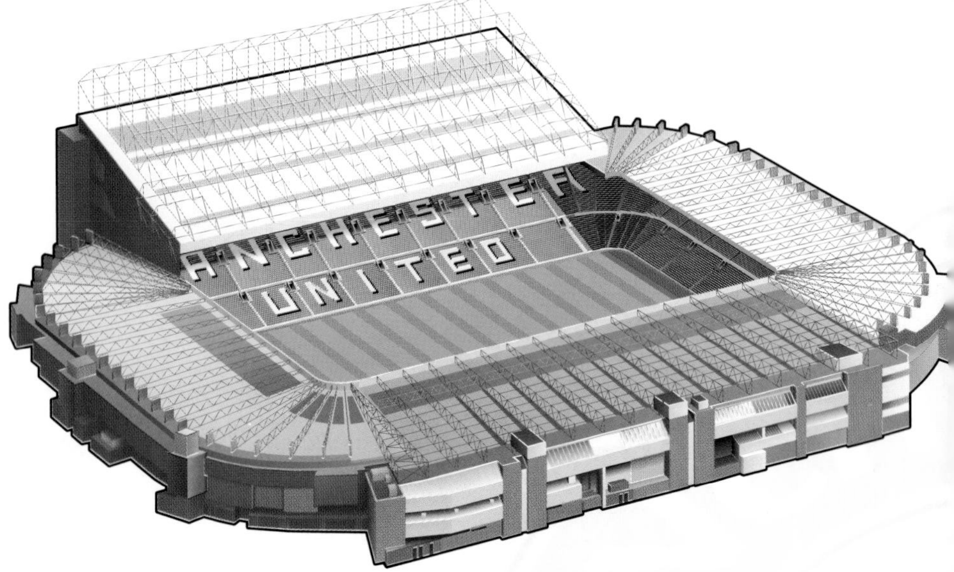

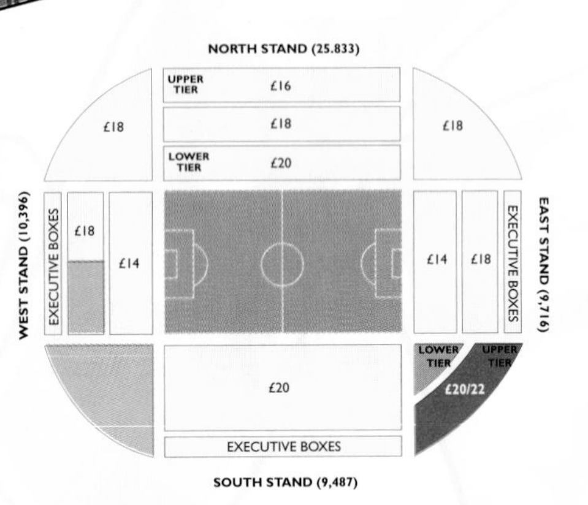

97/98 season points and league position by month

Goals for and against seasons 92/3 to 97/8

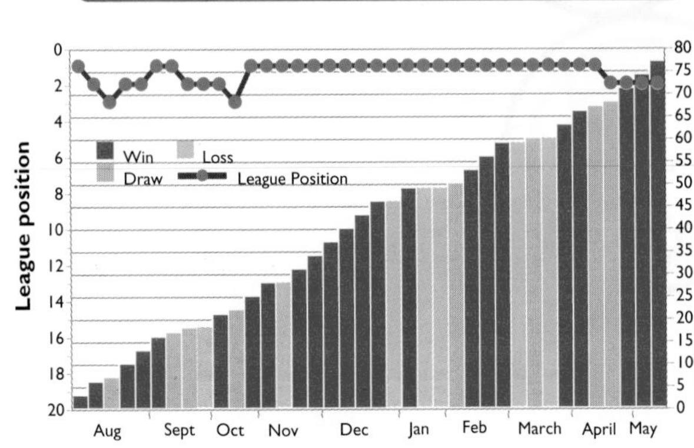

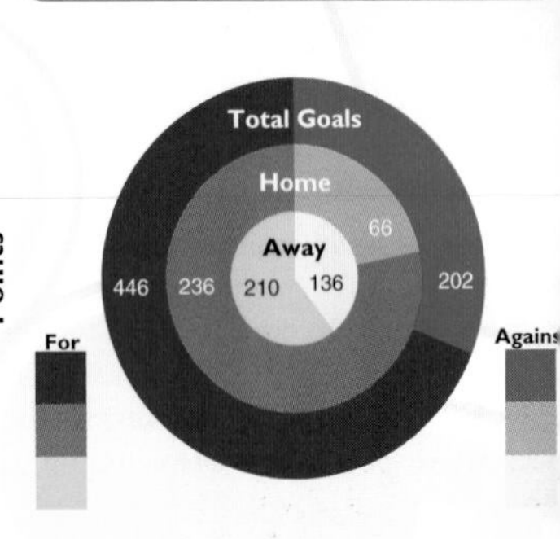

Goals scored by position by season

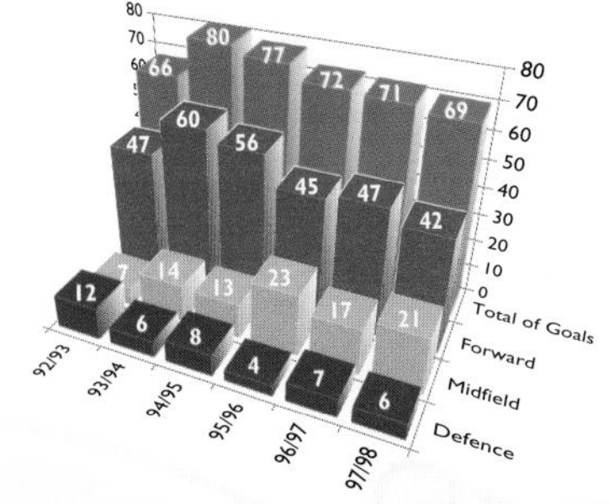

Bookings by position by season

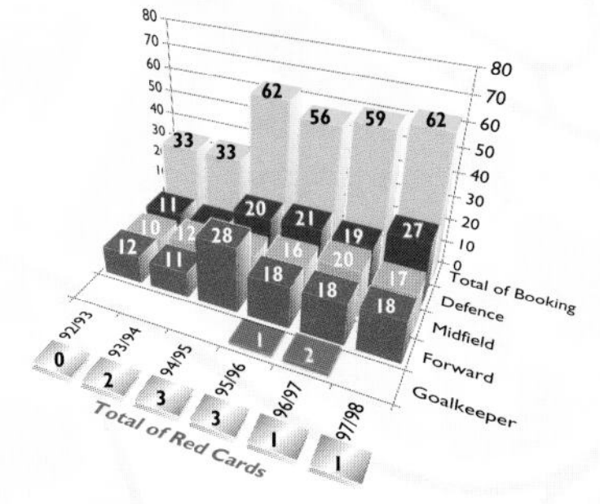

Goals scored by position by month 97/98

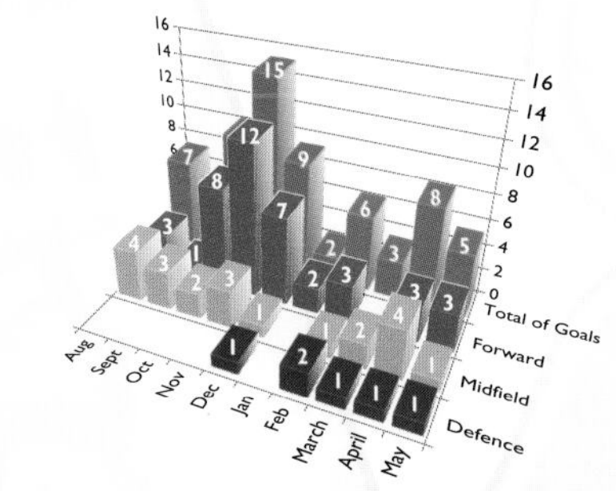

Final league position by season

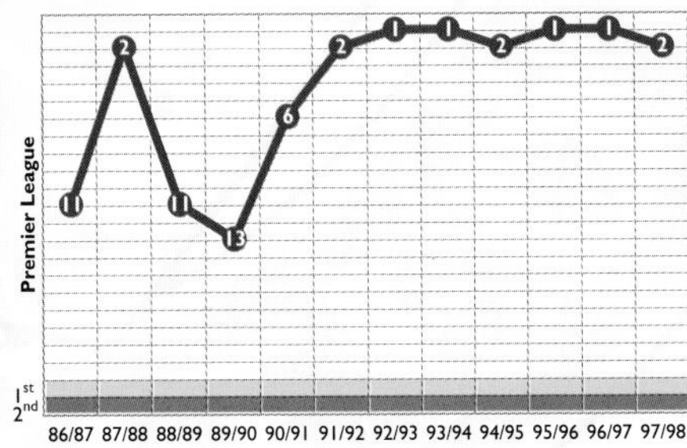

THE CARLING PREMIERSHIP FIXTURE LIST

HOME MATCH
AWAY MATCH
LAST SEASON: WIN
LAST SEASON: DRAW
LAST SEASON: LOSS

Opponent	Date	Last season
LEICESTER	15/8	0-1
WEST HAM	22/8	1-1
CHARLTON	8/9	N/A
COVENTRY	12/9	3-0
ARSENAL	19/9	2-3
CHELSEA	23/9	2-2
LIVERPOOL	26/9	1-1
SOUTHAMPTON	3/10	0-1
WIMBLEDON	17/10	2-0
DERBY	24/10	2-2
EVERTON	31/10	2-0
NEWCASTLE	7/11	1-1
BLACKBURN	14/11	4-0
SHEFF WED	21/11	0-2
LEEDS	28/11	3-0
ASTON VILLA	5/12	2-0
TOTTENHAM	12/12	2-0
MIDDLESBROUGH	19/12	N/A
NOTTM FOREST	26/12	N/A
CHELSEA	28/12	1-0
WEST HAM	9/1	2-1
LEICESTER	16/1	0-0
CHARLTON	30/1	N/A
NOTTM FOREST	6/2	N/A
ARSENAL	13/2	0-1
COVENTRY	20/2	2-3
SOUTHAMPTON	27/2	1-0
LIVERPOOL	6/3	3-1
NEWCASTLE	13/3	1-0
EVERTON	20/3	2-0
WIMBLEDON	3/4	5-2
DERBY	5/4	2-0
BLACKBURN	10/4	3-1
SHEFF WED	14/4	6-1
LEEDS	24/4	0-1
ASTON VILLA	1/5	1-0
MIDDLESBROUGH	8/5	N/A
TOTTENHAM	16/5	2-0

MANCHESTER UNITED FC

THE SQUAD

Goalkeeper · Defender · Midfield · Forward · No of goals · No of clean sheets · No of yellow cards · No of red cards

Player	Position	Goals / Clean sheets	Yellow cards	Red cards
P. Schmeichel	Goalkeeper	10		
R. Van Der Gouw	Goalkeeper	3		
G. Neville	Defender		2	
J. Curtis	Defender			
J. Stam	Defender			
D. May	Defender		3	
H. Berg	Defender	1	3	
C. Casper	Defender			
R. Johnsen	Defender	2	2	
R. Wallwork	Defender			
D. Irwin	Defender	2	3	
P. Neville	Defender	1	8	
M. Clegg	Defender			
D. Beckham	Midfield	9	6	
T. Cooke	Midfield			
R. Keane	Midfield	2	2	
N. Butt	Midfield	3	7	
J. Cruyff	Midfield		1	
R. Giggs	Midfield	8	1	
T. Sheringham	Forward	9	3	
A. Cole	Forward	16	5	
E. Nevland	Forward			
O. Solskjaer	Forward	6		1
P. Scholes	Forward	8	8	

Transfers after 15 July 1998:

David Pleat: *on the manager*

ALEX FERGUSON

He will be hurt by the way United were eased out of Europe and then displaced in the final furlong in the Premiership. With Jaap Stam brought in to control the defence allied to the unique talents of his youngsters, Alex is sure to be celebrating at least one trophy this coming season. He is a brainy, shrewd and sometimes dictatorial manager, but in a diplomatic way. He is a fighter for lesser colleagues' causes.

Trevor Brooking: *tactics*

One of the few clubs that have never varied their 4-4-2 system, and why should they when it has proved so effective for them? Up until Christmas last year it appeared they were unstoppable, but then injuries surfaced, and too many players had a dip in form at the same time. The arrival of Dutch defender Jaap Stam should prove interesting, and the need for additional cover down the left flank was another weakness last season. Whenever Ryan Giggs was unavailable the balance of the team was never as good without a naturally left-footed replacement.

Manchester United play at Old Trafford, two miles south-west of Manchester city centre. Parking is available at several paying car parks in the immediate vicinity of the ground.

DIRECTIONS

From The North:
Approaching on the M61, at Junction 1 continue onto the M602 and keep on this road for 4 miles. At Junction 3 turn right onto Trafford Road and after one mile turn right again into Trafford Park Road. Sir Matt Busby Way and Old Trafford are on the left.

From The South:
Take the M6 to Junction 19, turning onto the A556 Stockport Road which becomes the A56 at Altrincham. This becomes the Chester Road. After 9 miles, turn left onto the the A5063 Trafford Road, left onto the A5081 Trafford Park Road and left again into Sir Matt Busby Way. Old Trafford is on the right.

From The West:
Approaching on the M62, at Junction 12 continue on the M602, keeping to this road for 4 miles. Then as route for North.

From The East:
Get onto the M63 and at Junction 7 turn onto the A556. Then as route for South.

The nearest Metrolink stations are Old Trafford and Trafford Bar.

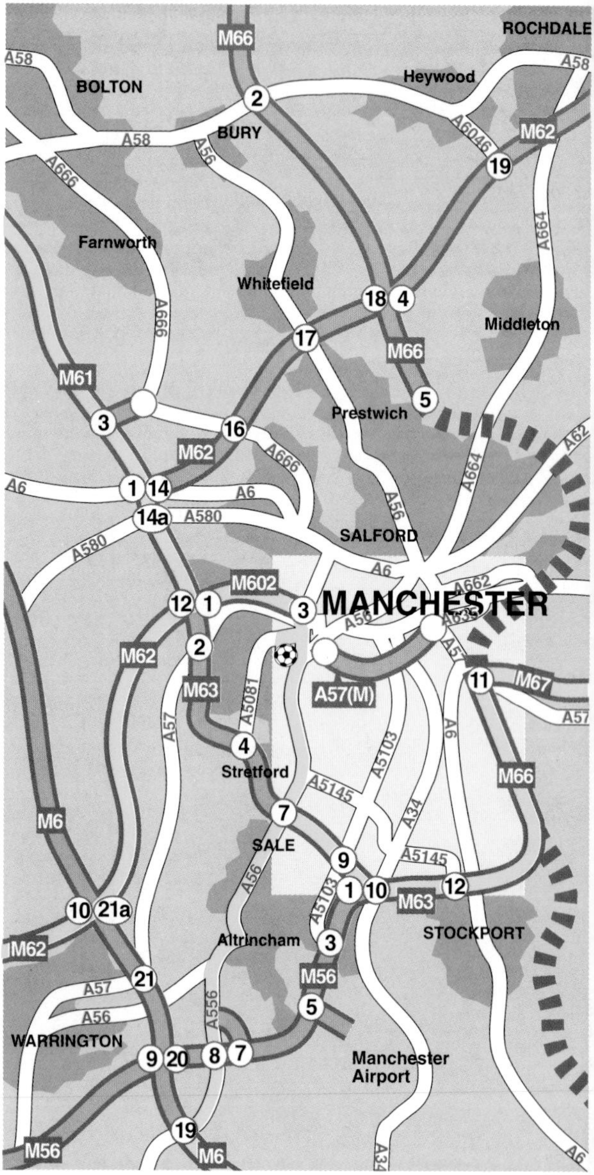

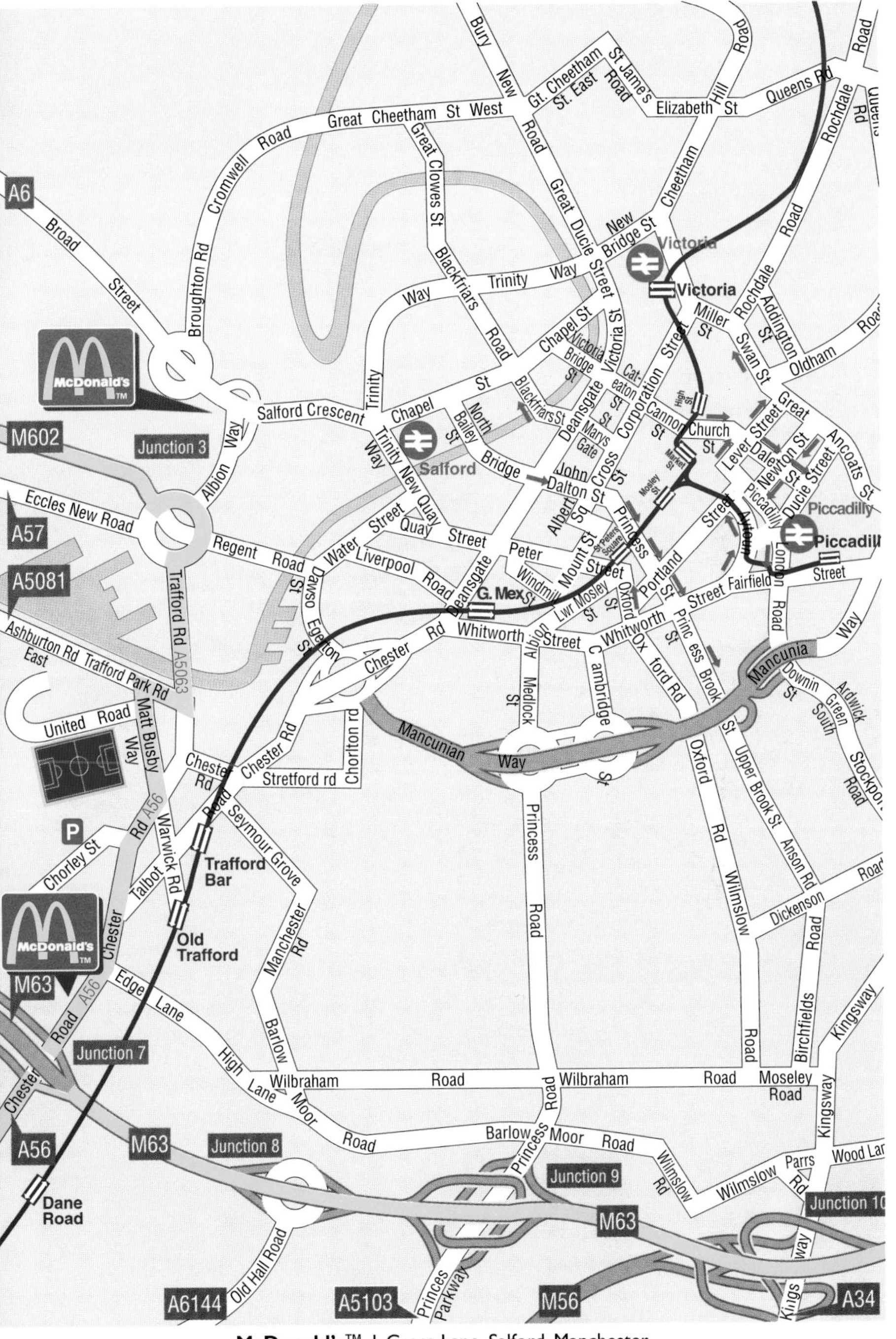

McDonald's™ I Cross Lane, Salford, Manchester
McDonald's™ Chester Road, Manchester

Middlesbrough FC

Middlesbrough FC
Cellnet Riverside Stadium
Middlesbrough
TS3 6RS

Club No: 01642·877700
Fax No: 01642·877840
Tickets: 01642·877745

AWAY

HOME

HOME

Bobby Robson: *view from abroad*

They will be fearfully aware of the fact that the last time they came up they returned pretty quickly. Bryan Robson will spend big but he will need to spend wisely and not waste the money if they are to keep their status this time around. They need to win their home matches at the Cellnet Riverside Stadium in front of their loyal 30,000 to be secure and put a smile on Bryan's face.

Bob Harris: *view in England*

Bryan Robson and Middlesbrough are back where they belong - in the top flight. Riverside Stadium, the fans who fill it, the free-spending chairman and the manager are Premier League calibre. They will have adjusted their values after the chastening experience of relegation which they scarcely deserved. They won't make the same mistakes again as Robson endeavours to build a team who play attractive football and can keep a clean sheet at the back. They must have a taste for the cup competitions but their priority this time around must be to secure a permanent foothold where it really matters and build from there. Robson will demand nothing less.

INFORMATION HOTLINES

ClubCall:	0891·12·11·81*
Recorded Information:	01642·877809*

**Calls cost 50p per minute at all times*
Club Call, Avalon House, 57-63 Scrutton St, London, EC2A 4PJ

CLUB SHOPS

THE MIDDLESBROUGH SHOP

Located at Cellnet Riverside Stadium, Middlesbrough

Opening Times:

Monday-Friday: 9.00am-5.00pm
Match Saturdays: 9.00am-2.45pm + 1hr after full time
Match Sundays: Closed
Match Evenings: 9.30am-7.30pm

Tel: 01642·877720

Mail Order Service: 01634·866622

THE MIDDLESBROUGH SHOP 2

Located at Cleveland Centre Middlesbrough

OPENING TIMES:

Monday-Saturday: 9.00am-5.30pm
Match Sundays: Closed
Match Evenings: 9.00am-5.30pm

Tel: 01642·877849

Mail Order Service: 01642·866622

BOOKING INFORMATION

General Enquiries:	01642·877745
Credit Card Bookings:	01642·877745
Travel Club:	01642·877745
Junior Club Line:	01642·877700

CATERING

FOOD

Burgers	£1.70
Hot Dogs	£1.60
Pizza	£1.70
Chips	£1.10
Crisps	£0.60
King Size Choc Bars	£0.60

BAR

Beer (Pint)	£1.80
Lager (Pint)	£1.90
Wine	£2.40
Cold Drinks	£1.00
Hot Drinks	£0.90

MISCELLANEOUS

West Stand Extensions
The filling in of the remaining two corners at the Cellnet Riverside Stadium, which will take the capacity to just under 35,000 for the start of 1998-99.

Boro TV
The first club in the country to set up their own cable television programme. Broadcast twice a week on Comcast Teesside's Channel 8, it has all the latest news from in and around the Riverside as well as fascinating features. Currently hosted by local radio personality Alistair Brownlee and former Boro Striker Bernie Slaven.

Rockliffe Park Training Ground is a new training complex situated in the picturesque village of Hurworth (about 18 miles from Middlesbrough). The first phase of building work, which will be complete in the autumn, is a training HQ and sports hall. The training HQ will include extensive changing facilities, steam rooms/sauna, a medical and sports science centre, a gym, offices and a restaurant. Total cost of £5 million.

ALUN ARMSTRONG

All that fuss and bother about Gazza and Merson, together with mixed views on the foreigners Beck, Ricard and Branca, served to overshadow the part Alun Armstrong played in Middlesbrough's promotion drive following his transfer from Stockport. The Gateshead born striker, released as a teenager by Newcastle, endeared himself to the Riverside fraternity by scoring two of the goals when Boro' beat Oxford to regain their Premiership status. Now they are back, Armstrong will be able to test his predatory skills in the highest company.

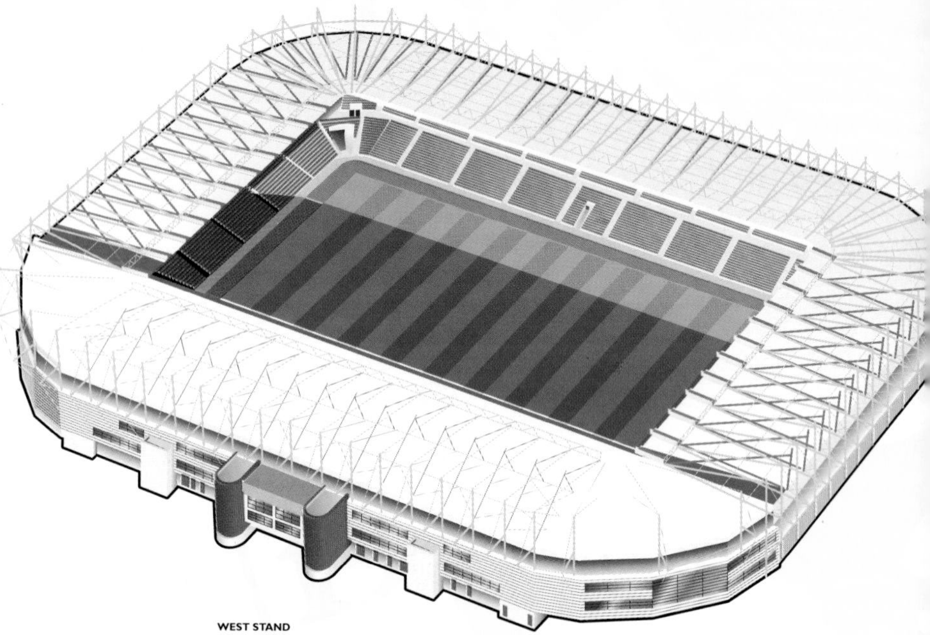

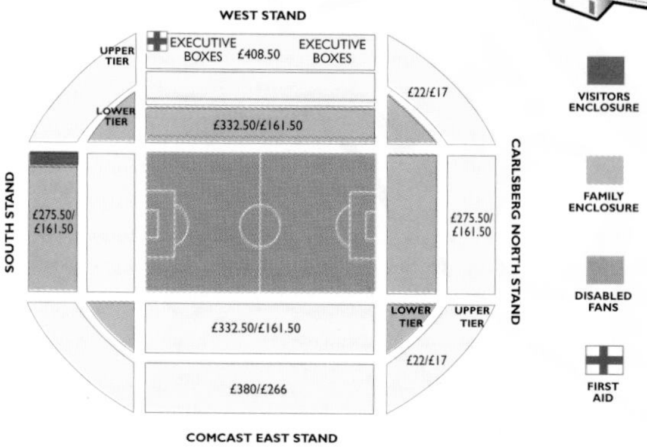

WEST STAND
UPPER TIER
EXECUTIVE BOXES
£408.50
EXECUTIVE BOXES
£22/£17
LOWER TIER
£332.50/£161.50
SOUTH STAND
£275.50/ £161.50
£275.50/ £161.50
CARLSBERG NORTH STAND
LOWER TIER
UPPER TIER
£332.50/£161.50
£22/£17
£380/£266
COMCAST EAST STAND
VISITORS ENCLOSURE
FAMILY ENCLOSURE
DISABLED FANS
FIRST AID

97/98 season points and league position by month

League position
Points
Win
Draw
Loss
League Position
0
2
4
6
8
10
12
14
16
18
20
95
90
85
80
75
70
65
60
55
50
45
40
35
30
25
20
15
10
5
0
Aug
Sept
Oct
Nov
Dec
Jan
Feb
March
April
May

Goals for and against seasons 92/3 to 97/8

Total Goals
Home
Away
352
226
126
194
129
323
For
Against

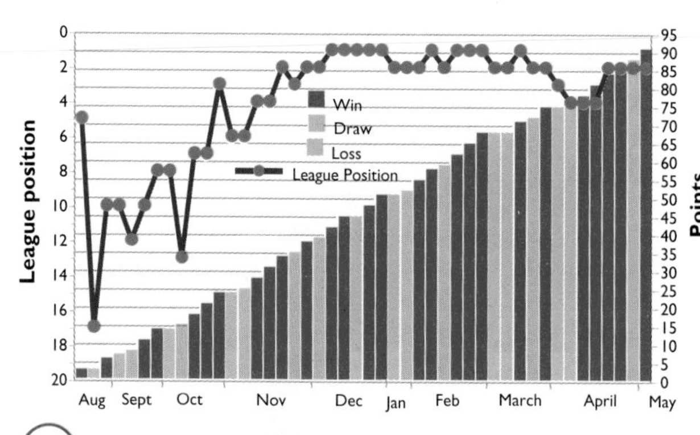

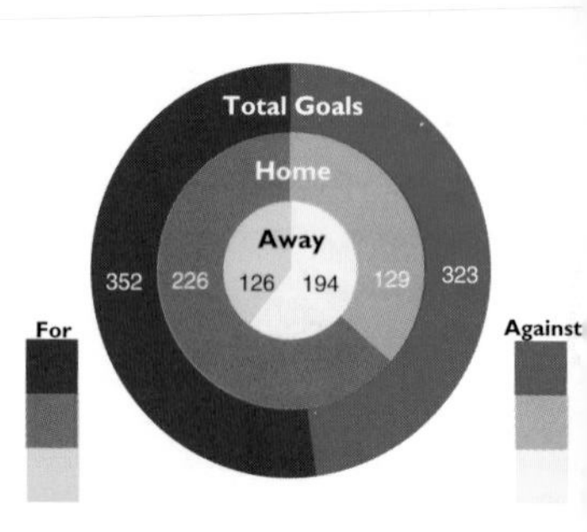

MIDDLESBROUGH FC

Goals scored by position by season

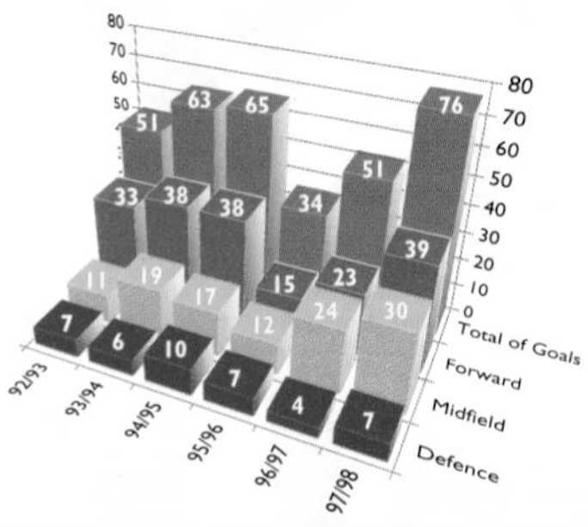

Bookings by position by season

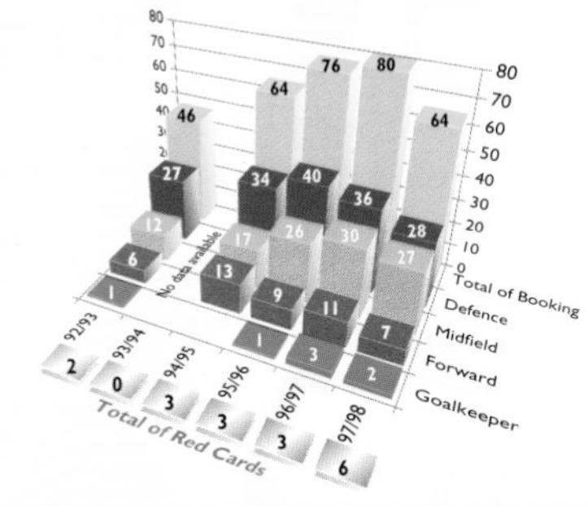

Goals scored by position by month 97/98

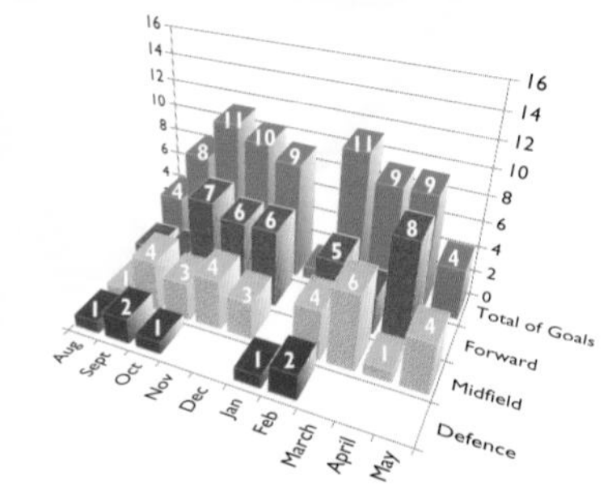

Final league position by season

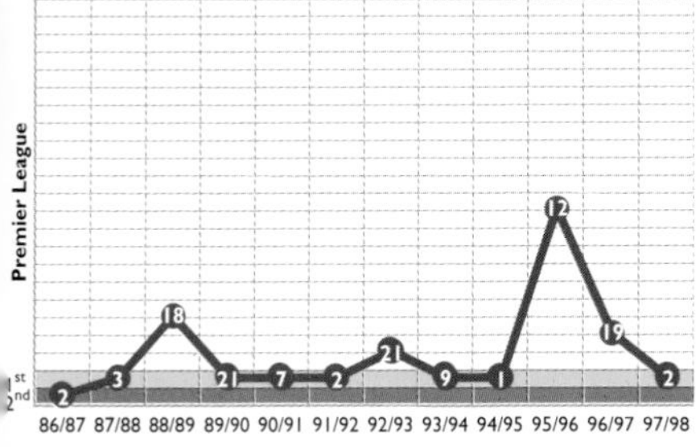

THE CARLING PREMIERSHIP FIXTURE LIST

HOME MATCH
AWAY MATCH
LAST SEASON: WIN
LAST SEASON: DRAW
LAST SEASON: LOSS

Club	Date	Last season
LEEDS UNITED	15/8	N/A
ASTON VILLA	23/8	N/A
DERBY COUNTY	29/8	N/A
LEICESTER CITY	9/9	N/A
TOTTENHAM HOTSPUR	13/9	N/A
EVERTON	19/9	N/A
CHELSEA	26/9	N/A
SHEFFIELD WEDNESDAY	3/10	N/A
BLACKBURN ROVERS	17/10	N/A
WIMBLEDON	24/10	N/A
NOTTINGHAM FOREST	1/11	0-0
SOUTHAMPTON	7/11	N/A
CHARLTON ATHLETIC	14/11	0-3
COVENTRY CITY	21/11	N/A
ARSENAL	29/11	N/A
NEWCASTLE UNITED	6/12	N/A
WEST HAM UNITED	12/12	N/A
MANCHESTER UNITED	19/12	N/A
LIVERPOOL	26/12	N/A
DERBY COUNTY	28/12	N/A
ASTON VILLA	9/1	N/A
LEEDS UNITED	16/1	N/A
LEICESTER CITY	30/1	N/A
LIVERPOOL	6/2	N/A
EVERTON	13/2	N/A
TOTTENHAM HOTSPUR	20/2	N/A
SHEFFIELD WEDNESDAY	27/2	N/A
CHELSEA	6/3	N/A
SOUTHAMPTON	13/3	N/A
NOTTINGHAM FOREST	20/3	0-4
BLACKBURN ROVERS	3/4	N/A
WIMBLEDON	5/4	N/A
CHARLTON ATHLETIC	10/4	2-1
COVENTRY CITY	17/4	N/A
ARSENAL	24/4	N/A
NEWCASTLE UNITED	1/5	N/A
MANCHESTER UNITED	8/5	N/A
WEST HAM UNITED	16/5	N/A

THE SQUAD

Key: Goalkeeper · Defender · Midfield · Forward · No of goals · No of clean sheets · No of yellow cards · No of red cards

Player	Position	Goals / Clean sheets	Yellow cards	Red cards
M.Beresford	Goalkeeper	3	1	
M.Schwarzer	Goalkeeper	14	1	
B.Roberts	Goalkeeper	1		
G.Pallister	Defender			
D.Gordon	Defender			
S.Baker	Defender		1	
R.Stockdale	Defender			
C.Harrison	Defender		2	
C.Fleming	Defender	1	5	
V.Kinder	Defender	2	4	
S.Vickers	Defender		3	1
G.Festa	Defender	2	4	2
C.Liddle	Defender			
R.Mustoe	Midfield	3	1	
P.Stamp	Midfield		1	
A.Moore	Midfield			
A.Townsend	Midfield	2	6	1
A.Ormerod	Midfield	3	1	
M.Summerbell	Midfield		1	
N.Maddison	Midfield	4	1	
P.Gascoigne	Midfield		1	
M.Beck	Forward	14	2	
P.Merson	Forward	12	2	
A.Campbell	Forward		1	
M.Branca	Forward	9	1	
A.Armstrong	Forward	7		
H.Ricard	Forward	2	1	

Transfers after 15 July 1998:

David Pleat: *on the manager*

BRYAN ROBSON

Has stuck by his troops after the humiliation of relegation despite those wonderful cup exploits. He has shown that he is not afraid to spend the money. Buys talent, sells talent and replaces talent. He can appear aloof within his own managerial circle but a winner who needs and wants to succeed. Who would bet against the fact that in two years time Old Trafford will beckon?

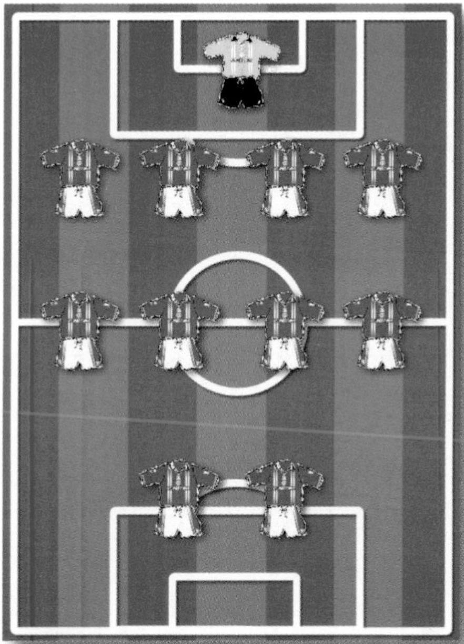

Trevor Brooking: *tactics*

Bryan Robson has certainly experienced a multitude of emotions since moving into managership with Cup Finals, relegation and promotion all part of the equation. He now has to guide his team into the new season with the harsh spotlight of the media focusing on Paul Gascoigne. Axed by England for the World Cup, "Gazza" now faces his greatest test as everyone awaits his reaction. The answer must have a significant bearing on how successful his club are to be this time round.

GETTING THERE
Middlesbrough is based in the Cellnet Riverside Stadium in the Middlehaven development area, 15 minutes walk from the town centre.

DIRECTIONS

DIRECTIONS

From the North:
Approaching Middlesbrough on the A19, cross over the River Tees. Turn left onto the A66 Middlesbrough bypass, continuing for 3 miles until the first roundabout. Turn left into Forest Road and the ground is straight ahead.

From the South:
Approaching from the South on the M1, exit where signposted to Teeside onto the A19. After 30 miles turn right onto the A66 Middlesbrough bypass. Then as route for north.

From the West:
From the A1(M) exit at Junction 57 onto the A66(M), following it until the end, turning onto the A66 for approximately 20 miles, turning left at the roundabout into Forest Road. The ground is straight ahead.

Middlesbrough Station is located on Albert Road, ten minutes walk from the ground.

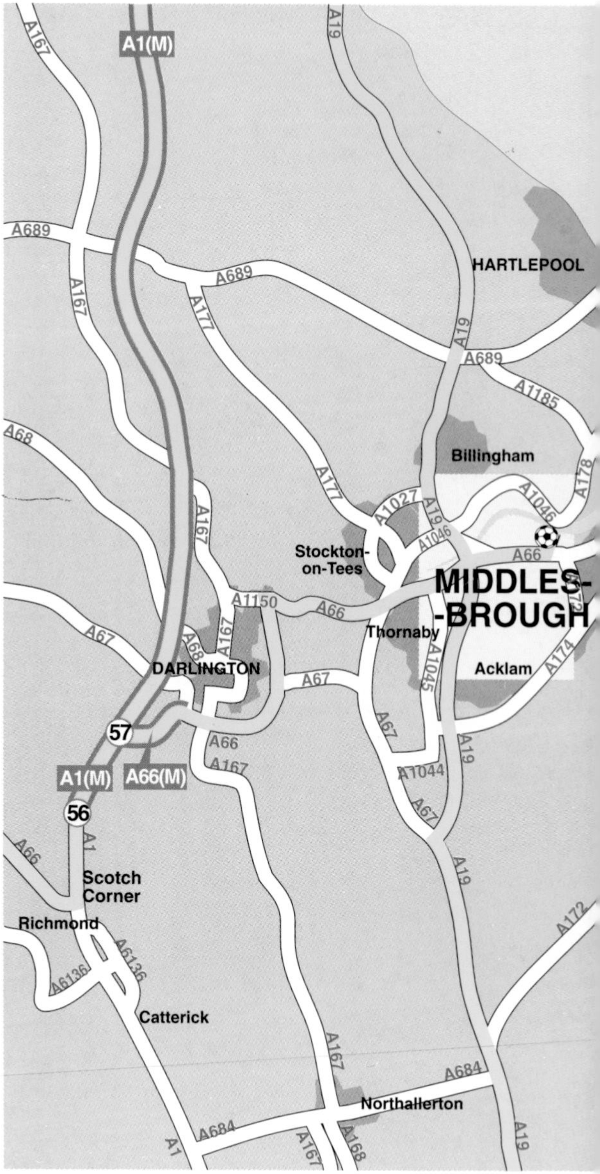

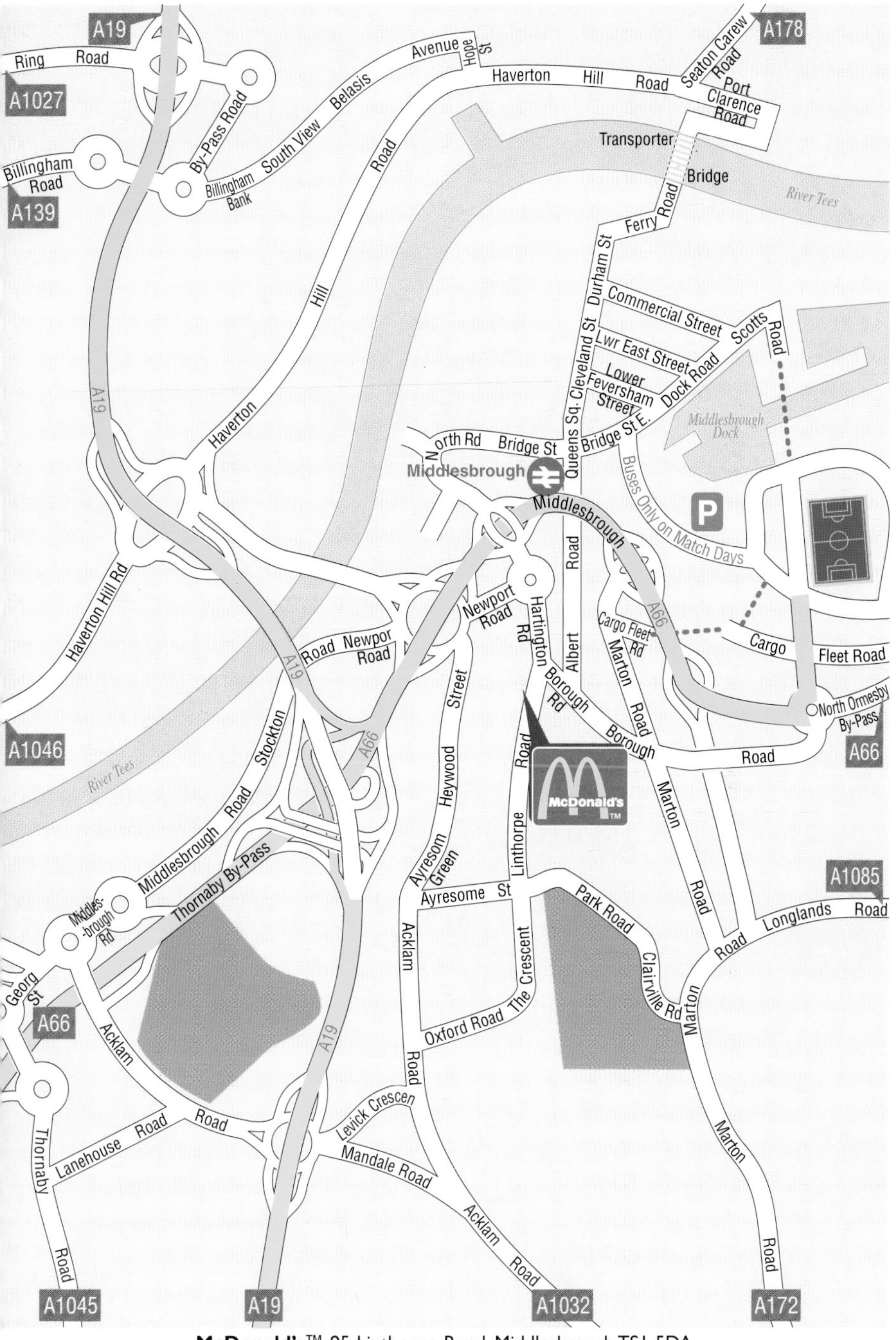

McDonald's™ 95 Linthorpe Road, Middlesbrough TS1 5DA

Newcastle United FC
St James' Park
Newcastle-Upon-Tyne
NE1 4ST

Club No: 0191·201·8401
Fax No: 0191·201·8600
Tickets: 0191·261·1571
Internet: www.nufc.co.uk

Bobby Robson: *view from abroad*

One of the greatest hotbeds of football fervour in Europe matching anything in Manchester or Madrid. Disappointing season even though they reached the F.A Cup final. It has taken a while to adjust from the departure of Keegan and his philosophy. Kenny is different, more conservative, but having been there for a while I now expect him to make dramatic strides forward this season. The crowd will demand it, making it a big year for Kenny and the club. The bonus is that, despite their poor season, they are back in Europe.

Bob Harris: *view in England*

Reaching the FA Cup Final was the highlight of a season to forget A few years age in the days before the Kevin Keegan revival, the loyal Newcastle fans would have given their eye teeth for such a "failure". Disappointing is a more apt word and only because expectations were at such a high level at the start of the season when there was talk of not only the Championship but even the Champions League, especially after that sensational win over Barcelona. A more settled board room will allow Kenny Dalgish to carry on rebuilding the side in his own image and the bonus is the place in the Cup Winners 'Cup alongside the holders Chelsea.

INFORMATION HOTLINES

ClubCall: 0891·12·11·90*

Calls cost 50p per minute at all times

Club Call, Avalon House, 57-63 Scrutton St, London, EC2A 4PJ

CLUB SHOPS

NEWCASTLE UNITED OFFICIAL STORE

St James' Park

Opening Times:

Monday-Saturday: 9.00am-5.00pm
Sundays: 11.00am-5.00pm
Match Saturdays: 9.00am-6.00pm
Match Sundays: 11.00am-6.00pm
Match Evenings: 9.00am-10.00pm

Tel: 0191·201·8426
Fax: 0191·201·8605
Mail Order Service: 0990·501892

NEWCASTLE UNITED OFFICIAL STORE

Monument Mall, Newcastle-Upon-Tyne

Opening Times:

Monday to Wednesday & Fridays: 9.00am-5.30pm
Thursdays: 9.00am-8.00pm
Sundays: 11.00am-4.00pm

Tel: 0191·232·4488
Fax: 0191·232·52298
Mail Order Service: 0990·501892

BOOKING INFORMATION

General Enquiries:	0191·201·8401
Credit Card Bookings:	0191·261·1571
Travel Club:	0191·201·8550
Recorded Info:	0191·201·8400
Junior Magpies:	0191·201·8472

CATERING

FOOD

Hamburger	£2.10
Cheeseburger	£2.25
Hot Dog	£2.10
Various Pies	£1.55
Cornish Pasty	£1.55
Cheese & Onion Pasty	£1.55
Mars/Snickers/Twix	£0.65
Crisps	£0.55

BAR

Lager	£2.15
Guinness	£2.25
Spirits	£3.00
Tea/Coffee/Chocolate/Bovril	£1.00
Coke/Fanta	from £1.00

MISCELLANEOUS

Stadium Tours
St James Park Ground Tours - Tel: 0191·201·8549
Corporate Hospitality
Tel: 0191·201·8424
Special matchday packages available. Entertain 6-40 guests in the relaxed and stylish surroundings of Newcastle United's Corporate Hospitality area.
Magpie Restaurant - Tel: 0191·201·8439
Business Club - Tel: 0191·201·8670
Literature
Programme price £2.00, Magazine 'Black&White' £2.30
Pre Match & Half Time Entertainment

John Motson: *one to watch*

NIKOLAOS DABIZAS

The signing of the Greek international defender from Olympiakos for £2 million was one of the saving graces in a season when Newcastle largely fell from grace. Dabizas displayed a fierce enthusiasm for the cause as well as confirming he is a redoubtable defender. His header clipped the Arsenal crossbar in the F.A Cup final, and he looks certain to feature in the realignment of a team that needs to make amends to their supporters for such a tame season in Premiership terms.

97/98 season points and league position by month

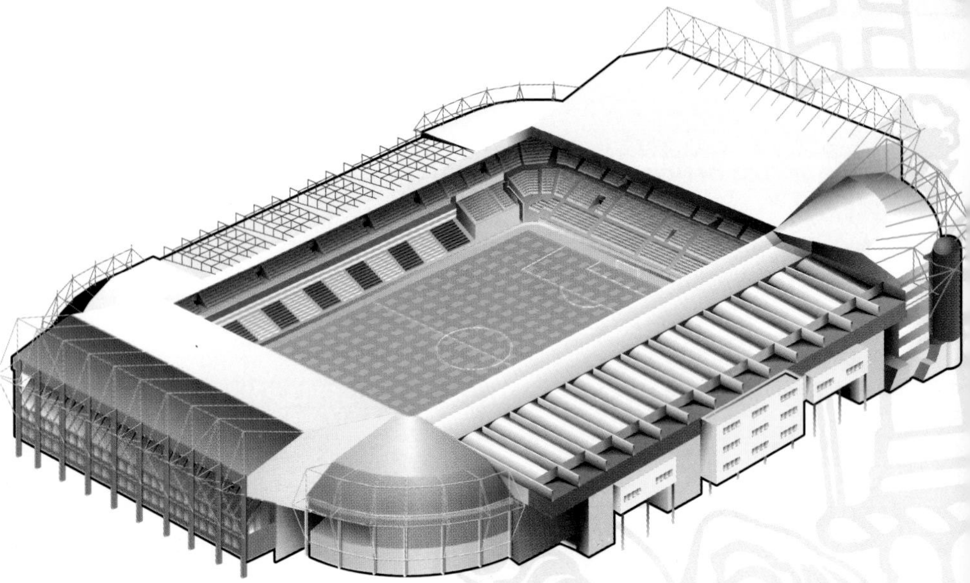

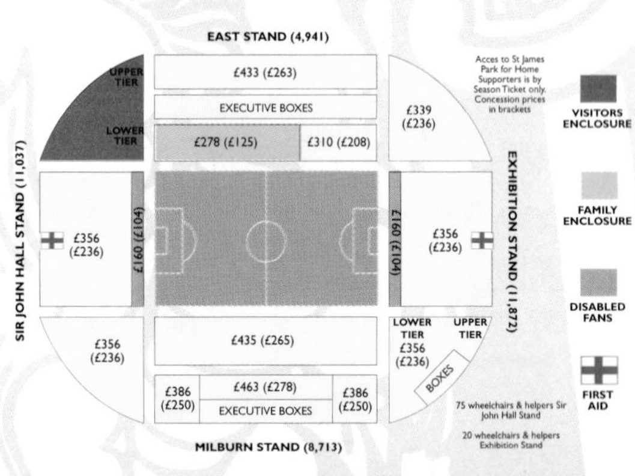

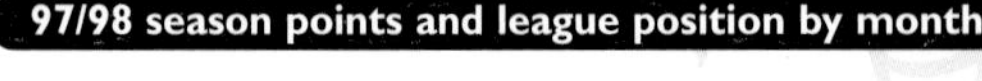

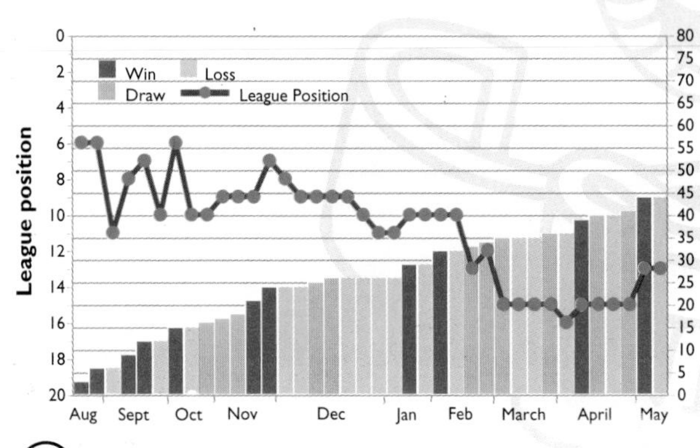

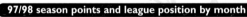

Goals for and against seasons 92/3 to 97/8

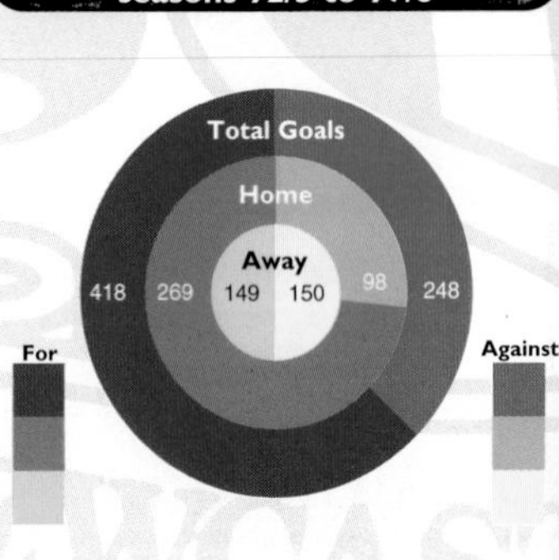

NEWCASTLE UNITED FC

Goals scored by position by season

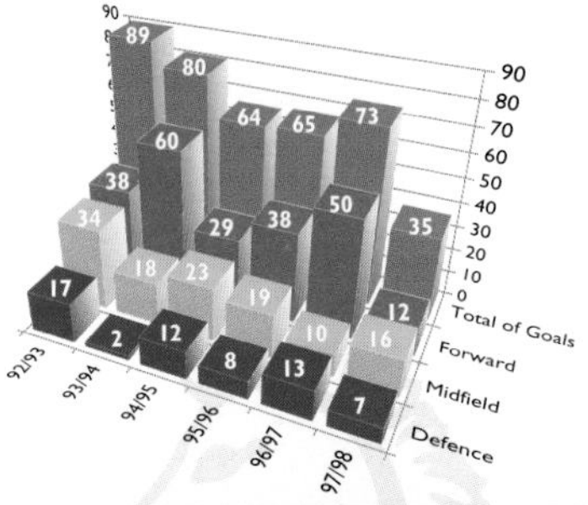

Bookings by position by season

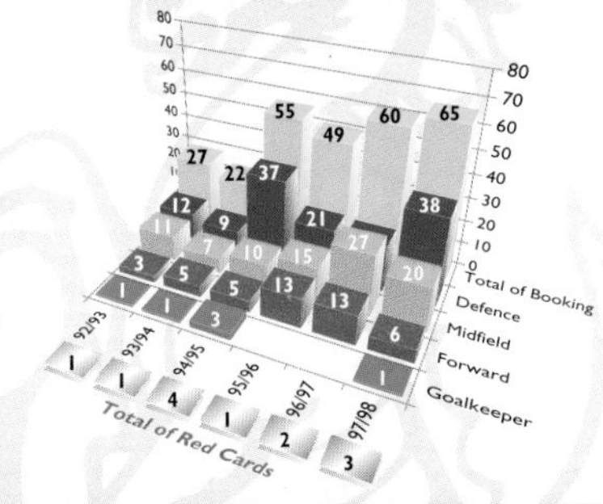

Goals scored by position by month 97/98

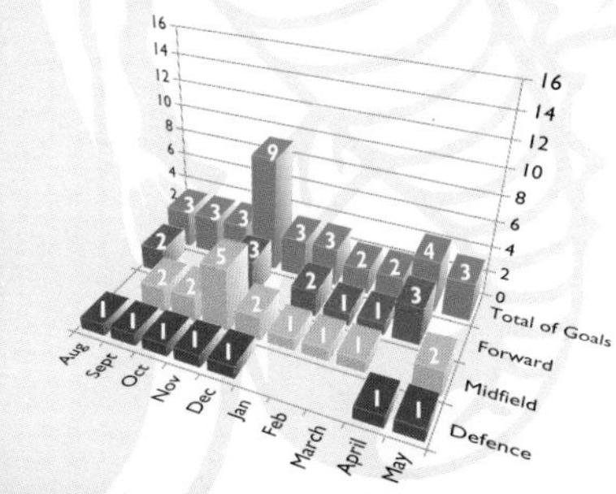

Final league position by season

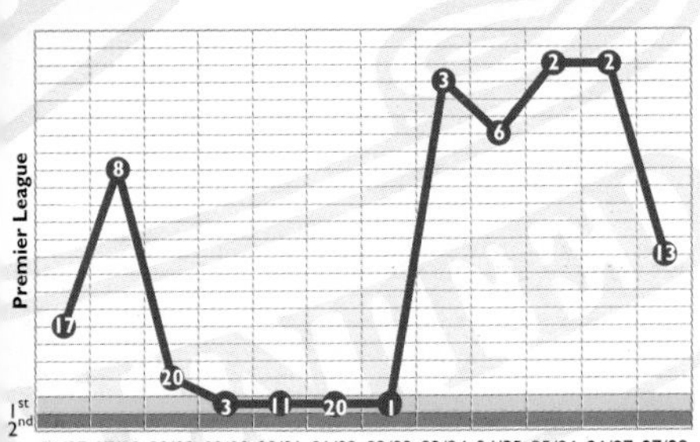

THE CARLING PREMIERSHIP FIXTURE LIST

HOME MATCH · AWAY MATCH · LAST SEASON: WIN · LAST SEASON: DRAW · LAST SEASON: LOSS

Opponent	Date	Last season
CHARLTON	15/8	N/A
CHELSEA	22/8	0-1
LIVERPOOL	29/8	1-2
ASTON VILLA	9/9	1-0
SOUTHAMPTON	12/9	2-1
COVENTRY	19/9	2-2
NOTTM FOREST	26/9	N/A
ARSENAL	3/10	1-3
DERBY	17/10	0-0
TOTTENHAM	24/10	0-2
WEST HAM	31/10	0-1
MAN UTD	7/11	1-1
SHEFF WED	14/11	2-1
EVERTON	21/11	0-0
WIMBLEDON	28/11	1-3
MIDDLESBROUGH	5/12	N/A
BLACKBURN	12/12	0-1
LEICESTER	19/12	3-3
LEEDS	26/12	1-1
LIVERPOOL	28/12	0-1
CHELSEA	9/1	3-1
CHARLTON	16/1	N/A
ASTON VILLA	30/1	1-0
LEEDS	6/2	1-4
COVENTRY	13/2	0-0
SOUTHAMPTON	20/2	1-2
ARSENAL	27/2	0-1
NOTTM FOREST	6/3	N/A
MAN UTD	13/3	0-1
WEST HAM	20/3	1-0
DERBY	3/4	0-1
TOTTENHAM	5/4	1-0
SHEFF WED	10/4	1-2
EVERTON	17/4	1-0
WIMBLEDON	24/4	0-0
MIDDLESBROUGH	1/5	N/A
LEICESTER	8/5	0-0
BLACKBURN	16/5	1-1

adidas®

THE SQUAD

Goalkeeper · Defender · Midfield · Forward · No of goals · No of clean sheets · No of yellow cards · No of red cards

Player	Position	Goals / Clean sheets	Yellow cards	Red cards
S. Given	Goalkeeper	8		1
L. Perez	Goalkeeper			
S. Watson	Defender		1	3
W. Barton	Defender	3	8	
N. Dabizas	Defender	1	2	
P. Albert	Defender		8	
A. Griffin	Defender			
S. Pearce	Defender		4	
S. Howey	Defender			
C. Serrant	Defender			
A. Hughes	Defender			
A. Pistone	Defender		6	
D. Hamilton	Defender			
K. Gillespie	Midfield	4	3	
G. Brady	Midfield			
G. Georgiadis	Midfield			
S. Glass	Midfield			
R. Lee	Midfield	4	3	
T. Ketsbaia	Midfield	3	3	
D. Batty	Midfield	1	10	3
G. Speed	Midfield	1	1	
J. Barnes	Midfield	6		
A. Shearer	Forward	2	2	
B. Gudjonsson	Forward			
S. Guivarc'h	Forward			
A. Andersson	Forward	2		

Transfers after 15 July 1998:

....

....

....

....

....

....

....

KENNY DALGLISH

Has taken some criticism and parried the blows with his doleful but occasionally funny retorts. Big test ahead with demands exceeding the current quality of the squad. Relying massively on Shearer, maybe changes in the backroom will promote and accelerate Kenny's return to honours. A sharp, canny man who has done it all on and off the pitch leaving you wondering if he really needs it.

Trevor Brooking: *tactics*

Getting through to the FA Cup Final tended to distract attention away from their poor league form. Alan Shearer must receive more support this season otherwise it is a waste of his finishing prowess if crosses are so few and far between. Although the initial priority was to make the defence more reliable, they have become too cautious in their approach, and this forward adjustment is vital if Newcastle are to improve their league form and position.

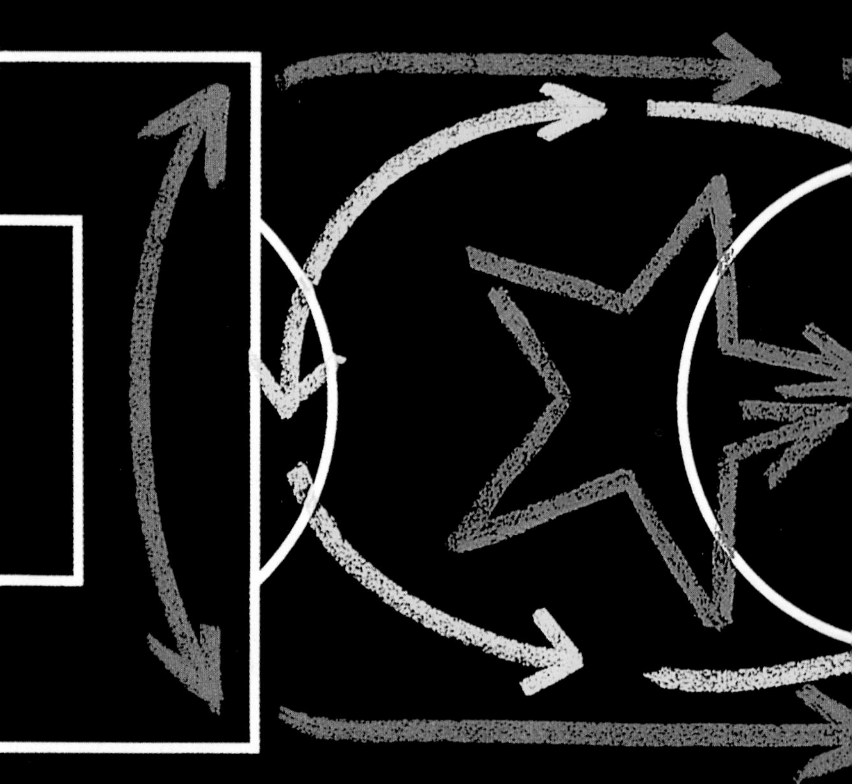

THE SECRET BEHIND NEWCASTLE'S FLUID FOOTBALL

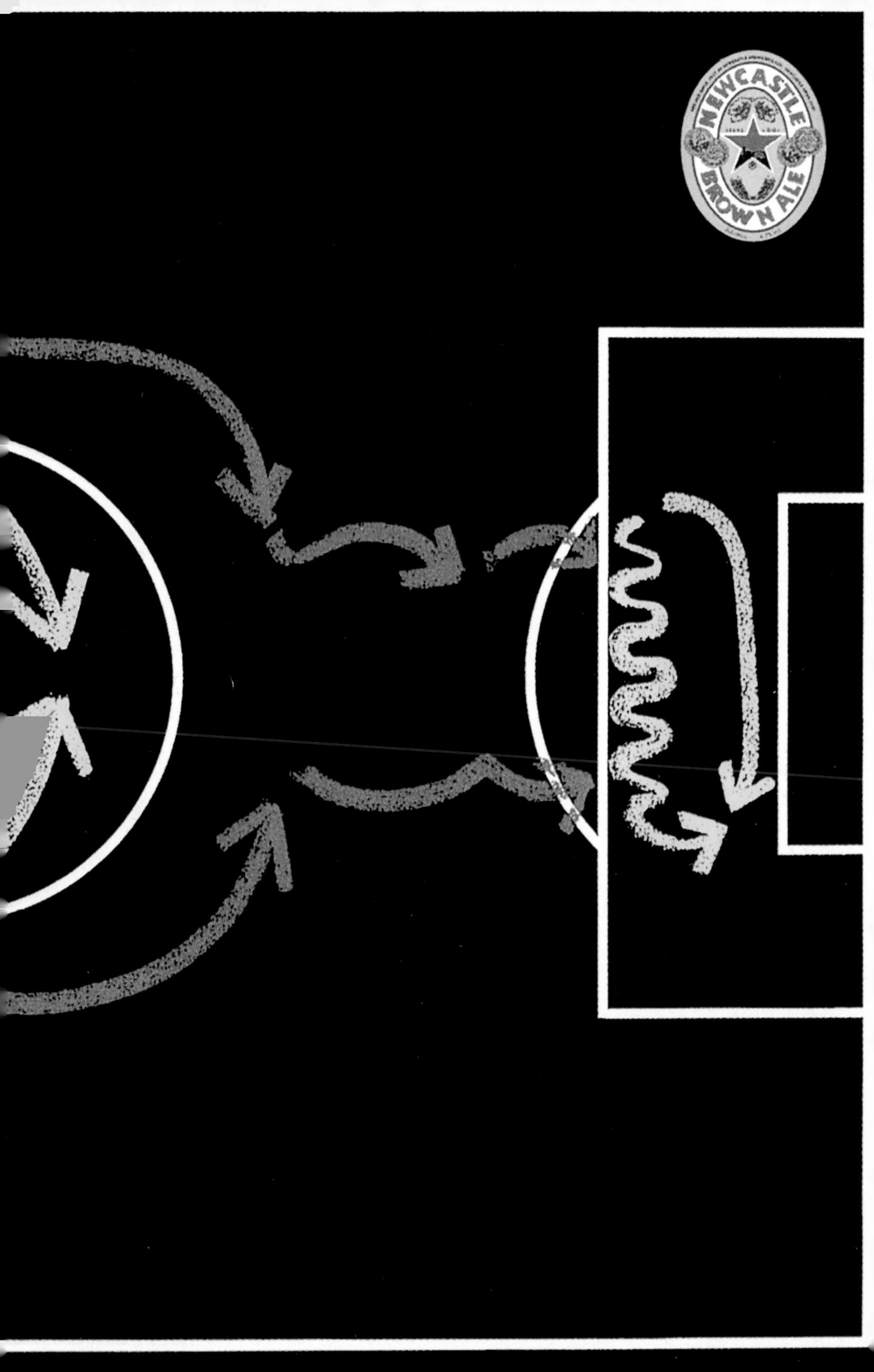

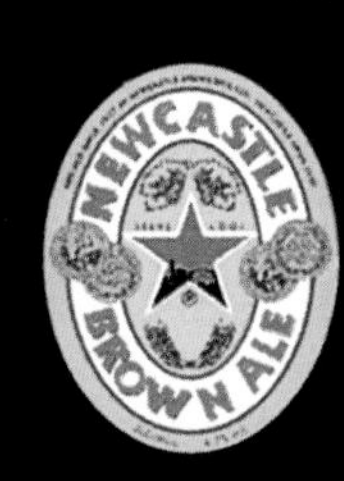

Newcastle United play at St James' Park, half a mile from Newcastle city centre. The metro system is very efficient and there is a station by the ground. Some car parking is available on Barrack Road.

DIRECTIONS

From the North:

Exit A1 onto the A167 Ponteland Road heading toward the city centre. At the fourth roundabout after approximately 1 1/2 miles, turn left onto Jedburgh Road. Take the first exit, turning right onto Grandstand Road and then left onto the A189 Ponteland Road. Keep on this road which becomes Barrack Road until the roundabout. The ground is on the left.

From the South:

From the A1(M) turn off at the junction with the A1 and continue on the A1 until the junction with the A184. Turn onto the the A184 and continue along this road, bearing left onto the A189. Continue over the River Tyne on the Redheugh Bridge, go straight over the roundabout onto Blenheim Street and continue until you meet Bath Lane. Turn left into Bath Lane, right into Corporation Street, and left at the roundabout into Gallowgate. At the next roundabout Barrack Road and the ground are straight ahead.

Newcastle Central Railway Station is half a mile from St James' park. The metro runs every 3-4 minutes to St James' Station.

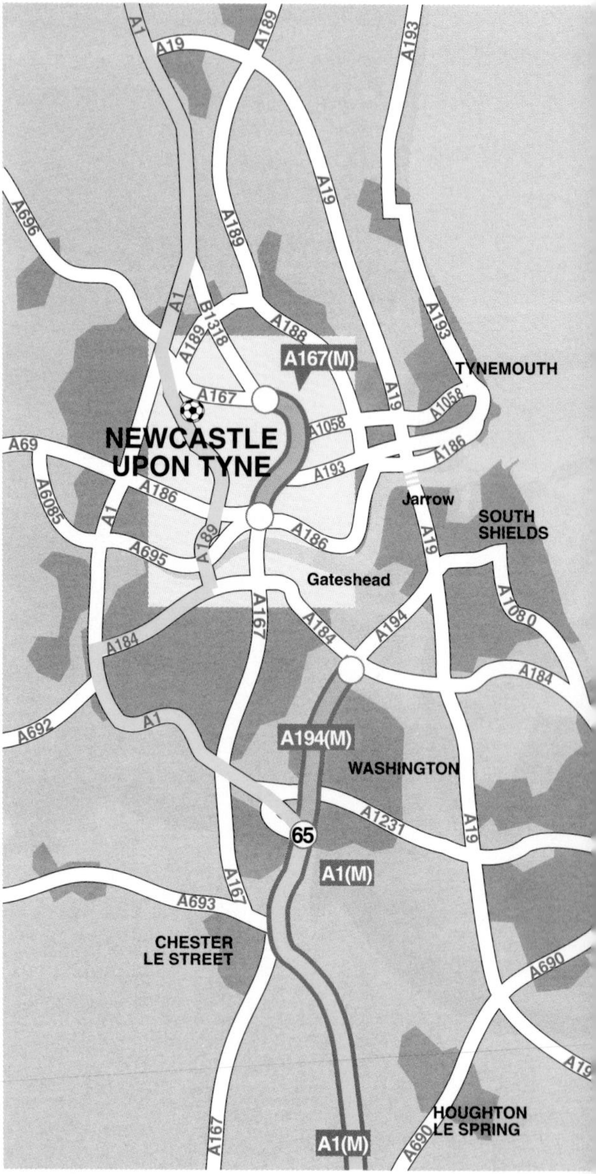

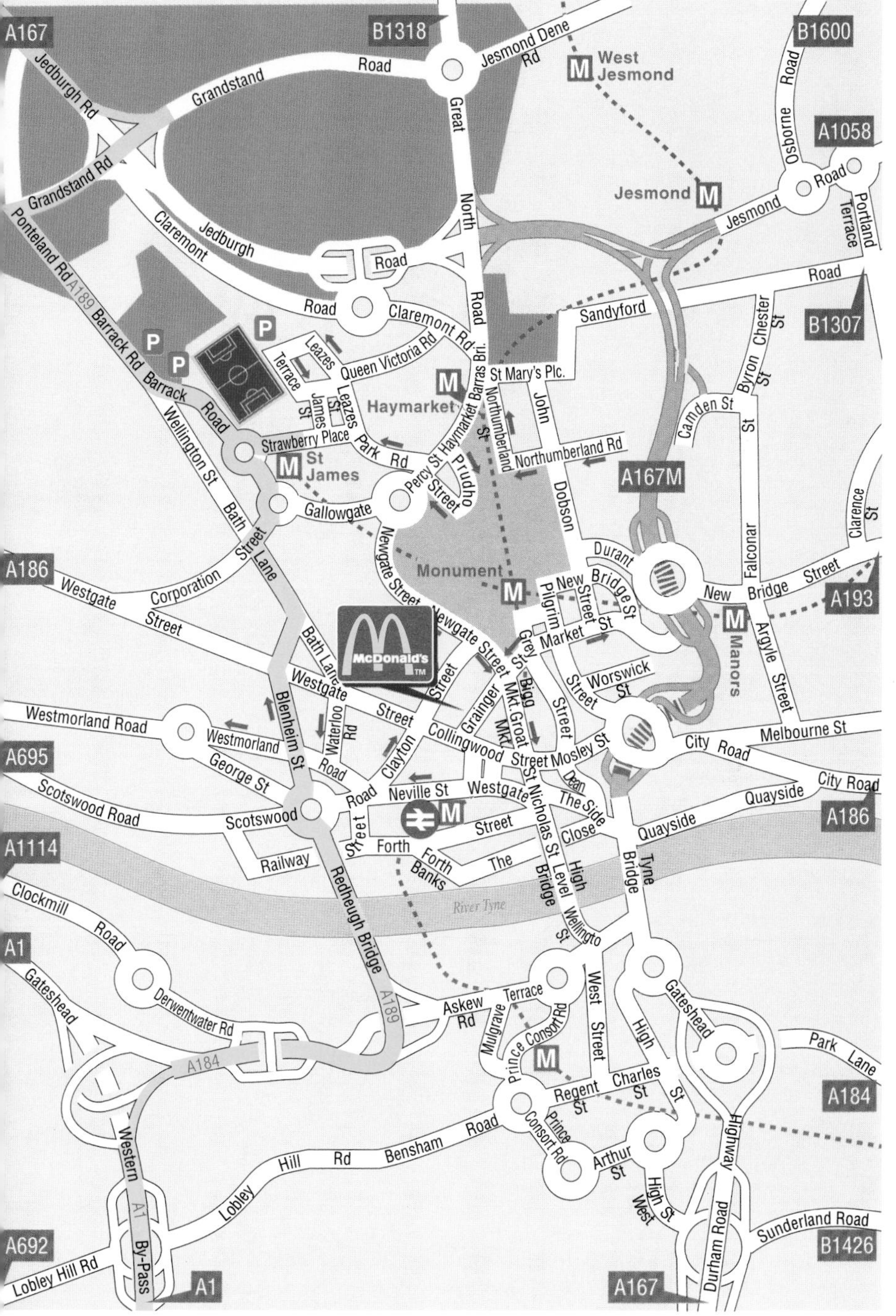

McDonald's™ 85-93 Grainger Street, Newcastle NE1 5AR

Nottingham Forest FC

FOREST

Nottingham Forest
Pavilion Road
The City Ground
Nottingham
NG2 5FJ

Club No: 0115·982·4444
Fax No: 0115·982·4455
Tickets: 0115·982·4445
Internet: www.nottinghamforest.co.uk

AWAY

HOME

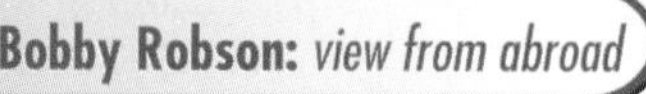

Bobby Robson: *view from abroad*

They will be glad to be back and they, like the other promoted clubs, will know what they have got to do. The first three months will be crucial to see if they can cope. The question is whether their Dutch World Cup striker Pierre van Hooijdonk can do it at this level. They have an experienced manager in Dave Bassett who knows how to scramble for points and they will probably have to do that in the top flight. He knows better than anyone that they are in a League where mistakes are punished unmercifully.

Bob Harris: *view in England*

Dave Basset has fought enough battles against relegation to know exactly what Forest must do this season to stop themselves going straight back down to Division One again. Passing Bolton, Palace and Barnsley going in the opposite direction is warning enough that goals and glory in the second grade is not enough to ensure a happy return. Goals were the problem for all three and Bassett must ensure that Pierre van Hooijdonk is kept happy and given the service he deserves. In that respect a fit again Steve Stone could prove to be every bit as valuable as the Dutchman.

INFORMATION HOTLINES

ClubCall:	0891·12·11·74*
Recorded Information:	0115·982·4446*

**Calls cost 50p per minute at all times*
Club Call, Avalon House, 57-63 Scrutton St, London, EC2A 4PJ

CLUB SHOPS

The Forest Superstore

Located on Pavilion Road, The City Ground, Nottingham

Opening Times:

Monday-Friday: 9.00am-5.00pm
Match Saturdays: 9.00am until Kick Off and 1/2hr after full time
Match Sundays: 12.00am until Kick Off and 1/2hr after full time
Match Evenings: 9.00am until Kick Off and 1/2hr after full time

Tel: 0115 982 4447

Mail Order Service: 0115 982 4343/4/5

BOOKING INFORMATION

General Enquiries:	0115·982·4445
Travel Club:	0115·982·4445
Recorded Information:	0115·982·4446

CATERING

Snackbars, soft drinks and alcohol are available throughout the ground, with the exception of the Main Stand side corner of the Bridgford stand where alcohol is not available. Snackbars do a variety of hot and cold drinks and food. Lindlay Catering handle snackbars and prices are still to be confirmed.

MISCELLANEOUS

Disabled Access

Bridgford Upper	£15
Trent End Lower	£14
Executive Stand	£12
Bridgford Lower	£22

*1 escort permitted per disabled Supporter

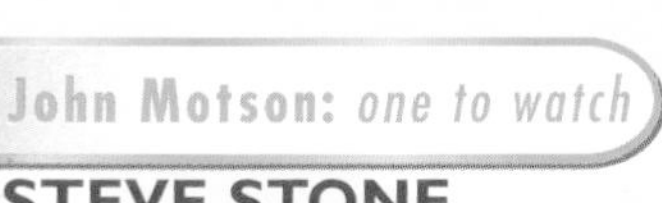

STEVE STONE

A freak injury put Steve Stone out of the game for a year just when he had established himself as an almost automatic England selection. While others looked towards the World Cup, the Forest winger knuckled down to regain not only his fitness, but the vibrant form which ultimately helped them win the Nationwide league. Stone's surging runs down the right flank, besides his eye for goal, will be pivotal in his club's desire to consolidate their place in the Premiership.

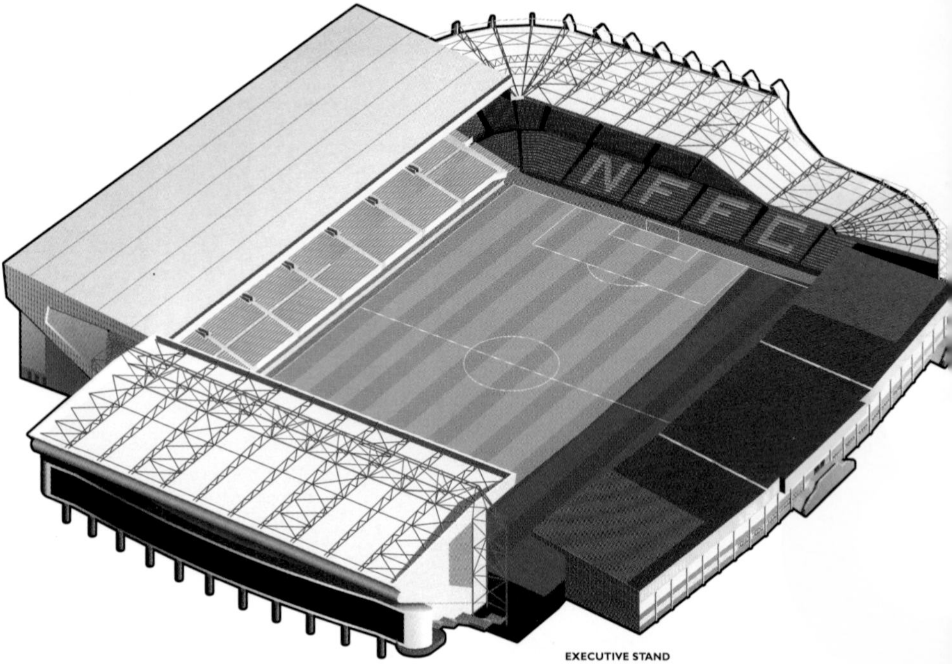

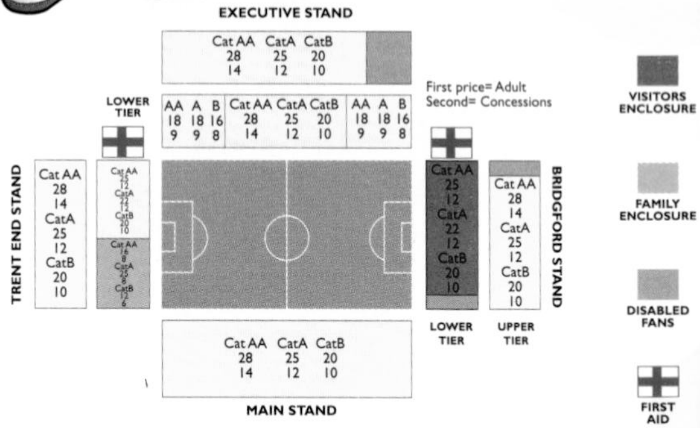

EXECUTIVE STAND

Cat AA 28 14 | CatA 25 12 | CatB 20 10

First price= Adult
Second= Concessions

LOWER TIER

AA 18 9 | A 18 9 | B 16 8 | Cat AA 28 14 | CatA 25 12 | CatB 20 10 | AA 18 9 | A 18 9 | B 16 8

TRENT END STAND

Cat AA 28 14
CatA 25 12
CatB 20 10

LOWER TIER

Cat AA 25 12
CatA 22 12
CatB 20 10

Cat AA 16 8
CatA 25 8
CatB 12 6

BRIDGFORD STAND

LOWER TIER

Cat AA 25 12
CatA 22 12
CatB 20 10

UPPER TIER

Cat AA 28 14
CatA 25 12
CatB 20 10

MAIN STAND

Cat AA 28 14 | CatA 25 12 | CatB 20 10

VISITORS ENCLOSURE

FAMILY ENCLOSURE

DISABLED FANS

FIRST AID

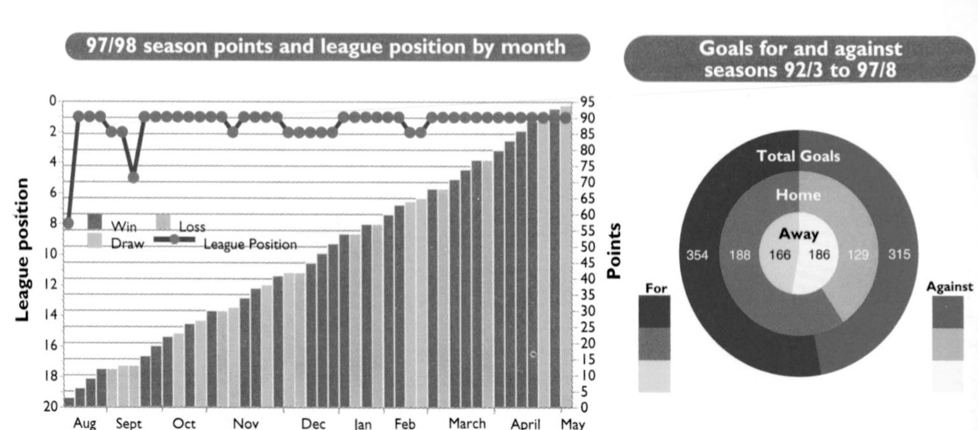

Goals scored by position by season

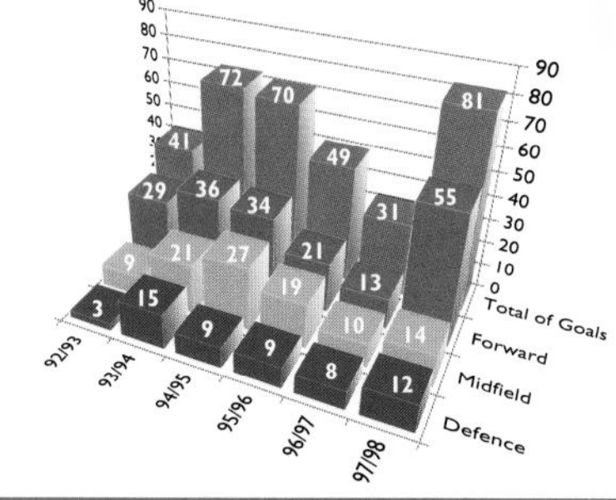

Bookings by position by season

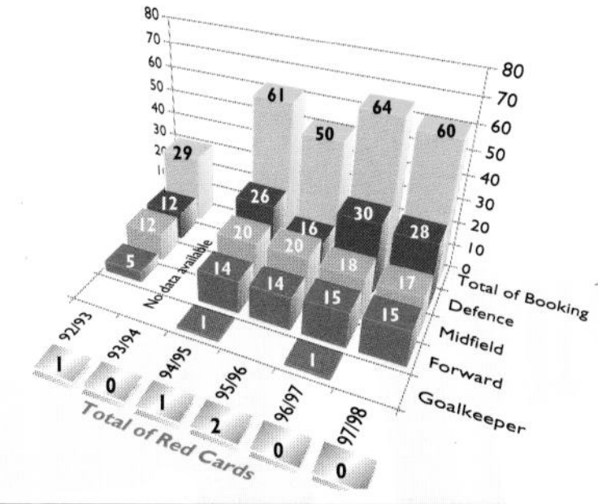

Goals scored by position by month 97/98

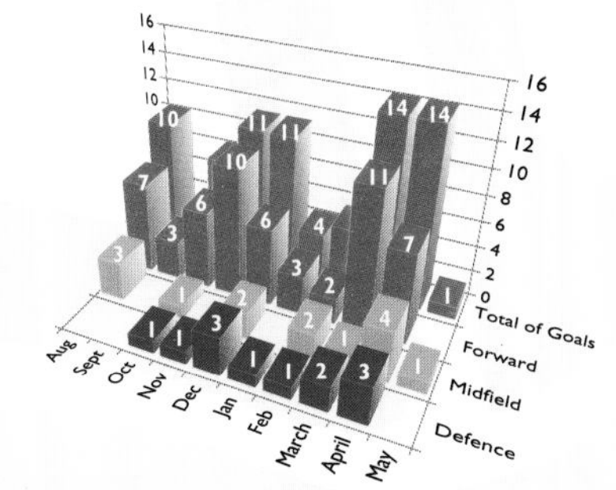

Final league position by season

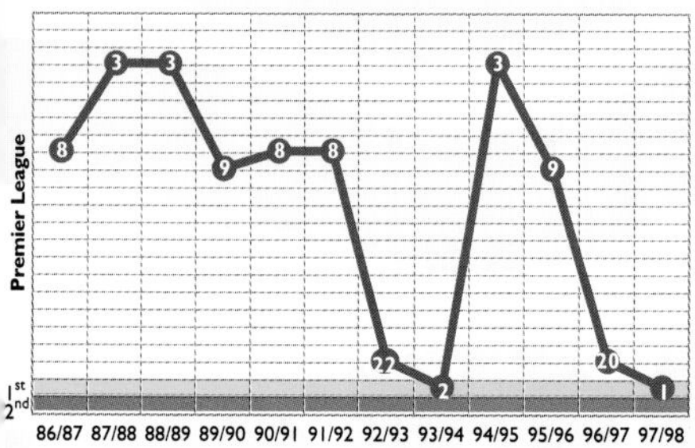

THE CARLING PREMIERSHIP FIXTURE LIST

HOME MATCH
AWAY MATCH
LAST SEASON: WIN
LAST SEASON: DRAW
LAST SEASON: LOSS

Opponent	Date	Last season
ARSENAL	17/8	N/A
COVENTRY CITY	22/8	N/A
SOUTHAMPTON	29/8	N/A
EVERTON	8/9	N/A
CHELSEA	12/9	N/A
WEST HAM UNITED	19/9	N/A
NEWCASTLE UNITED	26/9	N/A
CHARLTON ATHLETIC	3/10	5-2
LEEDS UNITED	17/10	N/A
LIVERPOOL	24/10	N/A
MIDDLESBROUGH	1/11	0-0
WIMBLEDON	7/11	N/A
DERBY COUNTY	16/11	N/A
TOTTENHAM HOTSPUR	21/11	N/A
ASTON VILLA	28/11	N/A
SHEFFIELD WEDNESDAY	7/12	N/A
LEICESTER CITY	12/12	N/A
BLACKBURN ROVERS	19/12	N/A
MANCHESTER UNITED	26/12	N/A
SOUTHAMPTON	28/12	N/A
COVENTRY CITY	9/1	N/A
ARSENAL	16/9	N/A
EVERTON	30/1	N/A
MANCHESTER UNITED	6/2	N/A
WEST HAM UNITED	13/2	N/A
CHELSEA	20/2	N/A
CHARLTON ATHLETIC	27/2	2-4
NEWCASTLE UNITED	6/3	N/A
WIMBLEDON	13/3	N/A
MIDDLESBROUGH	20/3	4-0
LEEDS UNITED	3/4	N/A
LIVERPOOL	5/4	N/A
DERBY COUNTY	8/10	N/A
TOTTENHAM HOTSPUR	17/4	N/A
ASTON VILLA	24/4	N/A
SHEFFIELD WEDNESDAY	1/5	N/A
BLACKBURN ROVERS	8/5	N/A
LEICESTER CITY	16/5	N/A

A team that's making headlines

THE SQUAD

Key: Goalkeeper (GK) · Defender (D) · Midfield (M) · Forward (F) · No of goals · No of clean sheets · No of yellow cards · No of red cards

Player	Position	Goals / Clean sheets	Yellow cards	Red cards
M. Pascolo	Goalkeeper	1 (clean sheets)		
M. Crossley	Goalkeeper			
D. Beasant	Goalkeeper	20 (clean sheets)		
C. Cooper	Defender	5	3	
S. Chettle	Defender	1	2	
D. Lyttle	Defender		6	
C. Armstrong	Defender		2	
A. Rogers	Defender	1	7	
J. Hjelde	Defender	1	5	
A. Johnson	Defender	4	3	
T. Bonalair	Midfield	2	4	
S. Stone	Midfield	2	2	
S. Gemmill	Midfield	2	2	
C. Bart-Williams	Midfield	4	6	
D. Johnson	Midfield		1	
G. Thomas	Midfield	3	2	
I. Woan	Midfield	1	3	
S. Guinan	Forward			
K. Campbell	Forward	23	7	
P. Van Hooijdonk	Forward	29	5	
I. Moore	Forward	1		
C. Allen	Forward			
P. McGregor	Forward			

Transfers after 15 July 1998:

DAVE BASSETT

A colourful character with a record of 17 years' aggravation that has seen him gain more promotions than suffer relegations. Always chirpy, never frightened to experiment, he handled his initial weeks at Forest, when Pearce was in temporary charge, diplomatically, calmly and knew exactly what he had to do when he was finally handed the managerial reins. Hard to argue with his record last season.

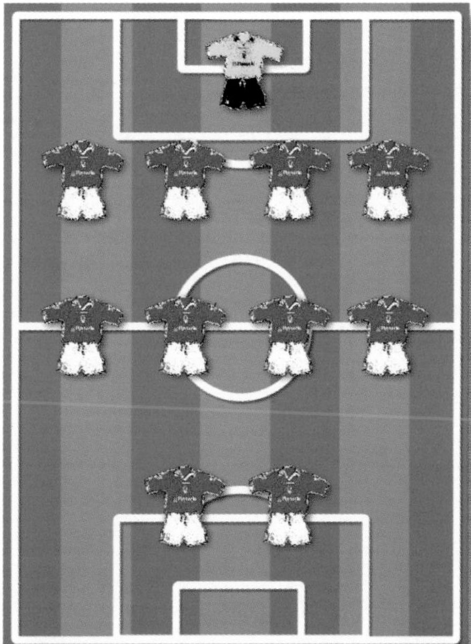

Trevor Brooking: *tactics*

Dave Bassett came up with the promotion formula again, but will be the first to acknowledge the huge contribution made by Pierre Van Hooijdonk, who fired goals in from all parts of the pitch. Their 4-4-2 system always looked better when Steve Stone was fit enough to provide the balance down the right flank. His absence was crucial when they were relegated previously, and with a limited transfer budget, need a good start to the season. Chris Bart-Williams will be a key player if those struggles are not to be repeated.

Nottingham Forest play at the city centre and the River Trent. Parking prohibitions are in force on match days but the council operates a paying car park on Victora Embankment - a 15 minute walk away.

DIRECTIONS

DIRECTIONS

From the North:

Exit M1 at Junction 26 heading for Nottingham on the A610. Stay on the A610 to the city centre, a distance of approximately 6 miles, and follow the one way system onto Lower Parliament Street heading for the A60 London Road. Once on this road, across the River Trent, turning into Pavilion Road for the City Ground.

From the South:

Exit at Junction 24 heading for Nottingham South on the A453. After approximately 7 miles keep to the left, avoiding the fly-over, and at the roundabout take the left exit to pass under the A52 onto the B679 Wilford Lane. Go to the end, turn left onto the A60, right onto Radcliffe Road and left into Colwick Road for the City Ground.

From the East:

Take the A52 until the roundabout with the A6011 Radcliffe Road, keeping left when the road splits and turning right into Colwick Road for the City Ground.

Nottingham Midland Railway Station is situated in the town centre, approximately half a mile from the ground.

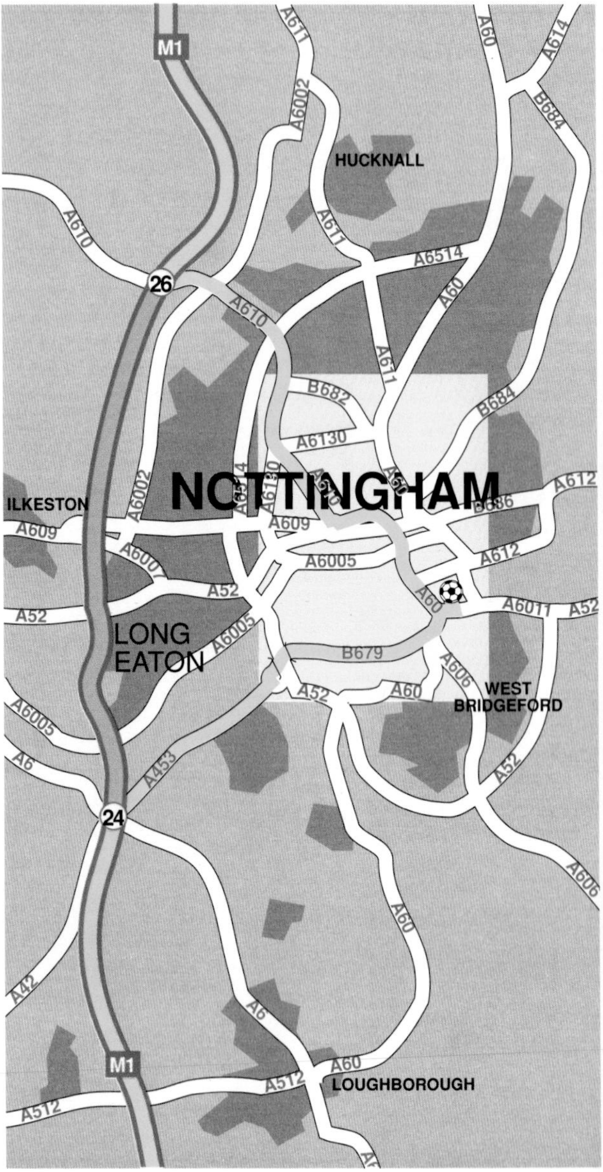

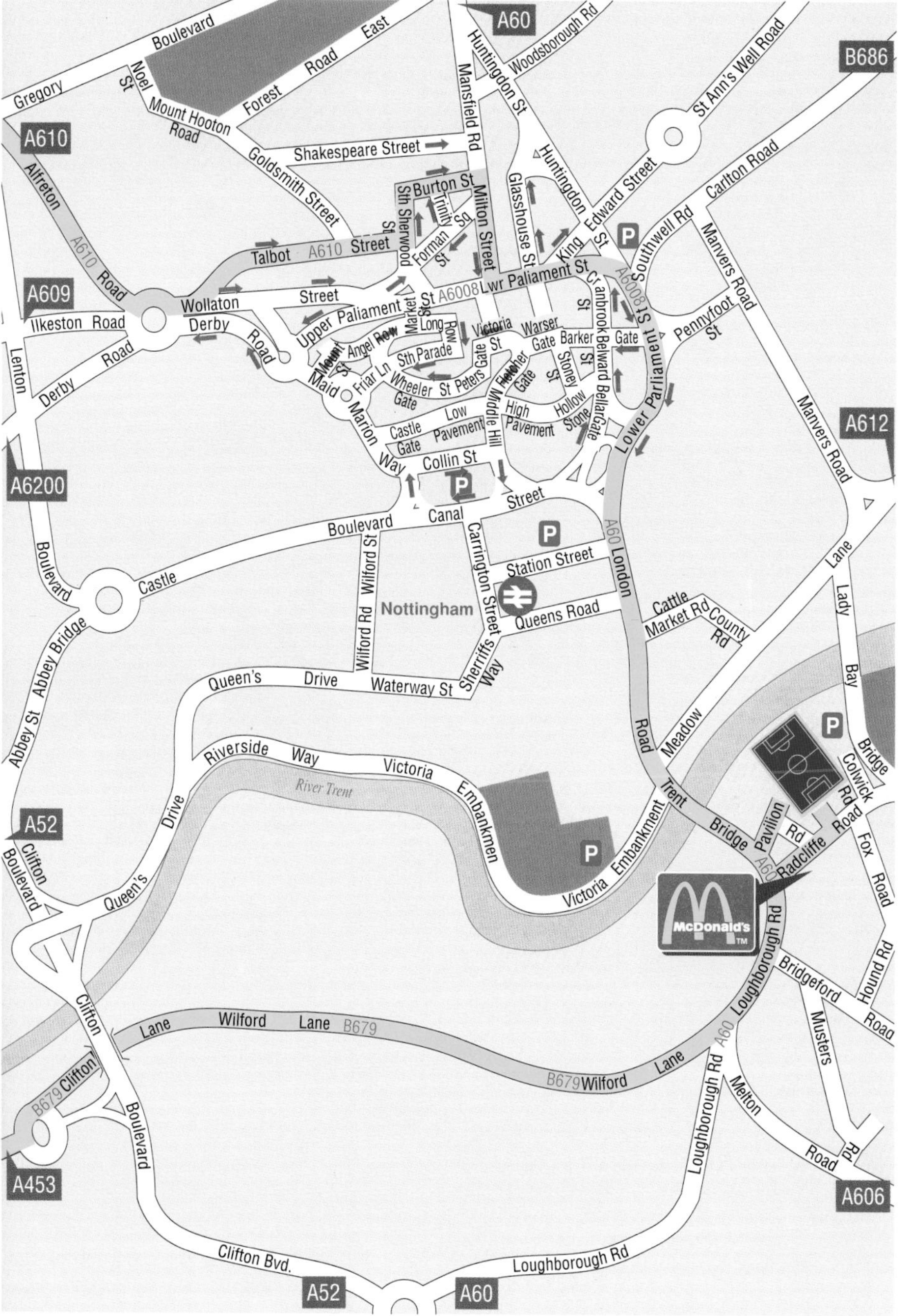

McDonald's™ 55a Radcliffe Road, Nottingham

Sheffield Wednesday FC

Sheffield Wednesday FC
Penistone Road
Hillsborough
Sheffield
S6 1SW

Club No: 0114·221·2121
Fax No: 0114·221·2122
Tickets: 0114·221·2400

Bobby Robson: *view from abroad*

One of the top Yorkshire clubs that never quite reaches the stars. They have a partisan crowd who love their football who deserve a good season to get their teeth into. Wednesday often promise a lot but then slip up along the way. They lose too many games to challenge for a place in Europe and for a good solid Premiership team they should be looking for a European place.

Bob Harris: *view in England*

The fact that Wednesday finished just four points clear of the relegation zone is warning enough that things must change this coming season. Having lost two of the biggest names in British Management, David Pleat and Ron Atkinson, in one season the whole club will be looking for stability this year. Facts show that when the first choice eleven were fit and well the results were there but, clearly, the squad is shallow and injuries could again wreck the season if they are not addressed. For a big club with a big support, not to mention their excellent ground Wednesday will look for and deserve better this season.

INFORMATION HOTLINES

ClubCall:	0891·12·11·86*
Prize Line:	0891·33·29·86*

Calls cost 50p per minute at all times
Club Call, Avalon House, 57-63 Scrutton St, London, EC2A 4PJ

CLUB SHOPS

THE OWLS SUPERSTORE

Located by North Stand, Hillsborough

Opening Times:

Monday-Friday: 9.00am-5.00pm
Tuesdays: 9.00am-7.00pm
Match Saturdays: 9.00am-Kick Off plus 45 mins at end
Match Sundays: 10.00am-Kick Off plus 45 mins at end
Match Evenings: 9.00am-Kick Off plus 45 mins at end
Non Match Saturdays: 9.00am-4.00pm

Tel: 0114·221·2345

Fax: 0114·221·2350

Mail Order Service: 0114·221·2345

WEDNESDAY GEAR

Orchard Square Shopping Centre, Sheffield

Opening Times:

Monday-Friday: 9.00am-5.30pm
Match Saturdays: 9.00am-5.30pm

Tel: 0114·221·2355

BOOKING INFORMATION

General Enquiries:	0114·221·2400
Credit Card Bookings:	0114·221·2400
Travel Club:	0114·221·2400
Recorded Info:	0114·221·2400
Owls Members Club:	0114·221·2407

CATERING

Food

Meat & Potato Pies	£tba
Cheese & Onion Pasties	£tba
Sausage Rolls	£tba
Hot Dogs	£tba
Burgers	£tba
Chips	£tba
Chip Butty	£tba
Pizza	£tba
Crisps	£tba
Mars/Snickers/Twix	£tba
Opal Fruits (Bag)	£tba

BAR

Coffee/Tea/Chocolate/Bovril/Soup	£tba
Pepsi/Tango/Lucozade/Slam Bottles (500ml)	£tba
Ribena (250ml)	£tba

MISCELLANEOUS

Stadium Tours
Contact Steve Adams - Tel: 0114·221·2377
Corporate Hospitality
Sales Department - Tel: 0114·221·2333
A range of Matchday hospitality packages, sponsorships and match ball sponsorship available through our commercial department.
For Conference and Banqueting opportunities call
Sales Department on 0114·221·2333, Fax 0114·221·2122.
Literature
Programme price £2.00
Pre Match & Half Time Entertainment
Still yet to be confirmed! Other than Ollie, Ozzie and Bazz owl Mascots.

SHEFFIELD WEDNESDAY FC

John Motson: *one to watch*

ANDY BOOTH

Wednesday's leading striker missed nine Premiership games with injury soon after the start of last season, and by the time he returned with a hat-trick against Bolton, Manager David Pleat had lost his job. Booth's scoring rate fell away in Wednesday's mild finish to the season which saw the departure of Ron Atkinson, so now he will want to prove to the new Hillsborough regime that he is a fearless and forthright centre forward who can score consistently.

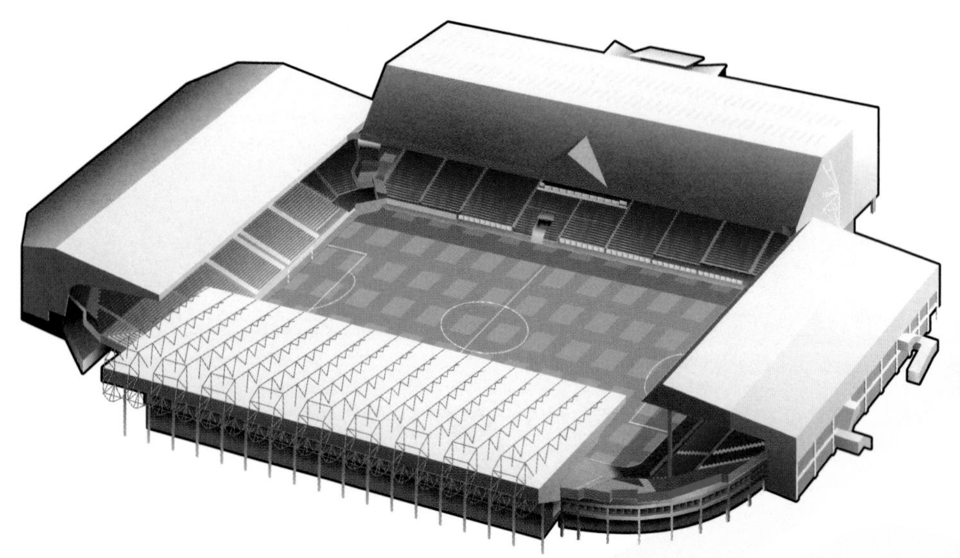

SOUTH STAND (8,000)

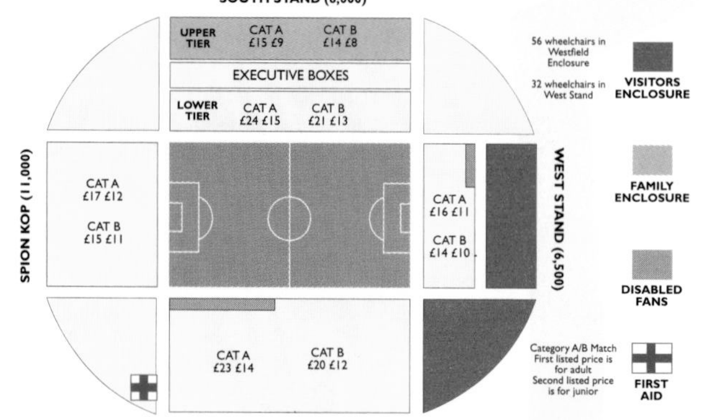

NORTH STAND (9,000)

97/98 season points and league position by month

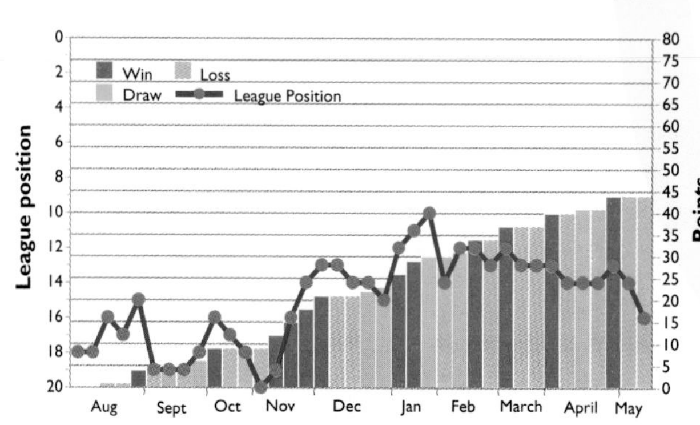

Goals for and against seasons 92/3 to 97/8

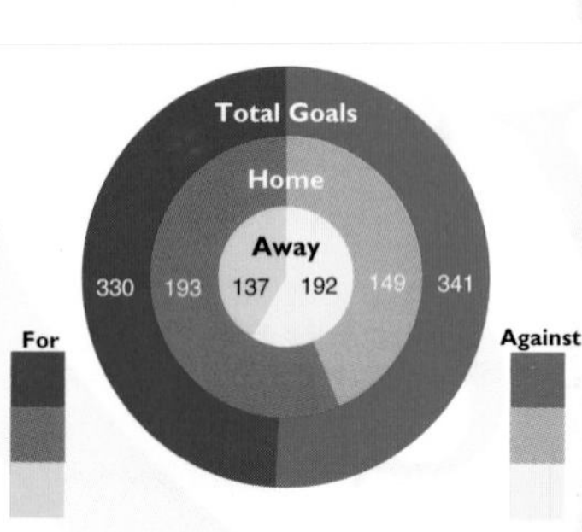

Goals scored by position by season

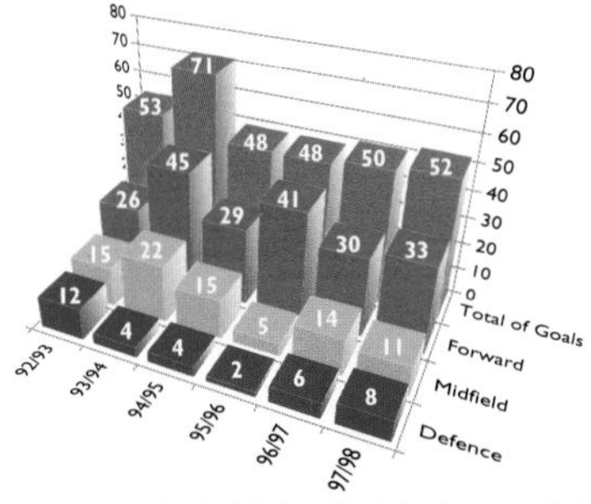

Bookings by position by season

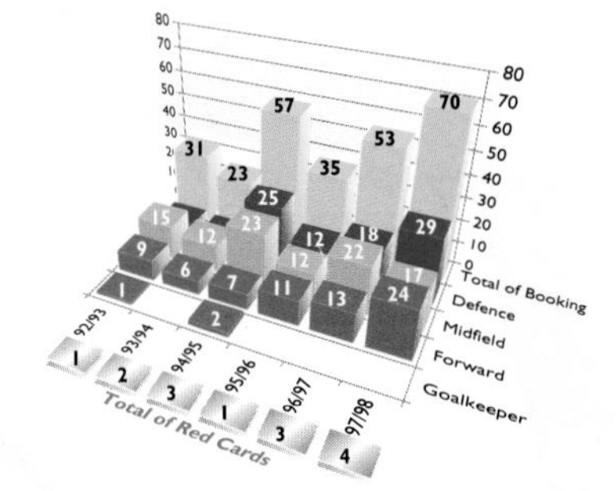

Goals scored by position by month 97/98

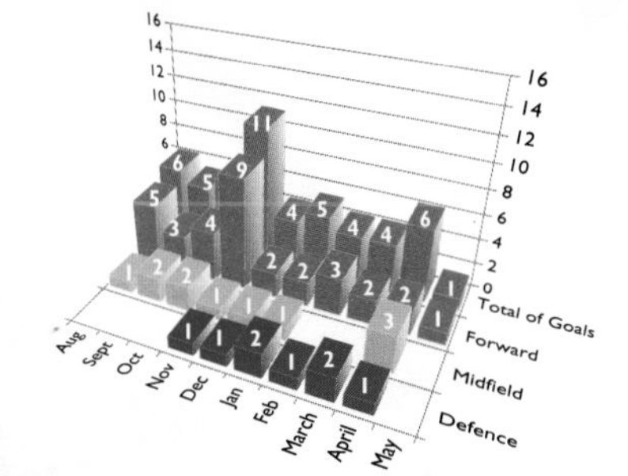

Final league position by season

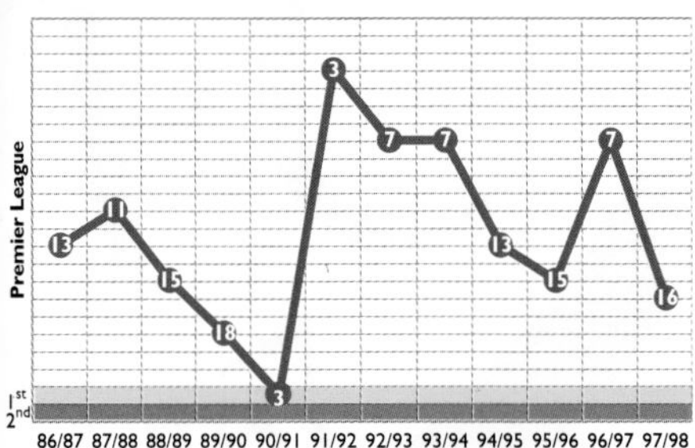

THE CARLING PREMIERSHIP FIXTURE LIST

HOME MATCH
AWAY MATCH
LAST SEASON: WIN
LAST SEASON: DRAW
LAST SEASON: LOSS

Opponent	Date	Last season
WEST HAM	15/8	1-1
TOTTENHAM	22/8	2-3
ASTON VILLA	29/8	1-3
DERBY	9/9	0-3
BLACKBURN	12/9	0-0
WIMBLEDON	19/9	1-1
ARSENAL	26/9	2-0
MIDDLESBROUGH	3/10	N/A
COVENTRY	17/10	0-1
EVERTON	24/10	3-1
SOUTHAMPTON	31/10	1-0
LEEDS	7/11	2-1
NEWCASTLE	14/11	1-2
MAN UTD	21/11	2-0
CHELSEA	28/11	0-1
NOTTM FOREST	5/12	N/A
CHARLTON	12/12	N/A
LIVERPOOL	19/12	1-2
LEICESTER	26/12	1-0
ASTON VILLA	28/12	2-2
TOTTENHAM	9/1	1-0
WEST HAM	16/1	0-1
DERBY	30/1	2-5
LEICESTER	6/2	1-1
WIMBLEDON	13/2	1-1
BLACKBURN	20/2	2-7
MIDDLESBROUGH	27/2	N/A
ARSENAL	6/3	0-1
LEEDS	13/3	1-3
SOUTHAMPTON	20/3	3-2
COVENTRY	3/4	0-0
EVERTON	5/4	3-1
NEWCASTLE	10/4	2-1
MAN UTD	17/4	1-6
CHELSEA	24/4	1-4
NOTTM FOREST	1/5	N/A
LIVERPOOL	8/5	3-3
CHARLTON	16/5	N/A

THE SQUAD

Goalkeeper · Defender · Midfield · Forward · No of goals · No of clean sheets · No of yellow cards · No of red cards

Player	Position	Goals / Clean sheets	Yellow cards	Red cards
K. Pressman	Goalkeeper	8		
M. Clarke	Goalkeeper			
E.Thome	Defender			
E. Barrett	Defender		4	
I. Nolan	Defender		2	
D. Walker	Defender			
G. Sedloski	Defender			
J. Newsome	Defender	2	3	
D. Stefanovic	Defender	2	7	1
A. Hinchcliffe	Defender	1		
L. Briscoe	Defender		1	
A.Quinn	Midfield			
K. Kotylo	Midfield			
B. Carbone	Midfield	9	8	1
S. Oakes	Midfield			
P. Atherton	Midfield	3	8	
G. Whittingham	Midfield	4	1	
G. Hyde	Midfield	1	8	
J. Magilton	Midfield	1	1	
P. Rudi	Midfield		2	
N. Alexandersson	Midfield			
A. Booth	Forward	7	1	1
P. Di Canio	Forward	12	9	
R. Humphreys	Forward		1	
M.Agogo	Forward			
F.Sanetti	Forward			

Transfers after 15 July 1998:

DANNY WILSON

Solid, determined and confident. Made progress through the tough lower league scenario as a player and has not lost his ideals. Down to earth, likes to be play the game properly and is popular because he doesn't try to be anything other than himself.

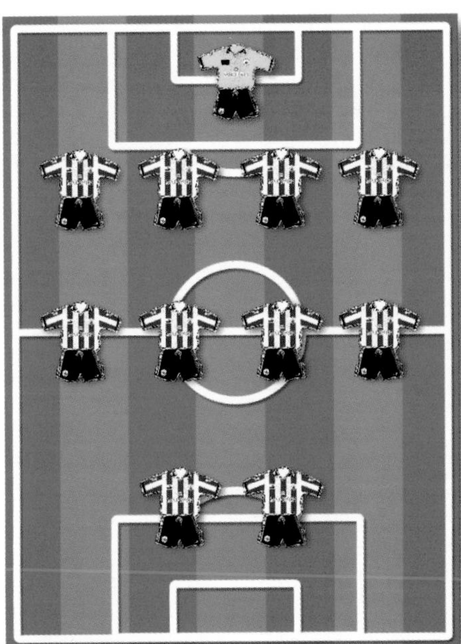

Trevor Brooking: *tactics*

Generally played 4-4-2 as well, but the Italian duo Paulo Di Canio and Benito Carbone were difficult to slot into any system when together in the starting line-up. Brilliant individuals who are natural entertainers, who can destroy any opposition, but can be equally frustrating as well. They must tighten up a defence that was always fragile, and the whole season fluctuated with alarming inconsistency.

Sheffield Wednesday's stadium is situated 2 miles from the city centre. All visitors are advised to approach via the M1/A61 route and avoid the city centre. Parking is possible in the area just north of Hillsborough around Doe Royd Lane as well as next to the stadium.

DIRECTIONS

All Routes:
Approaching on the M1, exit at Junction 36 onto the A61. Keep on this road for 7 miles, crossing over the roundabout onto Pennistone Road. The ground is on the right and some parking in Parkside Road.

Sheffield Railway Station is situated in the town centre, approximately 2 miles from the ground. Buses run to the ground from nearby Pond Street.

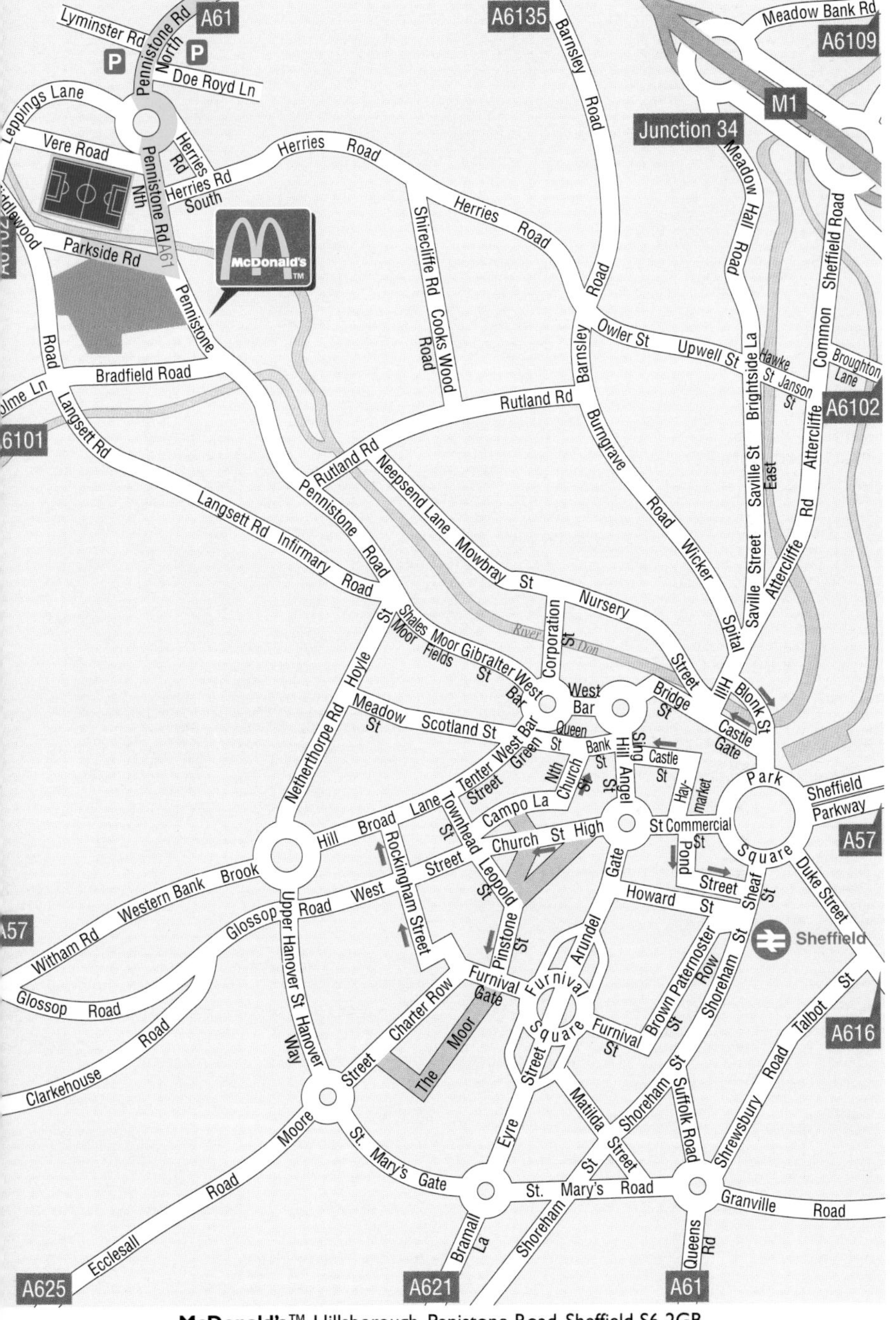

McDonald's™ Hillsborough, Penistone Road, Sheffield S6 2GB

Southampton FC

Southampton FC
The Dell
Milton Road
Southampton
SO15 2XH

Club Number: 01703·220505
Fax Number: 01703·330360
Tickets: 01703·337171
Internet: www.soton.ac.uk\~saints

Bobby Robson: *view from abroad*

Didn't they do well last season. Normally they are in a scrap right until the end of the season to retain their status but David Jones had them safe by March. It is a great achievement for a club of their size and he followed that by making a massive profit on selling Davies to Blackburn. Its a small town with a small club, small gates and a manager who keeps clubs like them up deserve al the credit they get. They are appreciated wher often a big club who finish in the middle of the tabl are dissatisfied with their manager.

Bob Harris: *view in England*

Until the Saints are able to move into their new stadium they are going to have to continue to live a hand to mouth existence and stop selling their top stars to balance the books. But, despite the loss of Davies, manager David Jones looks remarkably at home at the Dell. After his first season at the club they might well find it as difficult to hold onto him as their star players. This is also big season for Matthew Le Tissier and, having bee left out of the World Cup squad for France, he mus now show the character to bounce back an continue to play his massive part in the future of th Saints.

INFORMATION HOTLINES

ClubCall: 0891·12·11·78*

Calls cost 50p per minute at all times
Club Call, Avalon House, 57-63 Scrutton St, London, EC2A 4PJ

CLUB SHOPS

SAINTS SHOP

The Dell, Milton Road, Southampton

Opening Times:

Monday-Friday: 9.30am-5.00pm
Thursdays: 10.00am-5.00pm
Match Saturdays: 9.30am-Kick Off plus 20 mins at end
Match Sundays: 9.30am-Kick Off plus 20 mins at end
Match Evenings: 9.30am-Kick Off plus 15 mins at end

Tel: 01703·236400

Fax: 01703·336300

Mail Order Service: 01703·236400

SAINTS SHOP

Unit 29, The Bargate Centre, Southampton

Opening Times:
As above

Tel: 01703·333105

Mail Order Service: 01703·333105

BOOKING INFORMATION

General Enquiries:	01703·220505
Credit Card Bookings:	01703·337171
Travel Club:	01703·334172
Recorded Info:	01703·228575
Young Saints Line:	01703·334172

CATERING

FOOD

Quarter Pound Burger	£tba
Quarter Pounder Cheeseburger	£tba
Hot Dog	£tba
Chickenburger	£tba
Steak & Kidney Pie	£tba
Cornish Pasty	£tba
Sausage Roll	£tba
Chicken Curry & Rice	£tba
French Fries	£tba
Crisps	£tba

BAR

Soft Drinks	£tba
Tea	£tba
Coffee	£tba
Bovril	£tba
Hot Chocolate	£tba
Orange	£tba

MISCELLANEOUS

Stadium Tours
Available via prior booking - Tel: 01703·334172
Corporate Hospitality
Contact Kim Lawford - Tel: 01703·331417
Matchday Sponsorship including Ted Bates Suite for 10-12 persons. Executive Club for 170 persons. Matchball Sponsorship for 4 persons with complete Hospitality day and advertising.
Literature
Programme price £2.00
Pre Match & Half Time Entertainment
Interviews with players and management etc. Supersaint mascot presentations.

John Motson: *one to watch*

EGIL OSTENSTAD

The scale of Kevin Davies to Blackburn just a year after he arrived from Chesterfield did not please the majority of Saints supporters. Despite the fact their club made a handsome profit of around £7 million. It did confirm that their other much-envied striker would be staying at The Dell for the time being. Ostenstad was a member of Norway's squad in the World Cup, and if he can stay clear of the injuries which have plagued his time with Southampton, he is capable of taking on defences single-handed with his direct, thrustful style. He could also supply enough goals to lighten the effect of Davies departure.

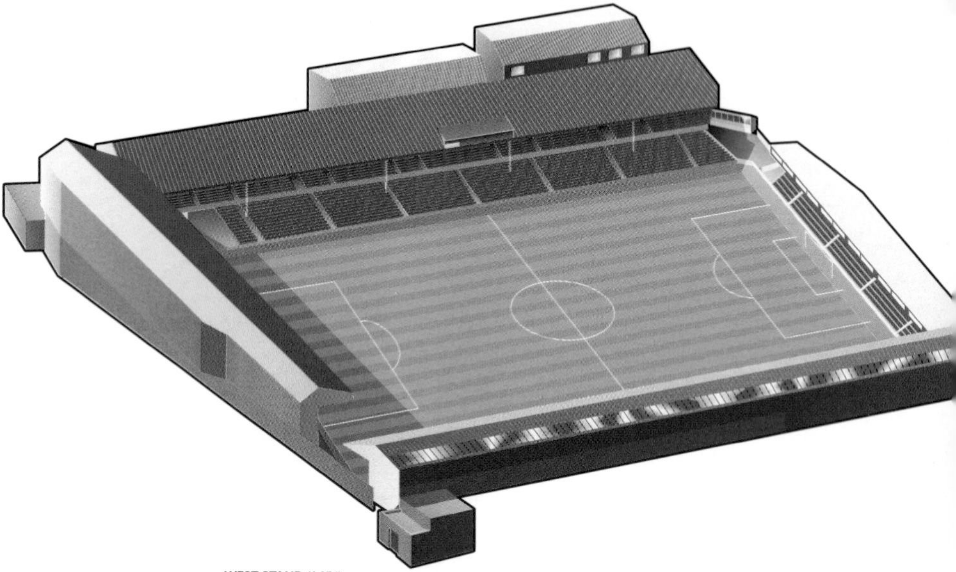

WEST STAND (6,074)

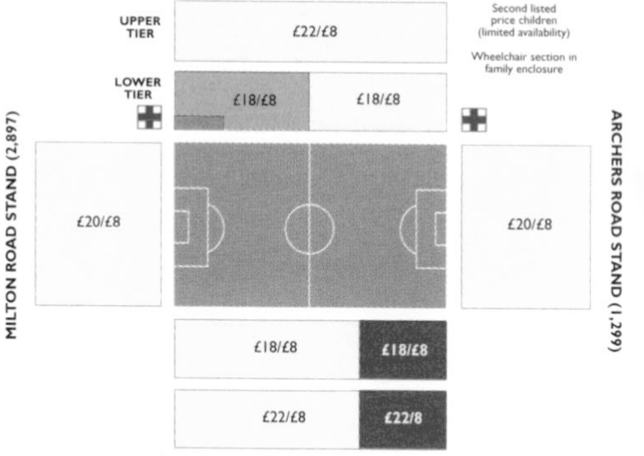

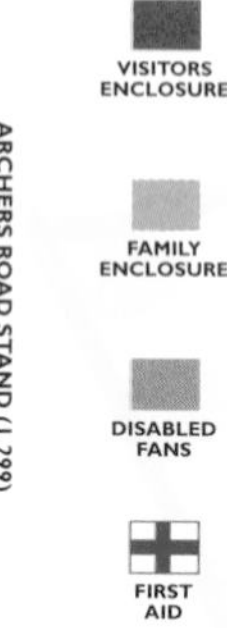

EAST STAND (4,882)

97/98 season points and league position by month

Goals for and against seasons 92/3 to 97/8

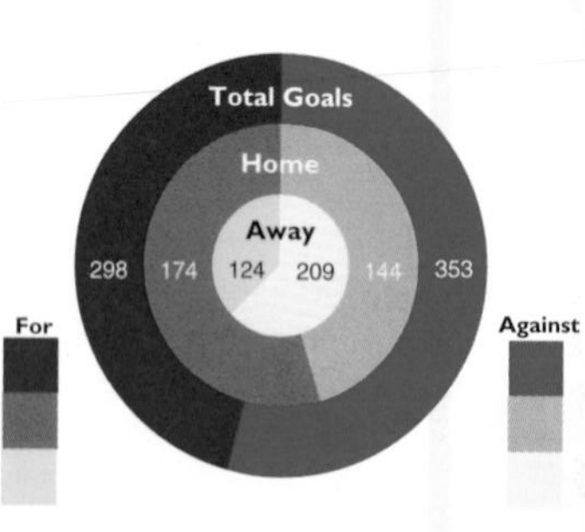

Goals scored by position by season

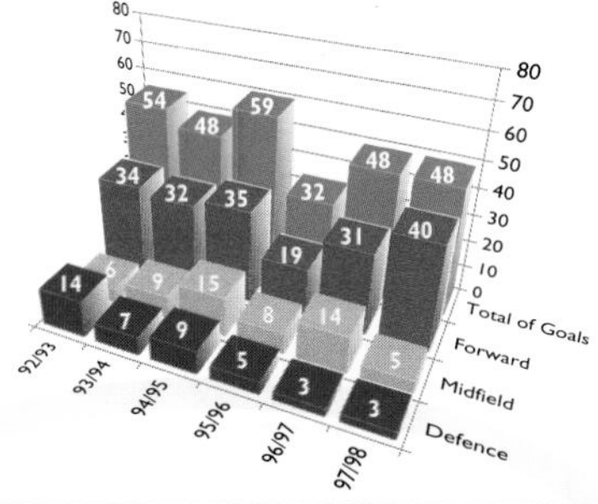

Bookings by position by season

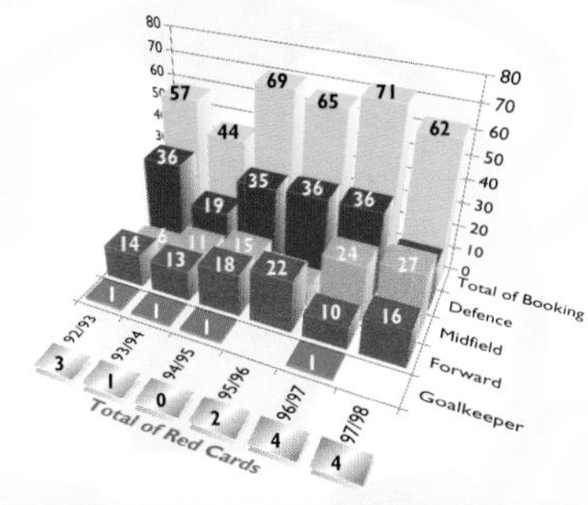

Goals scored by position by month 97/98

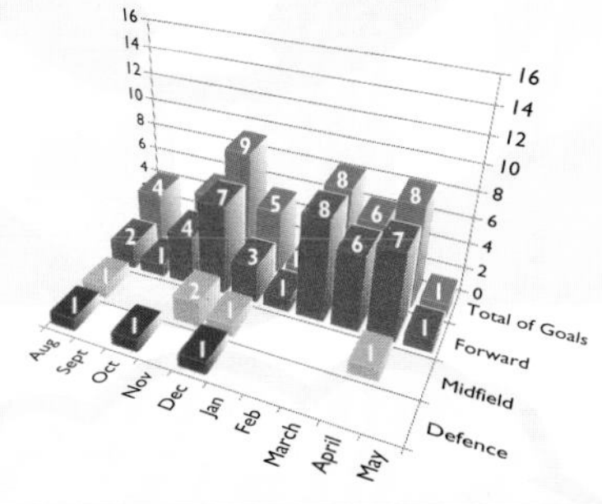

Final league position by season

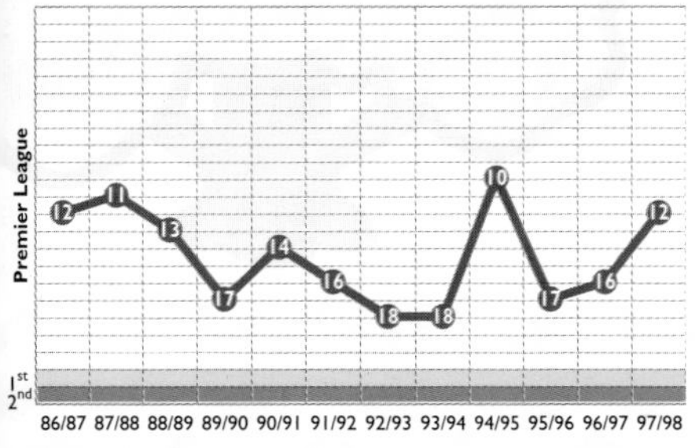

THE CARLING PREMIERSHIP FIXTURE LIST

HOME MATCH — AWAY MATCH — LAST SEASON: WIN — LAST SEASON: DRAW — LAST SEASON: LOSS

Opponent	Date	Last season
LIVERPOOL	16/8	1-1
CHARLTON	22/8	N/A
NOTTM FOREST	29/8	N/A
LEEDS	8/9	1-0
NEWCASTLE	12/9	1-2
TOTTENHAM	19/9	3-2
WEST HAM	28/9	4-2
MAN UTD	3/10	1-0
ARSENAL	17/10	0-3
COVENTRY	24/10	1-2
SHEFF WED	31/10	0-1
MIDDLESBROUGH	7/11	N/A
ASTON VILLA	14/11	1-2
BLACKBURN	21/11	3-0
DERBY	28/11	0-2
LEICESTER	5/12	3-3
EVERTON	12/12	2-0
WIMBLEDON	19/12	0-1
CHELSEA	26/12	1-0
NOTTM FOREST	28/12	N/A
CHARLTON	9/1	N/A
LIVERPOOL	16/1	3-2
LEEDS	30/1	0-2
CHELSEA	6/2	2-4
TOTTENHAM	13/2	1-1
NEWCASTLE	20/2	2-1
MAN UTD	27/2	0-1
WEST HAM	6/3	3-0
MIDDLESBROUGH	13/3	N/A
SHEFF WED	20/3	2-3
ARSENAL	3/4	1-3
COVENTRY	5/4	0-1
ASTON VILLA	10/4	1-1
BLACKBURN	17/4	0-1
DERBY	24/4	0-4
LEICESTER	1/5	2-1
WIMBLEDON	8/5	0-1
EVERTON	16/5	2-1

THE SQUAD

Goalkeeper · Defender · Midfield · Forward · No of goals · No of clean sheets · No of yellow cards · No of red cards

Player	Position	Goals / Clean sheets	Yellow cards	Red cards
P. Jones	Goalkeeper	8		
N. Moss	Goalkeeper			
J. Dodd	Defender	1	2	
D. Spedding	Defender			
K. Monkou	Defender	1	6	1
C. Lundekvam	Defender		8	
C. Palmer	Defender	3	7	1
R. Dryden	Defender		2	
F. Benali	Defender	1	2	2
L. Todd	Defender		1	
S. Marshall	Defender			
S. Ripley	Midfield			
M. Oakley	Midfield	1	3	
S. Basham	Midfield			
D.Howells	Midfield			
K. Richardson	Midfield		2	
M. Le Tissier	Midfield	11	6	
D. Hughes	Midfield		1	
J. Beresford	Midfield			
S. Ripley	Midfield			
D. Hirst	Forward	9	3	
S. Johansen	Forward		1	
E. Ostenstad	Forward	11	3	
A. Williams	Forward		3	
M. Hughes	Forward			
M. Paul	Forward			
J. Beattie	Forward			

Transfers after 15 July 1998:

David Pleat: *on the manager*

DAVID JONES

Won his spurs in his first season in the top grade. He still seems relaxed but maybe that is because he has yet to experience a really difficult time. Bought shrewdly but mainly ageing players. Sold brilliantly when he cashed in on young Davies. A big test awaits for this young man who suits the Dell so well that he could, with the right support, follow Lawrie McMenemy and become something of a permanent attachment.

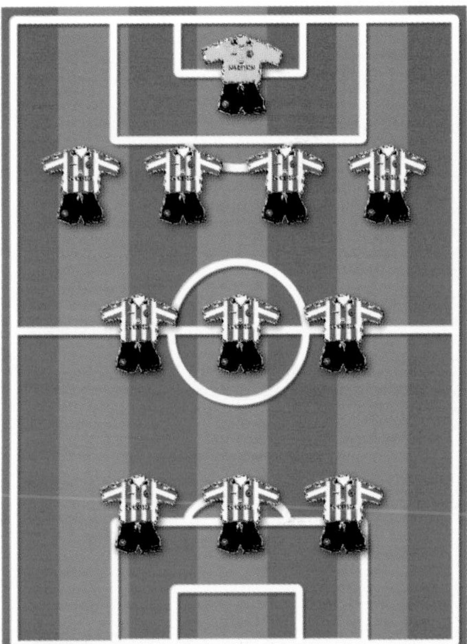

Trevor Brooking: *tactics*

Manager Dave Jones enjoyed a fine first season in charge, with a mixture of new faces and experience. Paul Jones was an outstanding goalkeeper and helped establish a new confidence in defence, which normally kept four at the back. Kevin Davies scored some spectacular goals, but has now moved on to Blackburn for £7.25 million, and will be sorely missed. This season will depend on how wisely that money has been invested, although no doubt Carlton Palmer will remain an important influence as he enjoyed a new lease of life down on the South Coast.

Southampton play at the Dell, situated half a mile from the city centre. It is usually possible to park near the ground.

DIRECTIONS

From The North:

Follow the M3 to the end exiting at Junction 4 onto The Avenue (A33). After 21/2 miles turn right into Northlands Road. Follow to the end T-junction with Archers Road. The Dell is opposite.

From The West:

From the M27 exit at Junction 3, turning right onto the M271. After 11/2 miles turn left at the roundabout onto the A3024, going over the flyover and turning left after approximately 2 miles into Central Station Bridge. Turn right at the roundabout into Commercial Road, left into Hill Lane and after approximately half a mile right into Archers Road. The Dell is on the right.

From The East:

From the M27 exit at Junction 5 left onto the Swaythling Link Road and on onto the High Road. Turn right where the road divides onto the A35 Burgess Road for 1 mile. Turn left onto The Avenue and right into Northlands Road. Follow to the end T-junction with Archers Road. The Dell is opposite.

Southampton Central Railway Station is a ten minute walk to the ground.

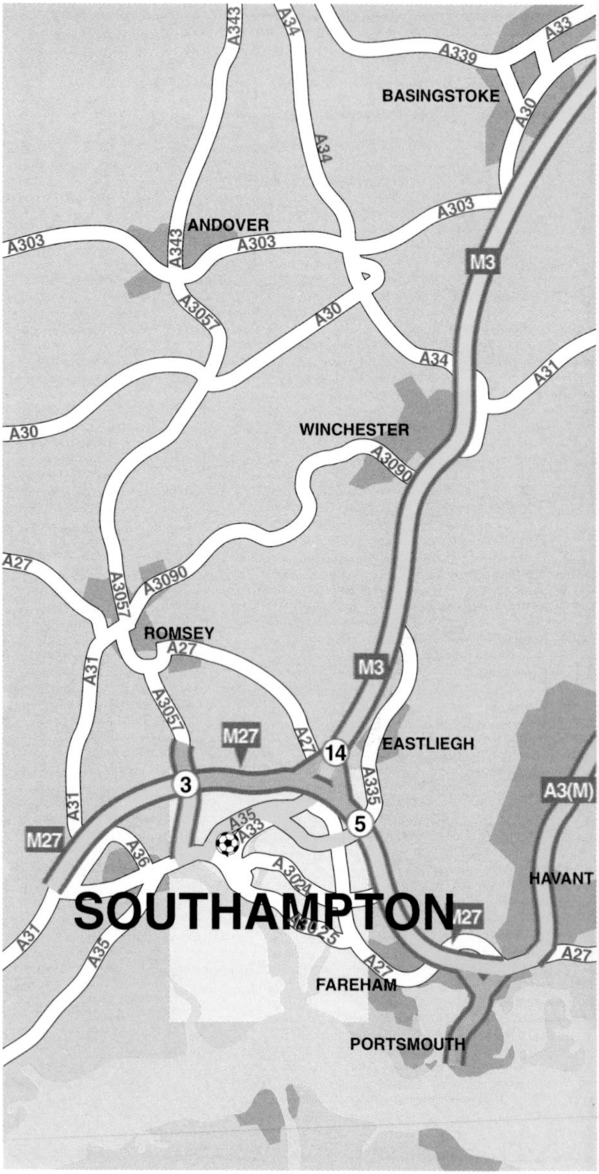

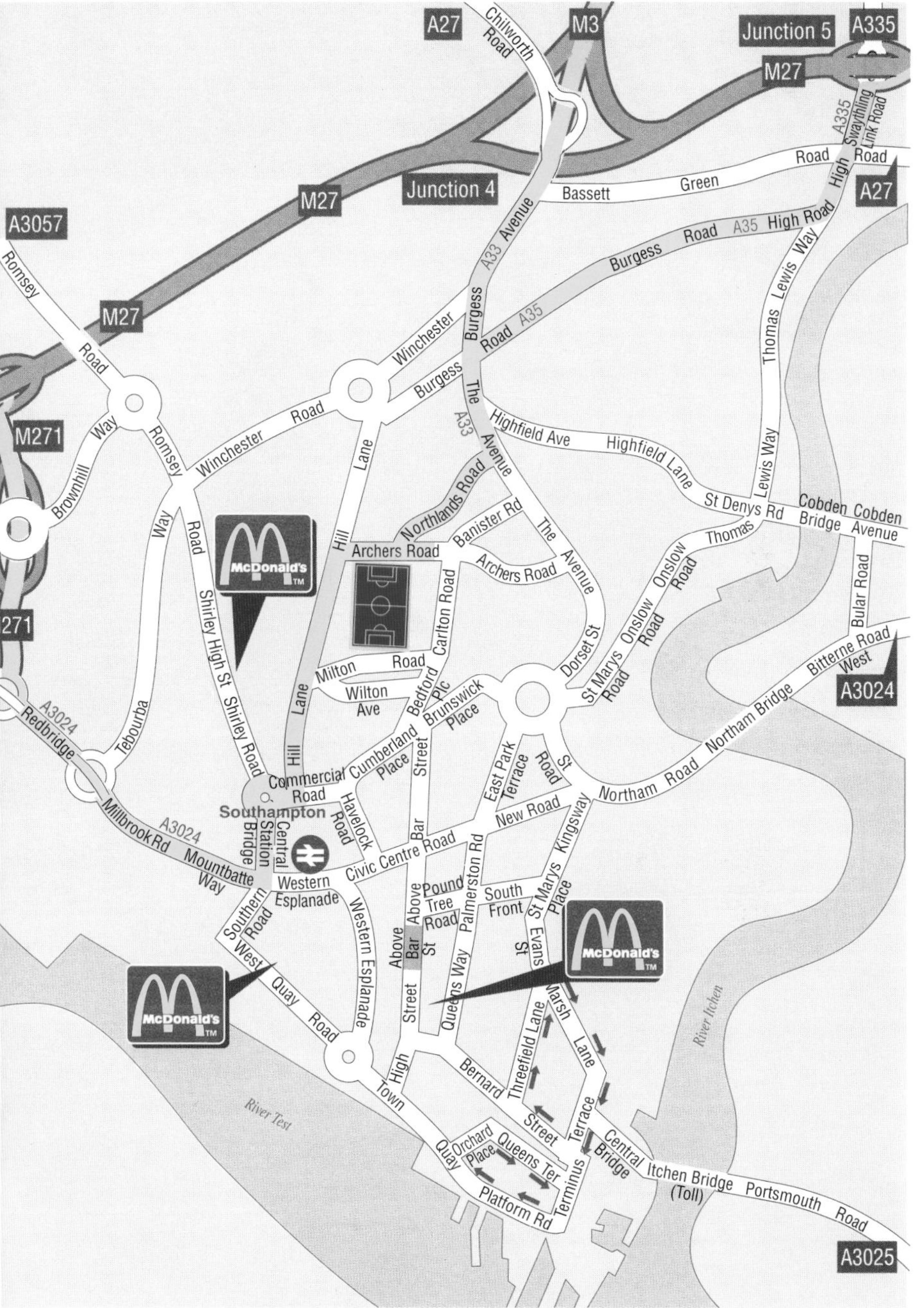

McDonald's™ 355 Shirley Road, Shirley SO15 3JD
McDonald's™ 1 Harbour Parade, Western Esplanade Retail Park SO1 5LB
McDonald's™ 12-16 Above Bar Street, Southampton SO1 0DQ

Tottenham Hotspur FC

Tottenham Hotspur FC
748 High Road
Tottenham
London N17 0AP

Club No:	0181·365·5000
Spurs Line:	0891·33·55·55
Tickets:	0181·365·5050
Internet:	**www.spurs.co.uk**

Bobby Robson: *view from abroad*

Injuries meant that these giants struggled for much of the season, in the doldrums only just avoiding relegation. They are one of our great clubs with a wonderful tradition in Europe and worldwide. They have gone for a foreign coach who took a while to settle but he has survived and will be looking forward to the challenge. They measure themselves with their next door neighbours Arsenal and last season will have wounded them deeply. Christian Gross will be under pressure to get results but the presence of Alan Sugar ensures stable foundations. They have a couple of great assets in David Pleat and my old friend Charlie Woods.

Bob Harris: *view in England*

Will be hoping that their troubles are behind them after grinding their way through an unimpressive season and only maintaining their status at the end of the campaign. Much will depend on how much Swiss coach Christian Gross learned after taking over from Gerry Francis and how much support he gets from the dressing room. A season free from injuries should see Spurs achieve respectability but their fans will be demanding so much more than that especially in view of what happened down the road at Highbury.

INFORMATION HOTLINES

Spurs Line:	0891·33·55·55*
Information Line:	0891·33·55·66*

**Calls cost 50p per minute at all times*
Spurs Line, The Information Service, Avalon House, 57-63 Scrutton St, London, EC2A 4PJ

CLUB SHOPS

SPURS SPORTSWEAR SHOP
762-776 High Road Tottenham, London, N17 OAP

Opening Times:

Monday-Friday: 9.30am-5.30pm
Match Saturdays: 9.30am-Kick off
Match Evenings: 9.30am-5.30pm

Tel: 0181·365·5041
Mail Order Service: 0181·808·5959

SPURS SOUVENIR SUPER STORE
1-3 Park Lane, Tottenham, London N17 OHJ

Opening Times:

Monday-Friday: 9.30am-5.30pm
Match Saturdays: 9.30am-Kick off
Match Evenings: 9.30am-5.30pm

Tel: 0181·366·5042
Mail Order Service: 0181·808·5959

Further shops at 61-62 Wood Green Shopping City and Pioneer Store, 6-7 Salisbury Hall Gardens, Chingford Road

BOOKING INFORMATION

General Enquiries:	0171·365·5050
Non-Members/ Credit Card Bookings:	0870·840·2468
Recorded Information:	0891·33·55·55
Members Ticket Bookings	0181·365·5100
Recorded Ticket Information	0891·33·55·66

MOUSSA SAIB

The Algerian international moved from Valencia to Tottenham for £2.3 million in February, but Spurs fans have yet to see the best or the most of him. Saib's early opportunities came in a wide left position, but he believes he is better in the centre of midfield and that is where Spurs have lacked an erudite passer in the Ardilles/Hoddle/Gascoigne mould for the last few years. Given the right framework around him, Saib could become a big favourite at White Hart Lane.

CATERING

FOOD

Soup	£tba
Hamburger	£tba
Chickenburger	£tba
Veggieburger	£tba
Pies	£tba
Pasties	£tba
Hot Dogs	£tba
Chips	£tba
Nachos	£tba
Crisps	£tba

BAR

Tea	£tba
Coffee	£tba
Soft Drinks	£tba

MISCELLANEOUS

Stadium Tours
Contact Main Reception - Tel: 0181·365·5000
Corporate Hospitality
Tel: 0181·365·5010
Corporate Hospitality facilities include 121 Executive Boxes of various sizes, 6 Executive Clubs with over 800 memberships available and selected match day sponsorship and hospitality packages.
Literature
Programme price £2, Spurs Monthly £2.50
Pre Match & Half Time Entertainment
Spurs TV on Jumbotron screen. One hour pre-match programme.

97/98 season points and league position by month

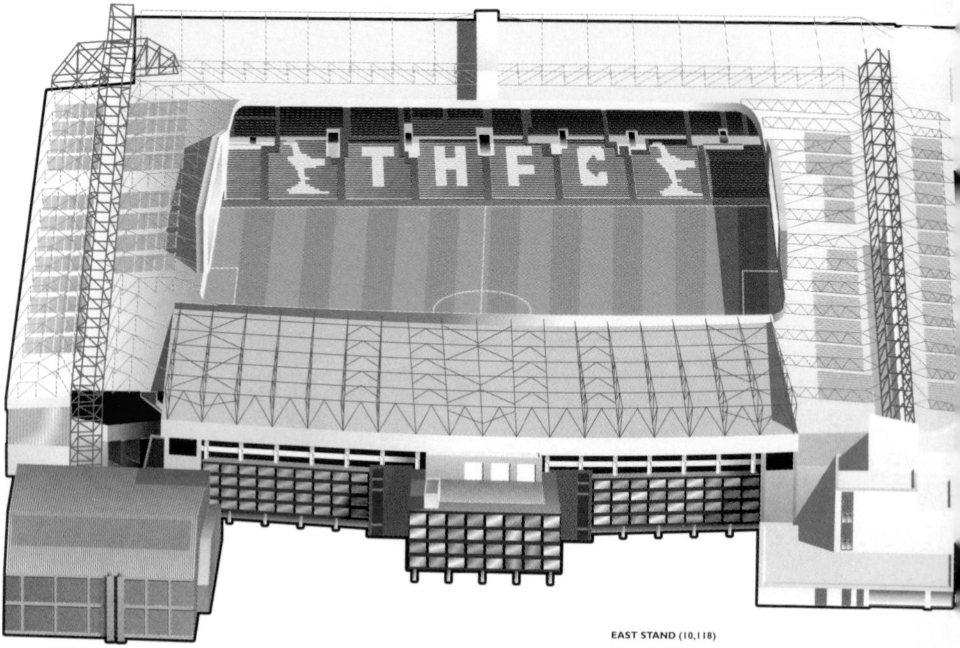

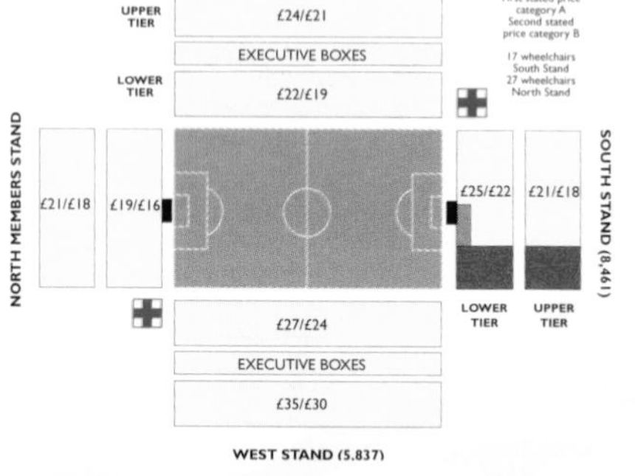

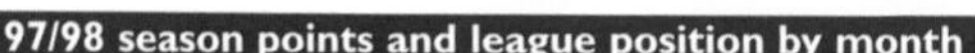

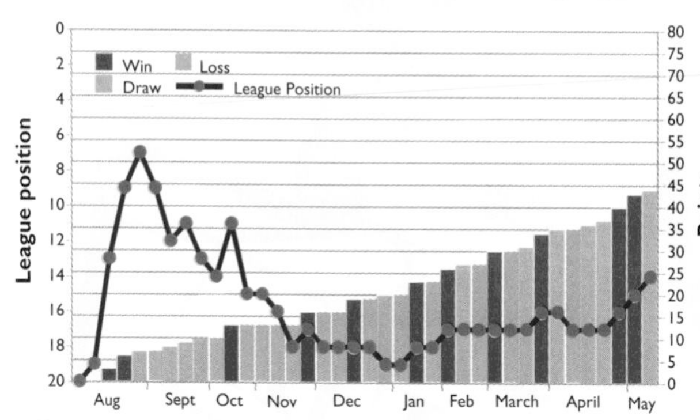

Goals for and against seasons 92/3 to 97/8

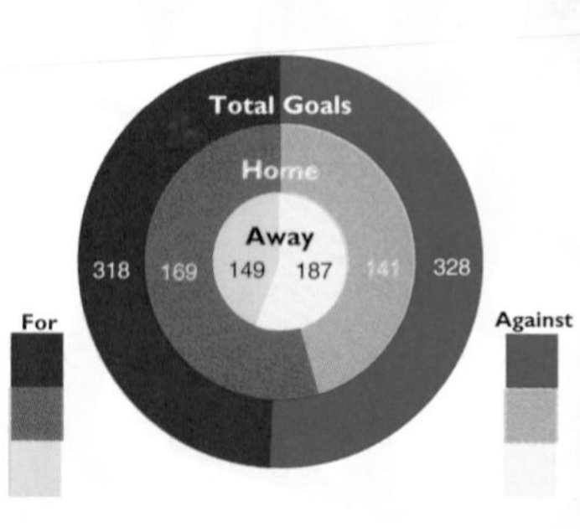

Goals scored by position by season

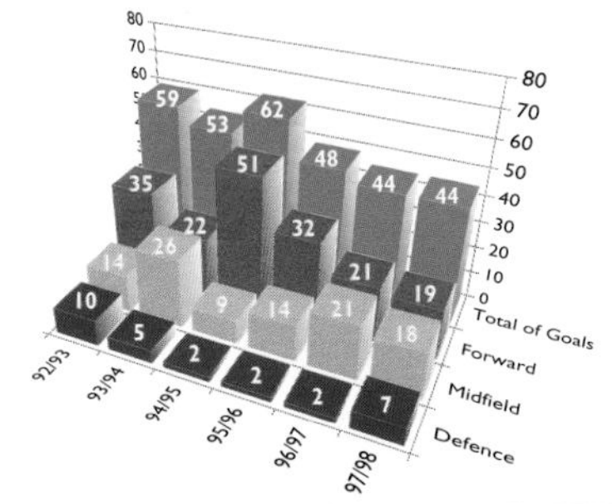

Bookings by position by season

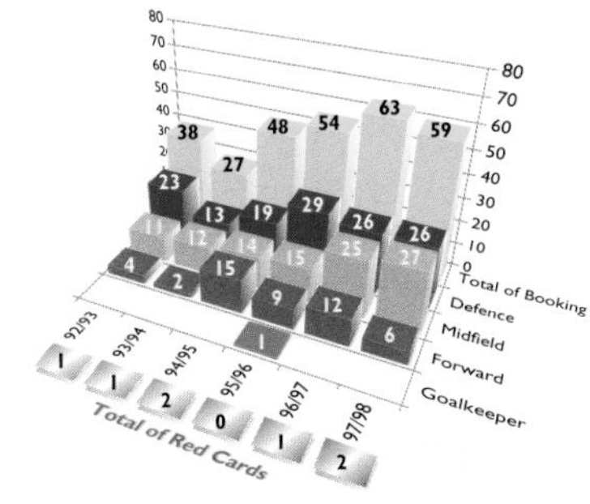

Goals scored by position by month 97/98

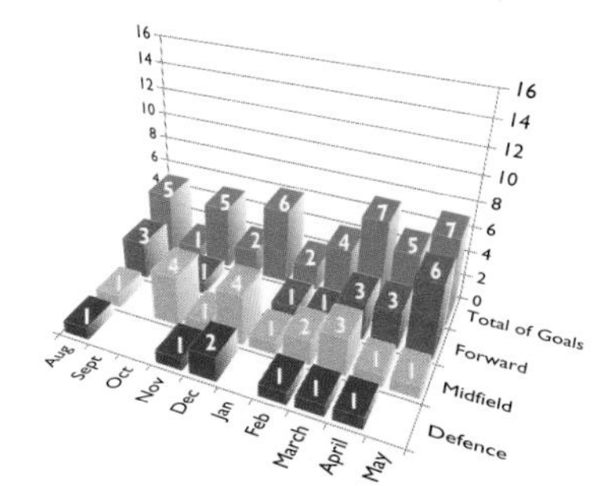

Final league position by season

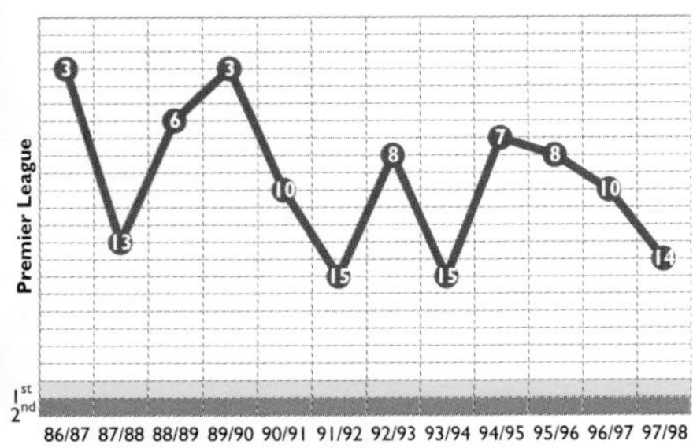

THE CARLING PREMIERSHIP FIXTURE LIST

HOME MATCH · AWAY MATCH · LAST SEASON: WIN · LAST SEASON: DRAW · LAST SEASON: LOSS

Opponent	Date	Last season
WIMBLEDON	15/8	6-2
SHEFF WED	22/8	3-2
EVERTON	29/8	2-0
BLACKBURN	9/9	0-0
MIDDLESBROUGH	12/9	N/A
SOUTHAMPTON	19/9	2-3
LEEDS	26/9	0-1
DERBY	3/10	1-2
LEICESTER	17/10	0-3
NEWCASTLE	24/10	2-0
CHARLTON	31/10	N/A
ASTON VILLA	7/11	1-4
ARSENAL	14/11	0-0
NOTTM FOREST	21/11	N/A
WEST HAM	28/11	1-2
LIVERPOOL	5/12	3-3
MAN UTD	12/12	0-2
CHELSEA	19/12	0-2
COVENTRY	21/12	0-4
EVERTON	28/12	1-1
SHEFF WED	9/1	0-1
WIMBLEDON	16/1	0-0
BLACKBURN	30/1	3-0
COVENTRY	6/2	1-1
SOUTHAMPTON	13/2	1-1
MIDDLESBROUGH	20/2	N/A
DERBY	27/2	1-0
LEEDS	6/3	0-1
ASTON VILLA	13/3	3-2
CHARLTON	20/3	N/A
LEICESTER	3/4	1-1
NEWCASTLE	5/4	0-1
ARSENAL	10/4	1-1
NOTTM FOREST	17/4	N/A
WEST HAM	24/4	1-0
LIVERPOOL	1/5	0-4
CHELSEA	8/5	1-6
MAN UTD	16/5	0-2

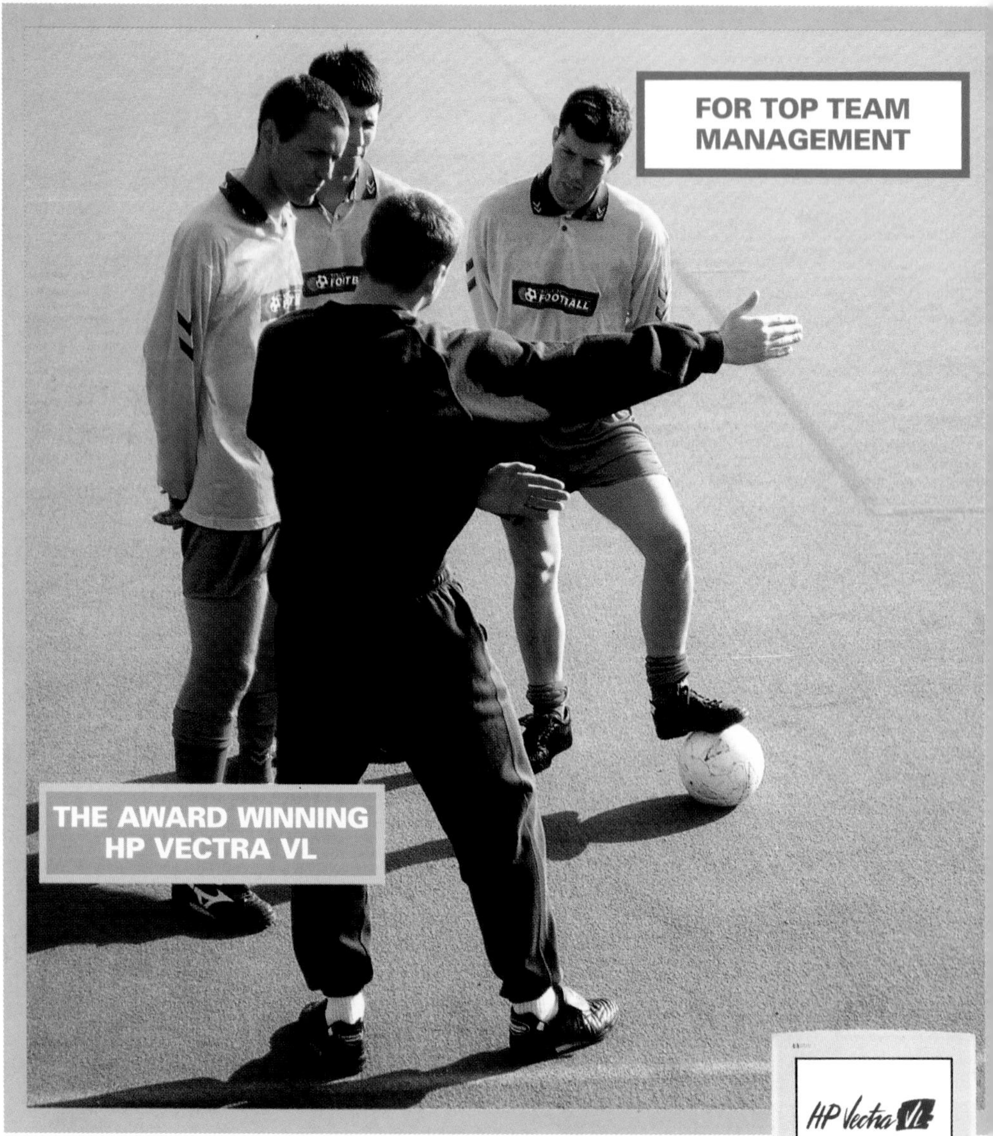

THE SQUAD

Goalkeeper · Defender · Midfield · Forward · No of goals · No of clean sheets · No of yellow cards · No of red cards

Player	Position	Goals / Clean sheets	Yellow cards	Red cards
I. Walker	Goalkeeper	7		
E. Baardsen	Goalkeeper	3		
F. Grodas	Goalkeeper			
P. Tramezzani	Defender			
J. Scales	Defender		1	
R. Vega	Defender	3	6	1
C. Calderwood	Defender	4	3	
S. Campbell	Defender		5	
C. Wilson	Defender		1	
J. Edinburgh	Defender		4	1
D. Anderton	Midfield			
R. Fox	Midfield	3	3	
S. Clemence	Midfield		1	
N. Berti	Midfield	3	5	
A. Sinton	Midfield		1	
M. Saib	Midfield	1		
A. Nielsen	Midfield	3	3	
S. Carr	Midfield		3	
D. Ginola	Midfield	6	7	
J. Domingues	Midfield	2	4	
C. Armstrong	Forward	5	2	
R. Allen	Forward			
L. Ferdinand	Forward	5	2	
S. Iversen	Forward		1	
N. Fenn	Forward			

Transfers after 15 July 1998:

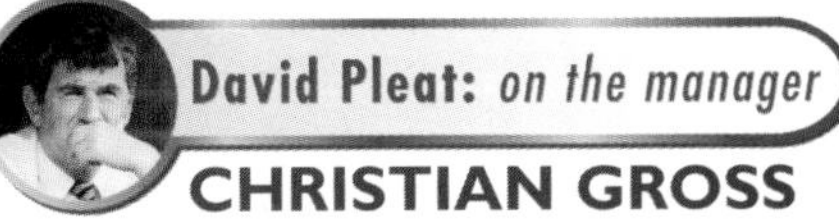

CHRISTIAN GROSS

Is learning the language quickly and beginning to understand the football humour, the pressures of the need to succeed and the media negativity that can be gained if not successful. He will be more determined than ever to build on the end of season improvement that saw Spurs pull away from relegation. A hard worker who is focused and prepared to stand up to difficult situations.

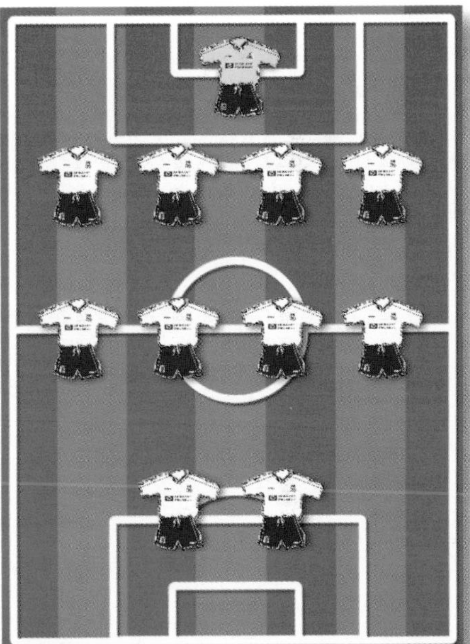

Trevor Brooking: *tactics*

Surely they cannot struggle as badly this time. They abandoned the three central defenders halfway through as Christian Gross went 4-4-2. David Ginola was their outstanding player through all the difficulties, but his wandering excursions around the pitch does often unbalance the shape of the side. I expect them to start much better this season but still cannot see their defence being strong enough to take them too far into the top half of the Premiership.

White Hart Lane is situated in North London, 6 miles from the centre. Limited parking is available near the ground.

DIRECTIONS

From The North:
From the M1, turn off onto the A1 at Junction 2/3. Join the A406 North Circular Road eastbound and continue for 7 miles. At the Edmonton traffic lights turn right onto the A1010 Fore Street. Continue for 1 mile and White Hart Lane is on the left.

From The North West:
Approaching London on the M40, at Junction 1 stay on the A40 for 10 miles before turning onto the A406 North Circular Road for 13 miles until reaching the Edmonton traffic lights. Then as route for North.

From The West:
Approaching London on the M4, turn off onto the A406 North Circular Road at Junction 1 and continue for 16 miles until reaching the Edmonton traffic lights. Then as route for North.

From The South West:
From the M3 turn off onto the M25 at Junction 2. Continue for 10 miles until you reach Junction 15 at which point turn off onto the M4. Then as route for the West.

From The East:
From the M11 turn off onto the A406 at Junction 4 and continue for 6 miles. At the Edmonton traffic lights turn left onto the A1010 Fore Street. Continue for 1 mile and White Hart Lane is on the left.

Seven Sisters tube station is 1.5 miles away. White Hart Lane Main Line is 3 minutes walk, Northumberland Park, 7 minutes.

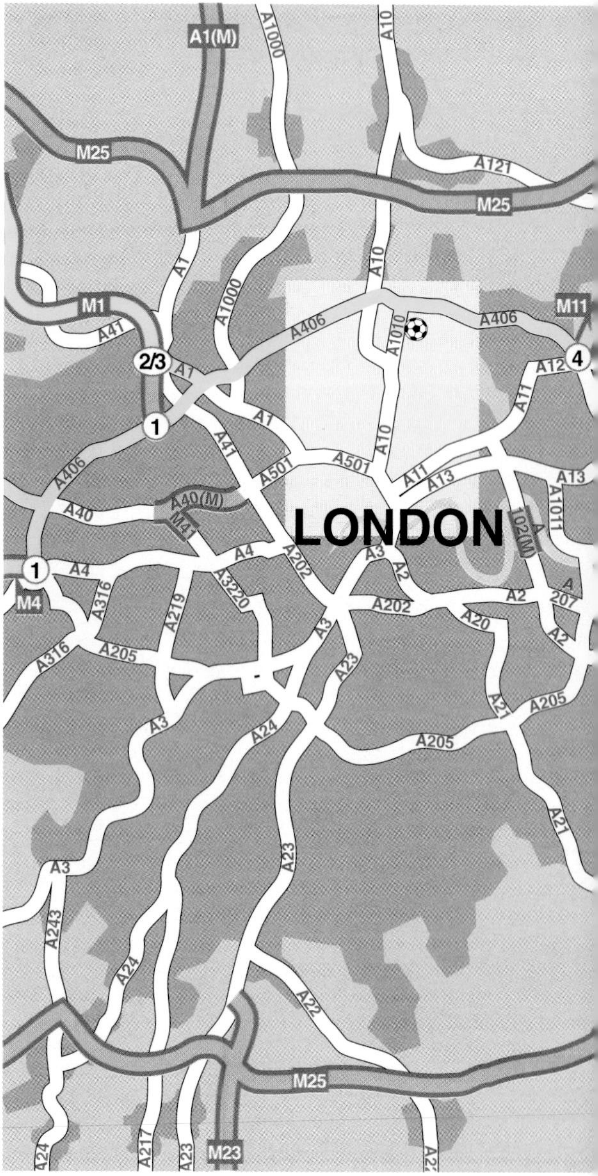

LONDON

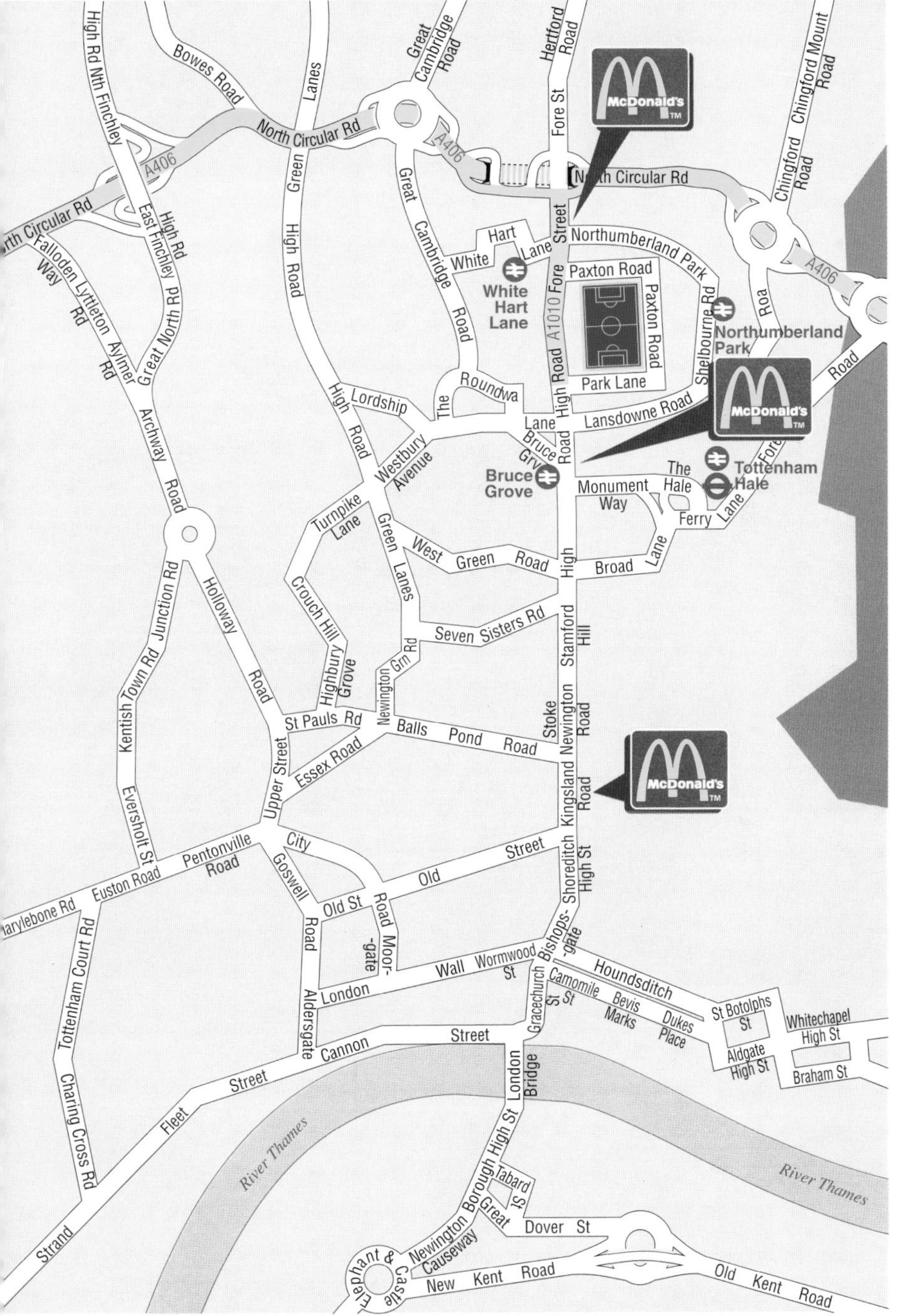

McDonald's™ 500 High Road, Tottenham, London N17 9JF
McDonald's™ 112-118 Fore Street, Edmonton, London N18 2XA
McDonald's™ 36-42 Kingsland High Street, Dalston London E8 2JP

West Ham United FC

West Ham United
Boleyn Ground
Green Street
Upton Park
London E13 9AZ

Club No: 0181·548·2748
Fax No: 0181·548·2758
Tickets: 0181·548·2700
Internet: www.westhamunited.co.uk

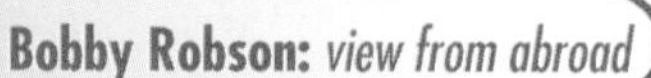

Bobby Robson: *view from abroad*

Harry Redknapp does a great job for a club who don't have quite the same potential as their big London rivals. But Harry is following on from Ron Greenwood and John Lyall bringing on the traditional youth policy and mixing it with a sprinkling of foreign names. They need to spend their money on the development of the young players and we are all waiting with baited breath to see how good young Joey Cole is.

Bob Harris: *view in England*

Harry Redknapp seems to have come to terms with his foreign imports and their integration into his team. It is the British players who continue to catch the eye at Upton Park and this season could see the emergence of young Rio Ferdinand as a player of real class after his experience of travelling to France for the World Cup. The whole football world is also waiting to see how soon Harry dares introduce young Joey Cole who has already been likened to a young Maradona, in strictly football terms that is!

INFORMATION HOTLINES

ClubCall: 0891·12·11·65*

Calls cost 50p per minute at all times
Club Call, Avalon House, 57-63 Scrutton St, London, EC2A 4PJ

CLUB SHOPS

HAMMERS MERCHANDISE - STADIUM SHOP

Boleyn Ground, Green Street, Upton Park

Opening Times:

Monday-Friday: 9.30am-5.00pm
Match Saturdays: 9.30am-Kick Off, plus after game
Non-Match Saturday: 9.30am-1.00pm
Match Sundays: 9.30am-Kick Off, plus after game
Match Evenings: 9.30am-Kick Off, 30 minutes at end

Tel: 0181·548·2722

Fax: 0181·472·0616

Mail Order Service: 0181·548·2730

SHOP 2

39-41 Barking Road, London E6

Opening Times:

Monday-Friday: 9.30am-5.00pm
Match Saturdays: 9.30am-6.00pm
Match Sundays: As Saturday
Match Evenings: 9.30am-Kick Off, 30 minutes at end.
Tel: 0181·548·4453

Further shops at
81 South Street, Romford.
Tel: 01708 766111
Savacentre, Eastgate Shopping Centre, Basildon.
Tel: 01268 521212
18 Clifftown Road Southend-on-sea
Tel: 01702 393 799

BOOKING INFORMATION

General Enquiries:	0181·548·2700
Credit Card Bookings:	0181·548·2700
Travel Club:	0181·548·2700
Recorded Info:	0181·548·2761
Junior Club Info:	0181·548·2727
Ticket Master:	0171·413·9013

CATERING

FOOD

Jumbo Frankfurter ..... £tba
Sausage Roll ..... £tba
Pasties ..... £tba
Pies ..... £tba

BAR

Coffee ..... £tba
Tea ..... £tba
Chocolate ..... £tba
Cold Drinks ..... £tba

MISCELLANEOUS

Stadium Tours
Contact Wally Morris - Tel: 0181·548·2777
Last Thursday in every month
Corporate Hospitality
Contact Promotions Department - Tel: 0181·548·2777
Corporate Hospitality in the Executive Suite, Academy Suite and '66' Club.
Matchday Sponsorship in the Trevor Brooking Suite.
Matchball Sponsorship for 4 people.
Programme Sponsorship for 4 people.
Literature
Programme price £2, Hammers News £2.50
Pre match and Half time entertainment
Hammerettes & Cheerleaders

TREVOR SINCLAIR

With seven goals in 14 Premiership games after his January transfer from Queens Park Rangers, the elusive Sinclair demonstrates his right to be on the big stage. A one-in-two strike rate from a swift, clever ball player who can also act as provider is not easily come by, and at 25 Sinclair now has the platform to steer his upwardly mobile club to bigger things and to further his own international prospects.

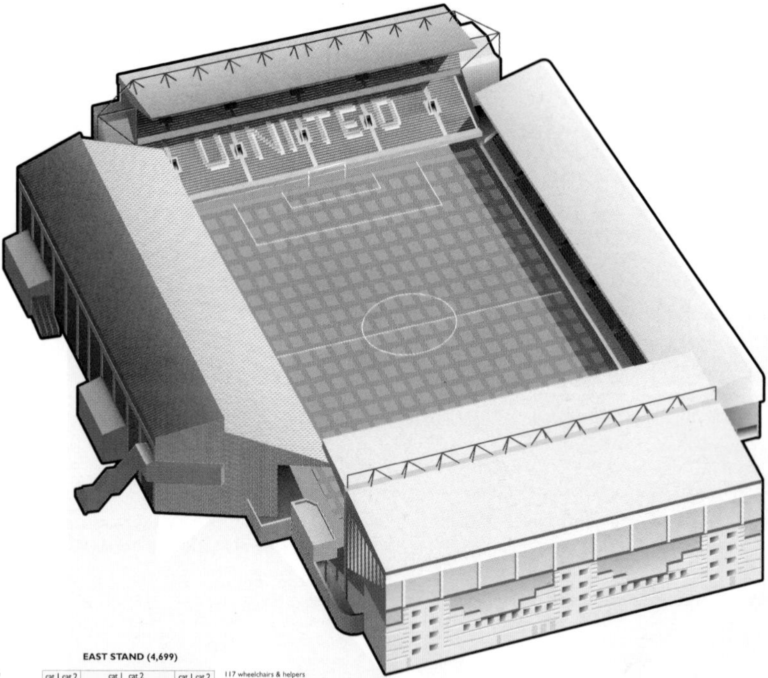

UNITED

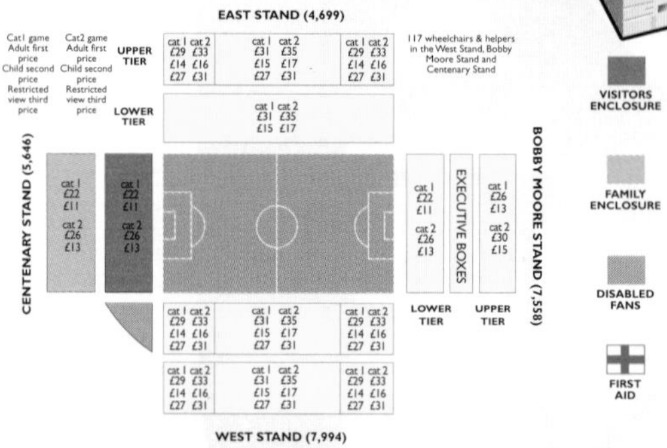

EAST STAND (4,699)
Cat1 game Adult first price Child second price Restricted view third price
Cat2 game Adult first price Child second price Restricted view third price
UPPER TIER
cat 1 cat 2 £29 £33 £14 £16 £27 £31
cat 1 cat 2 £31 £35 £15 £17 £27 £31
cat 1 cat 2 £29 £33 £14 £16 £27 £31
117 wheelchairs & helpers in the West Stand, Bobby Moore Stand and Centenary Stand
LOWER TIER
cat 1 cat 2 £31 £35 £15 £17
CENTENARY STAND (5,646)
cat 1 £22 £11 cat 2 £26 £13
cat 1 £22 £11 cat 2 £26 £13
cat 1 £22 £11 cat 2 £26 £13
EXECUTIVE BOXES
cat 1 £26 £13 cat 2 £30 £15
LOWER TIER
UPPER TIER
BOBBY MOORE STAND (7,558)
cat 1 cat 2 £29 £33 £14 £16 £27 £31
cat 1 cat 2 £31 £35 £15 £17 £27 £31
cat 1 cat 2 £29 £33 £14 £16 £27 £31
cat 1 cat 2 £29 £33 £14 £16 £27 £31
cat 1 cat 2 £31 £35 £15 £17 £27 £31
cat 1 cat 2 £29 £33 £14 £16 £27 £31
WEST STAND (7,994)
VISITORS ENCLOSURE
FAMILY ENCLOSURE
DISABLED FANS
FIRST AID

97/98 season points and league position by month

League position
0
2
4
6
8
10
12
14
16
18
20
Points
80
75
70
65
60
55
50
45
40
35
30
25
20
15
10
5
0
Win
Loss
Draw
League Position
Aug
Sept
Oct
Nov
Dec
Jan
Feb
March
April
May

Goals for and against seasons 92/3 to 97/8

Total Goals
Home
Away
311
196
115
174
131
305
For
Against

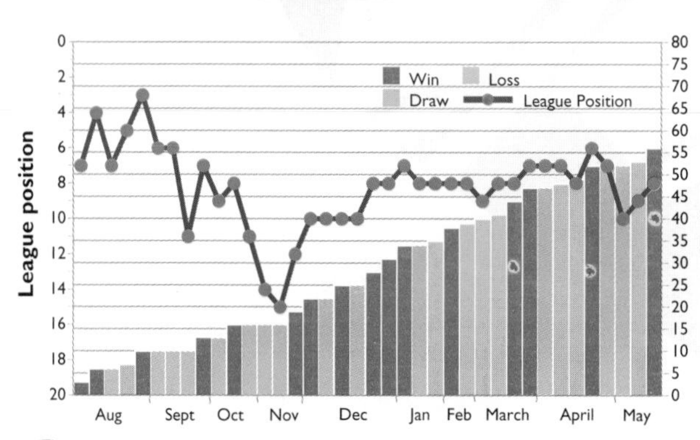

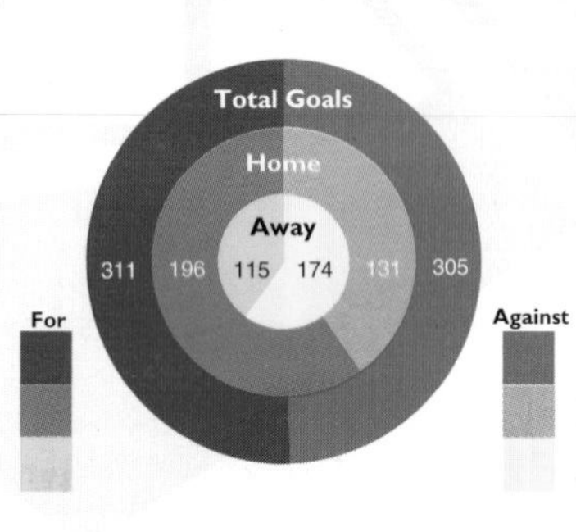

Goals scored by position by season

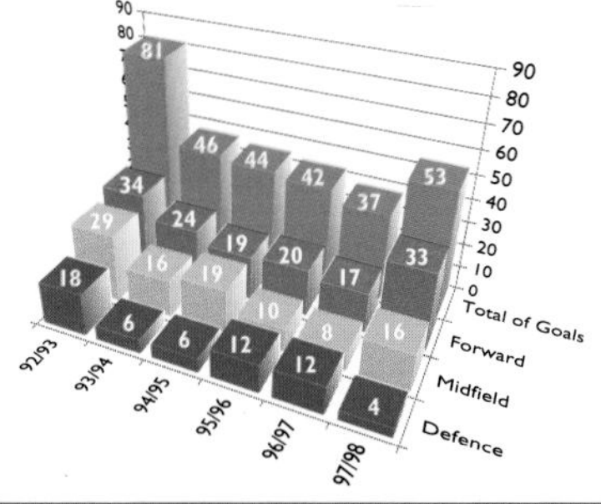

Bookings by position by season

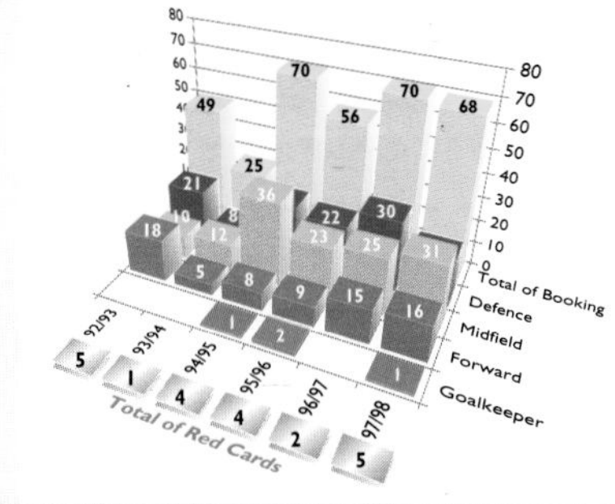

Goals scored by position by month 97/98

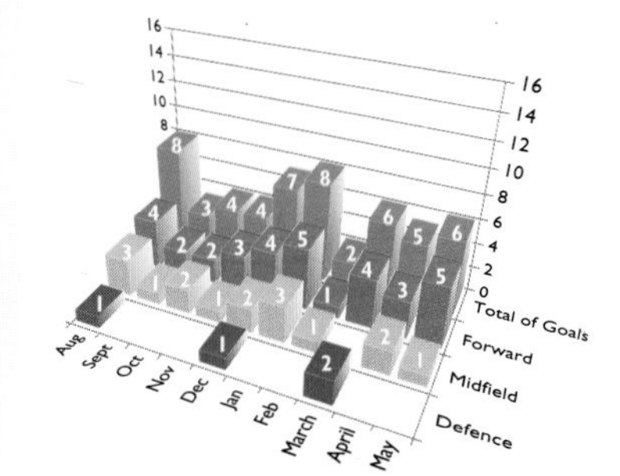

Final league position by season

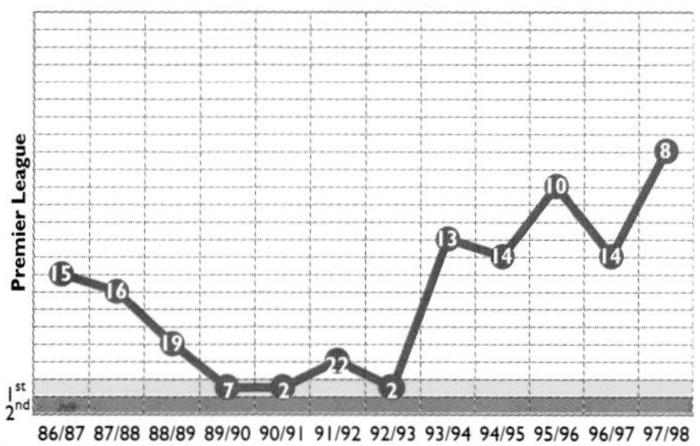

THE CARLING PREMIERSHIP FIXTURE LIST

HOME MATCH
AWAY MATCH
LAST SEASON: WIN
LAST SEASON: DRAW
LAST SEASON: LOSS

Opponent	Date	Last season
SHEFF WED	15/8	1-1
MAN UTD	22/8	1-1
COVENTRY	29/8	1-1
WIMBLEDON	9/9	3-1
LIVERPOOL	12/9	2-1
NOTTM FOREST	19/9	N/A
SOUTHAMPTON	28/9	2-4
BLACKBURN	3/10	0-3
ASTON VILLA	17/10	2-1
CHARLTON	24/10	N/A
NEWCASTLE	31/10	1-0
CHELSEA	8/11	2-1
LEICESTER	14/11	4-3
DERBY	22/11	0-2
TOTTENHAM	28/11	2-1
LEEDS	5/12	1-3
MIDDLESBROUGH	12/12	N/A
EVERTON	19/12	2-2
ARSENAL	26/12	0-4
COVENTRY	28/12	1-0
MAN UTD	9/1	1-2
SHEFF WED	16/1	1-0
WIMBLEDON	30/1	2-1
ARSENAL	6/2	0-0
NOTTM FOREST	13/2	N/A
LIVERPOOL	20/2	0-5
BLACKBURN	27/2	2-1
SOUTHAMPTON	6/3	0-3
CHELSEA	13/3	1-2
NEWCASTLE	20/3	0-1
ASTON VILLA	3/4	0-2
CHARLTON	5/4	N/A
LEICESTER	10/4	1-2
DERBY	17/4	0-0
TOTTENHAM	24/4	0-1
LEEDS	1/5	3-0
EVERTON	8/5	1-2
MIDDLESBROUGH	16/5	N/A

THE SQUAD

Key: Goalkeeper · Defender · Midfield · Forward · No of goals · No of clean sheets · No of yellow cards · No of red cards

Player	Position	Goals / Clean sheets	Yellow cards	Red cards
Shaka Hislop	Goalkeeper	2		
L. Miklosko	Goalkeeper			
C. Forrest	Goalkeeper	5		
T. Breacker	Defender		3	
D. Unsworth	Defender	2	8	1
R. Ferdinand	Defender		4	
I. Pearce	Defender	1	2	
R. Hall	Defender			
J. Dicks	Defender			
S. Potts	Defender		2	
E. Berkovic	Midfield	7	2	
A. Impey	Midfield		1	
S. Lomas	Midfield	2	7	1
M. Keller	Midfield			
J. Moncur	Midfield	1	9	
F. Lampard	Midfield	4	6	
T. Sinclair	Midfield	7	5	
S. Lazaridis	Midfield	2	2	
P. Kitson	Forward	4	1	
S. Abou	Forward	5	2	1
J. Hartson	Forward	15	3	2
M. Omoyinmi	Forward	2		
I. Wright	Forward			

Transfers after 15 July 1998:

David Pleat: *on the manager*

HARRY REDKNAPP

Enjoyed a shrewdly successful season in the transfer market but he will need to hang on to his best players if he is to keep it going forward. A genuine, determined character but with an endearing touch of nerves about him. Knows only too well the meaning of the safety margin and it will be no easy task to repeat the success of last season.

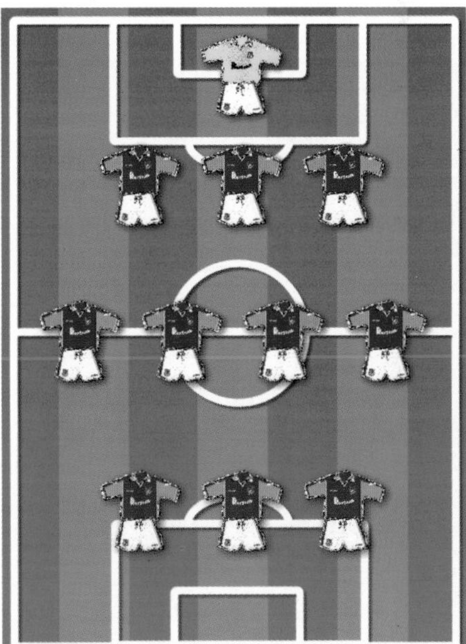

Trevor Brooking: *tactics*

A far happier season last year for my old team, who played like Championship contenders at home, but struggled for goals away from Upton Park. Nearly always played with three central defenders and it was a system that suited the constructive skills of Rio Ferdinand, and helped him to book his World Cup place. John Hartson continued his fine goalscoring record, but the latter months of the season were disrupted by a decline in his discipline. Other young players like Frank Lampard Junior are emerging from the youth ranks, and this should ensure another steady season of progress.

Upton Park is in London's East End, approximately 7 miles from London's city centre. There is usually ample parking in the streets around the ground.

DIRECTIONS

From The North:

From the M1, turn off onto the A1 at Junction 2/3. Join the A406 North Circular Road and continue east for 17 miles until the junction with the A214 Barking Road. Turn right into Barking Road and continue for 2 miles, turning right into Green Street. Upton Park is on the right.

From The North West:

Approaching London on the M40, at Junction 1 stay on the A40 for 10 miles before turning onto the A406 North Circular Road eastbound. Stay on this road for 23 miles until the junction with the A214 Barking Road. Then as route for North.

From The West:

Approaching London on the M4, turn off onto the A406 North Circular Road eastbound. Stay on this road for 26 miles until the junction with the A214 Barking Road. Then as route for North.

From The South West:

From the M3 turn off onto the M25 at Junction 2. Continue for 10 miles until you reach Junction 15 at which point turn off onto the M4. Then as route for the West.

From The East:

From the M11 turn off onto the A406 at Junction 4 for 4 miles until the junction with the A214 Barking Road. Then as route for North.

The nearest tube stations are Upton Park and East Ham.

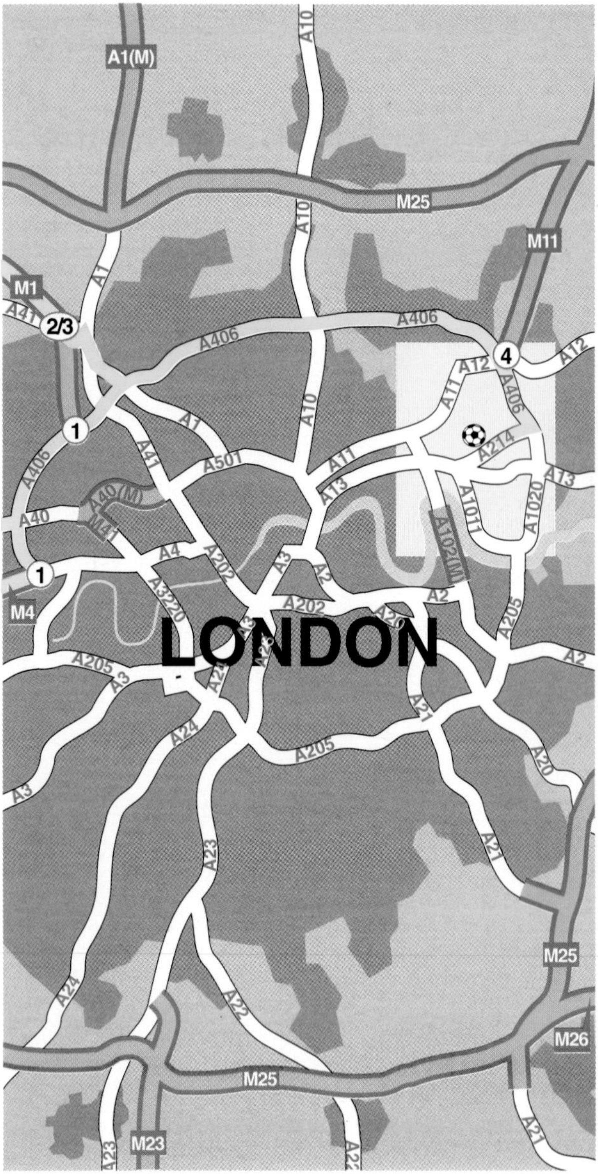

McDonald's™ 28 High Street North, London E6 2HJ
McDonald's™ Drive Thru, 322 Romford Road, London E7 8BD
McDonald's™ Drive Thru, 164 Barking Road, London E16

Wimbledon FC

Wimbledon FC
Selhurst Park Stadium
South Norwood
London
SE25 6PY

Club No: 0181·771·2233
Fax No: 0181·768·0641
Tickets: 0181·771·8841
Internet: www.wimbledonfc.co.uk

Bobby Robson: *view from abroad*

Joe Kinnear and Sam Hammam do one of the most fantastic jobs in the country to achieve what they have done on their gates. It is nothing short of miraculous. They wave the magic wand in transfers, buying players that no one else fancies at the time and then selling them on for huge profits. They do it regularly so it can't be luck. It is good, sound, shrewd judgement. Joe Kinnear should be Chancellor of the Exchequer for what he does.

Bob Harris: *view in England*

0Find goals or go down! That is the harsh reality for outstanding manager Joe Kinnear at the most remarkable club in the country. Homeless and with a minimal fan base it seems every year the Dons must go down. They just survived with four points to spare having scored only 18 goals at home and 16 away. But the chances of doing that twice are remote. There is nothing they like better than being written off and you can bet that Joe and his chairman Sam Hammam have something up their sleeves again this year.

INFORMATION HOTLINES

ClubCall: 0891·12·11·75*

Calls cost 50p per minute at all times
Club Call, Avalon House, 57-63 Scrutton St, London, EC2A 4PJ

CLUB SHOPS

SHOP 1

Selhurst Park Stadium

Opening Times:

Monday-Friday: 9.30am-5.00pm
Match Saturdays: 9.30am-kick off & half an hour after game
Match Sundays: 9.30am-kick off & half an hour after game
Match Evenings: 9.30am-kick off & half an hour after game

Tel: 0181·768·6100

Fax: 0181·653·4708

Mail Order Service: 0181·768·6100

BOOKING INFORMATION

General Enquiries:	0181·771·8841
Credit Card Bookings:	0181·771·8841
Travel Club:	0181·771·8841
Junior Club Line:	0181·771·2233
Football in the Community:	0181·771·1772

CATERING

FOOD

Hot Dog	£2.00
Burger	£2.00
Veggie Burger	£2.00
Pies/Pasties	£1.40
Sausage Rolls	£1.20
Pizza	£1.60
Jacket Potato	£1.70
Ice Cream	£1.50
Chips	£1.00
Pop Corn	£1.00
Nachos	£1.30
Sweets	from £0.30

BAR

Tea	£0.80
Coffee	£1.00
Bovril	£1.00
Chocolate	£1.00
Lucozade	£1.00

MISCELLANEOUS

Stadium Tours
Football in the Community - Tel: 0181·771·1772
Corporate Hospitality/Sponsorship
Sharon Sillitoe, Marketing Department
Tel: 0181·771·2233
Matchday hospitality packages from £70 per head
Sponsorship and Matchball Sponsorship available.
Executive boxes - match to match '6 pack'.
Restaurant facilities
Call Catering on 0181·771·2233
Literature
Programme price £2 (mail order available contact Reg Davis 0181 771 2233)
Pre match and half time entertainment
Selhurst Park Television
Selhurst Super Lottery Draw
Music and Dedications
Occasional Live Acts

MARK KENNEDY

Regarded by many in the game as a frustrating and unfulfilled talent, Mark Kennedy can point to the fact that he is still only 22, and in three years at Liverpool was given the chance to start only 15 Premiership Games. The Dublin-born winger has natural flair and a sharp turn of pace, which could catch on in the more modest environment in which he now finds himself.

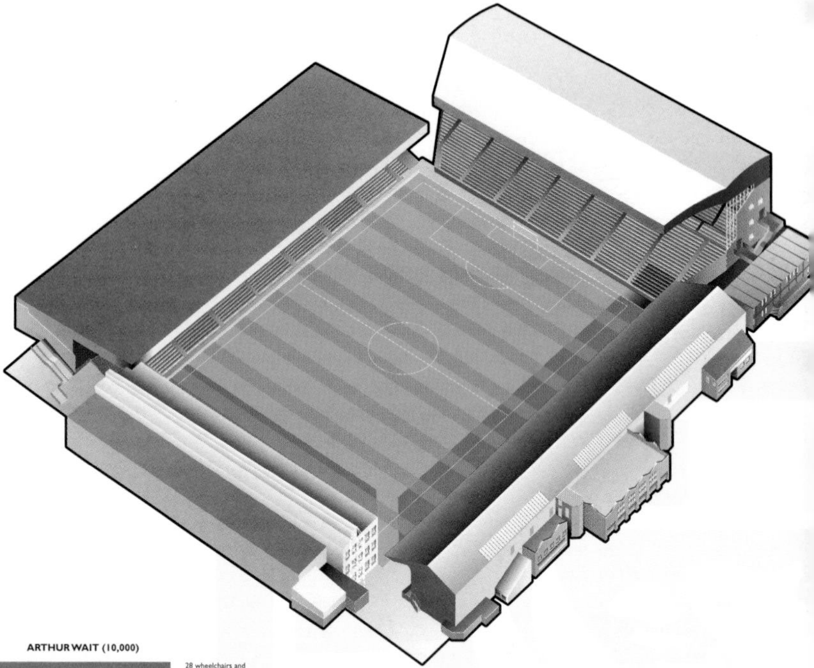

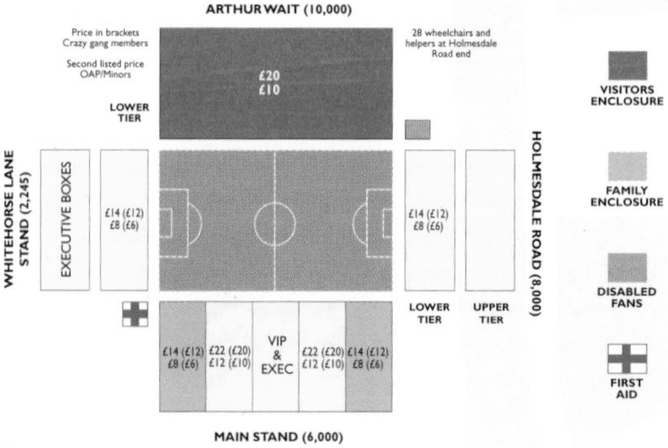

ARTHUR WAIT (10,000)
Price in brackets Crazy gang members
Second listed price OAP/Minors
LOWER TIER
£20
£10
28 wheelchairs and helpers at Holmesdale Road end
WHITEHORSE LANE STAND (2,245)
EXECUTIVE BOXES
£14 (£12)
£8 (£6)
£14 (£12)
£8 (£6)
LOWER TIER
UPPER TIER
HOLMESDALE ROAD (8,000)
£14 (£12)
£8 (£6)
£22 (£20)
£12 (£10)
VIP & EXEC
£22 (£20)
£12 (£10)
£14 (£12)
£8 (£6)
MAIN STAND (6,000)
VISITORS ENCLOSURE
FAMILY ENCLOSURE
DISABLED FANS
FIRST AID

97/98 season points and league position by month

Win
Loss
Draw
League Position
League position
Points
0
2
4
6
8
10
12
14
16
18
20
80
75
70
65
60
55
50
45
40
35
30
25
20
15
10
5
0
Aug
Sept
Oct
Nov
Dec
Jan
Feb
March
April
May

Goals for and against seasons 92/3 to 97/8

Total Goals
Home
Away
297
166
131
185
149
334
For
Against

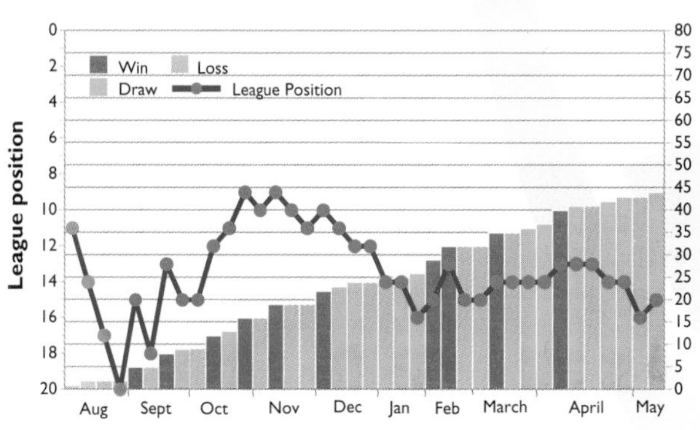

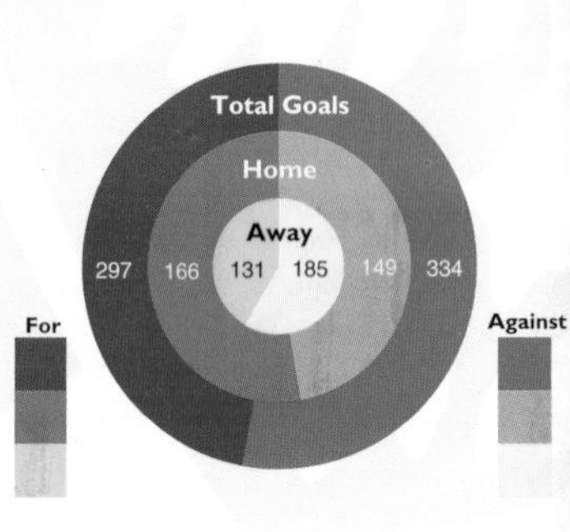

Goals scored by position by season

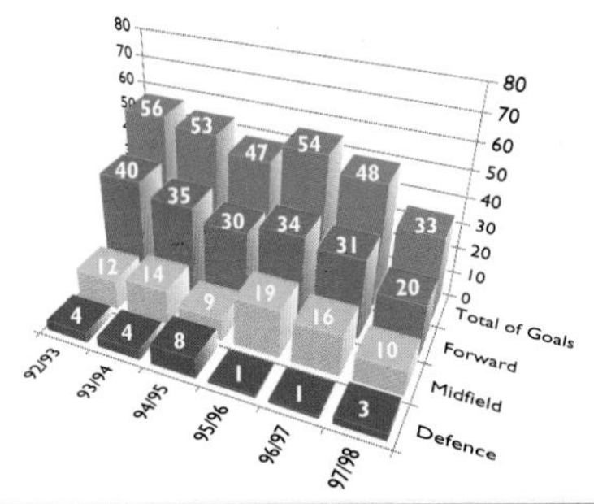

Bookings by position by season

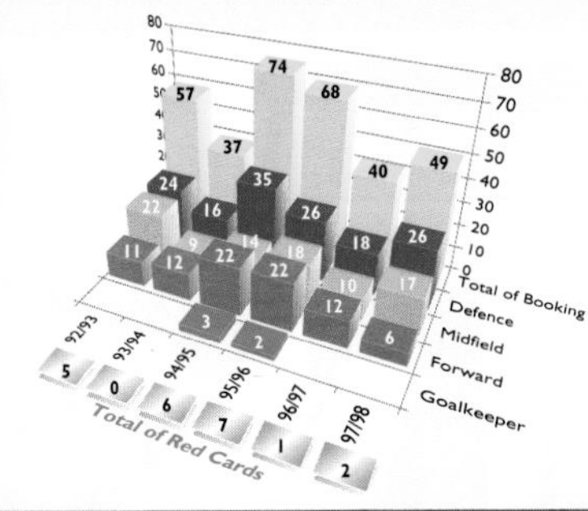

Goals scored by position by month 97/98

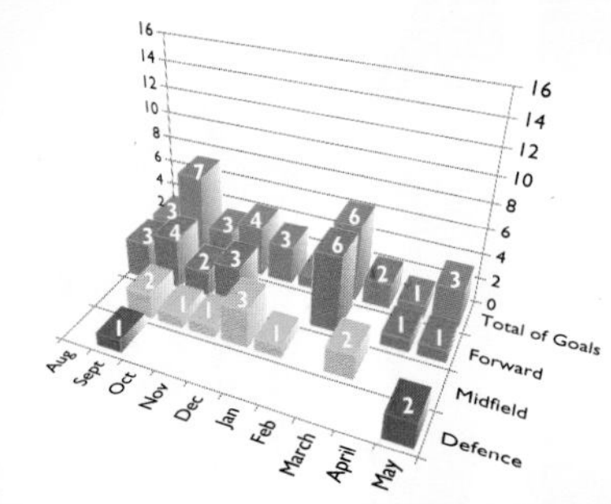

Final league position by season

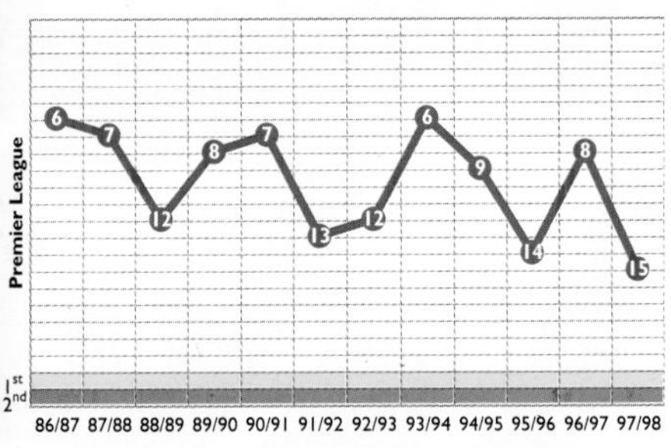

THE CARLING PREMIERSHIP FIXTURE LIST

HOME MATCH
AWAY MATCH
LAST SEASON: WIN
LAST SEASON: DRAW
LAST SEASON: LOSS

Opponent	Date	Last season
TOTTENHAM	15/8	2-6
DERBY	22/8	1-1
LEEDS	29/8	1-0
WEST HAM	9/9	1-3
ASTON VILLA	12/9	2-1
SHEFF WED	19/9	1-1
LEICESTER	27/9	1-0
EVERTON	3/10	0-0
MAN UTD	17/10	0-2
MIDDLESBROUGH	24/10	N/A
BLACKBURN	31/10	0-1
NOTTM FOREST	7/11	N/A
CHELSEA	14/11	1-1
ARSENAL	21/11	0-5
NEWCASTLE	28/11	3-1
COVENTRY	5/12	1-2
LIVERPOOL	13/12	1-1
SOUTHAMPTON	19/12	1-0
CHARLTON	26/12	N/A
LEEDS	28/12	1-1
DERBY	9/1	0-0
TOTTENHAM	16/1	0-0
WEST HAM	30/1	1-2
CHARLTON	6/2	N/A
SHEFF WED	13/2	1-1
ASTON VILLA	20/2	2-1
EVERTON	27/2	0-0
LEICESTER	6/3	2-1
NOTTM FOREST	13/3	N/A
BLACKBURN	20/3	0-0
MAN UTD	3/4	2-5
MIDDLESBROUGH	5/4	N/A
CHELSEA	10/4	0-2
ARSENAL	17/5	0-1
NEWCASTLE	24	0-0
COVENTRY	1/5	0-0
SOUTHAMPTON	8/5	0-1
LIVERPOOL	16/5	0-2

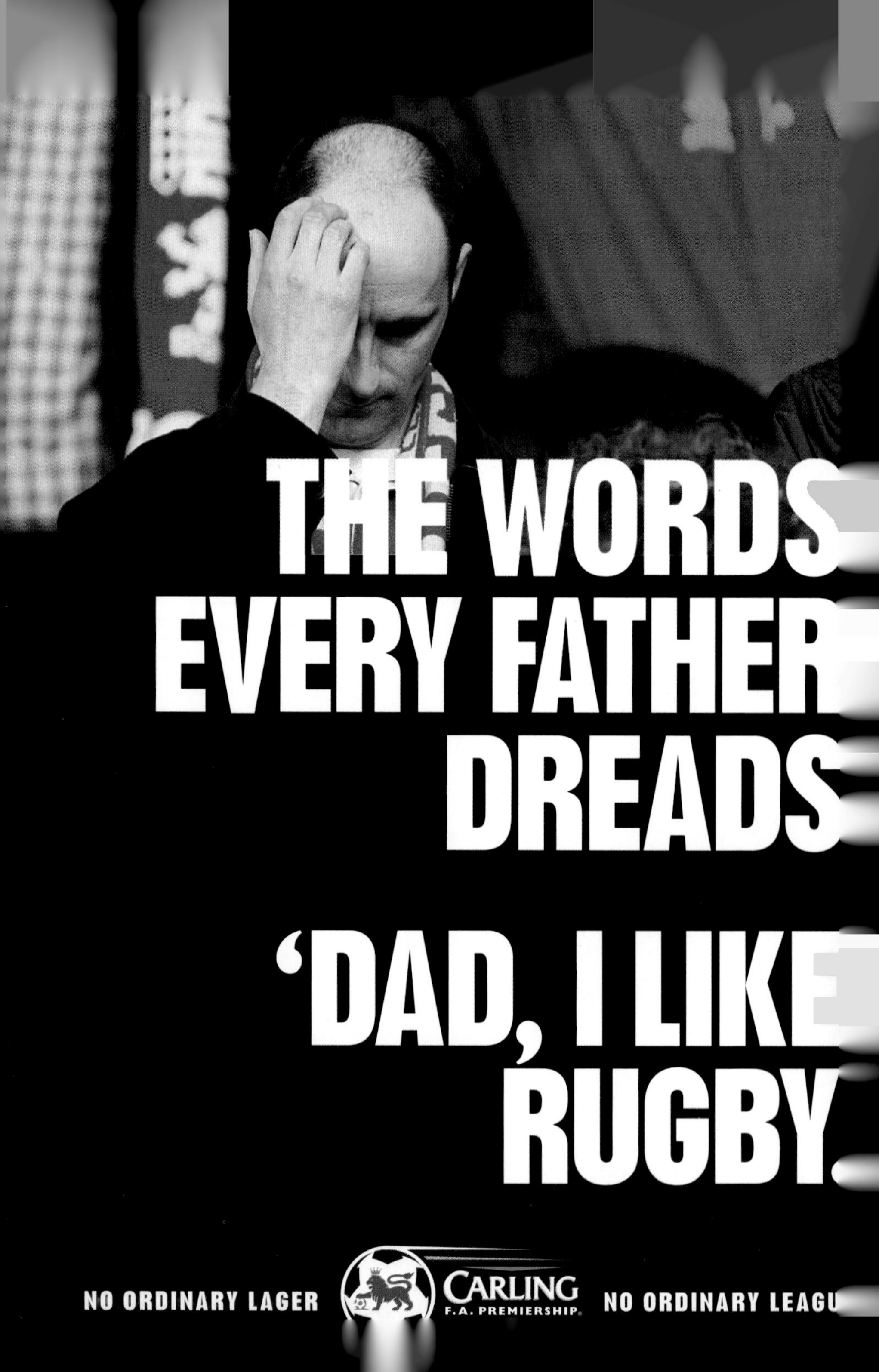

THE WORDS EVERY FATHER DREADS

'DAD, I LIKE RUGBY.

NO ORDINARY LAGER

NO ORDINARY LEAGU

THE SQUAD

Key: Goalkeeper · Forward · No of yellow cards · Defender · No of goals · No of red cards · Midfield · No of clean sheets

Player	Position	Goals / Clean sheets	Yellow cards	Red cards
N. Sullivan	Goalkeeper			
P. Heald	Goalkeeper			
B. Thatcher	Defender		2	2
K. Cunningham	Defender		2	
D. Jupp	Defender		2	
B. McAllister	Defender			
C. Perry	Defender	1	7	
A. Pearce	Defender			
A. Kimble	Defender		7	
D. Blackwell	Defender		4	
A. Roberts	Defender	1	3	
A. Clarke	Midfield			
S. Castledine	Midfield		1	
C. Hughes	Midfield	1	4	
P. Fear	Midfield	2	2	
R. Earle	Midfield	3		
M. Hughes	Midfield	4	4	
J. Euell	Midfield	4	1	
N. Ardley	Midfield	2	1	
M. Kennedy	Midfield			
D. Francis	Midfield			
M. Gayle	Forward	2	1	
E. Ekoku	Forward	4		
C. Leaburn	Forward		4	
J. Goodman	Forward			
C. Court	Forward	4		

Transfers after 15 July 1998:

David Pleat: *on the manager*

JOE KINNEAR

Will bubble and bounce and roll along with the Crazy Gang. But he will be aware that every year they beat the odds is a year closer to that dreaded problem when they flirt near the bottom group. A super front man for a club directed by Sam Hammam, performing wonders in retaining their status.

Trevor Brooking: *tactics*

Another team set with their 4-4-2 system, which gives them a solid defensive base for the team to build on. Kenny Cunningham and Chris Perry continue to improve but it gets tougher for Manager Joe Kinnear to sign 'bargains' from the lower ranks. Scoring goals was much harder as injuries and loss of form affected both regular strikers Efan Ekoku and Marcus Gayle. It gets even harder for them to keep away from the relegation threat now and once again a limited transfer fund will not help stem the tide.

Wimbledon play at Selhurst Park in South London, nine miles from the city centre. Parking is allowed in most of the neighbourhood streets and it is usually possible to leave the car quite close to the stadium.

DIRECTIONS

From the North:

Approaching on the M1, exit at Junction 1 onto the A406 North Circular Road. Keep on the North Circular until Chiswick roundabout, then take the A205 South Circular which joins the A3 to Wandsworth. Follow the one-way system and turn right onto the A214 Trinity Road, through Tooting Bec to Streatham. Turn onto the A23 Streatham High Road and left onto the A214 Crown Lane. At the junction turn right onto the A215 Beulah Hill and then right into Whitehorse Lane. The ground is on the left.

From the North West:

Approaching on the M40, continue straight onto the A40 until you meet the A406 North Circular. Then as route for North.

From the West:

Approaching on the M4, exit at Junction 1 Chiswick Roundabout onto the A205 South Circular. Then as route for North.

From the South West:

Approaching on the M3, continue onto the A316 until the junction with the A205 South Circular. Then as route for North.

There are two train stations nearby - Selhurst and Norwood. Both are about five minutes walking distance from Selhurst Park.

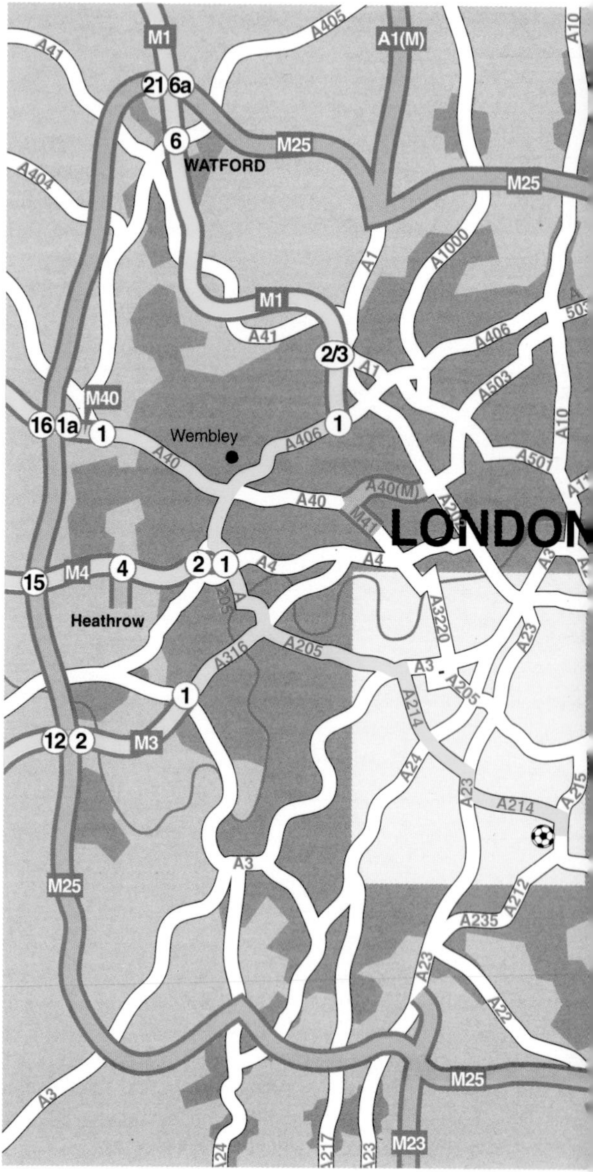

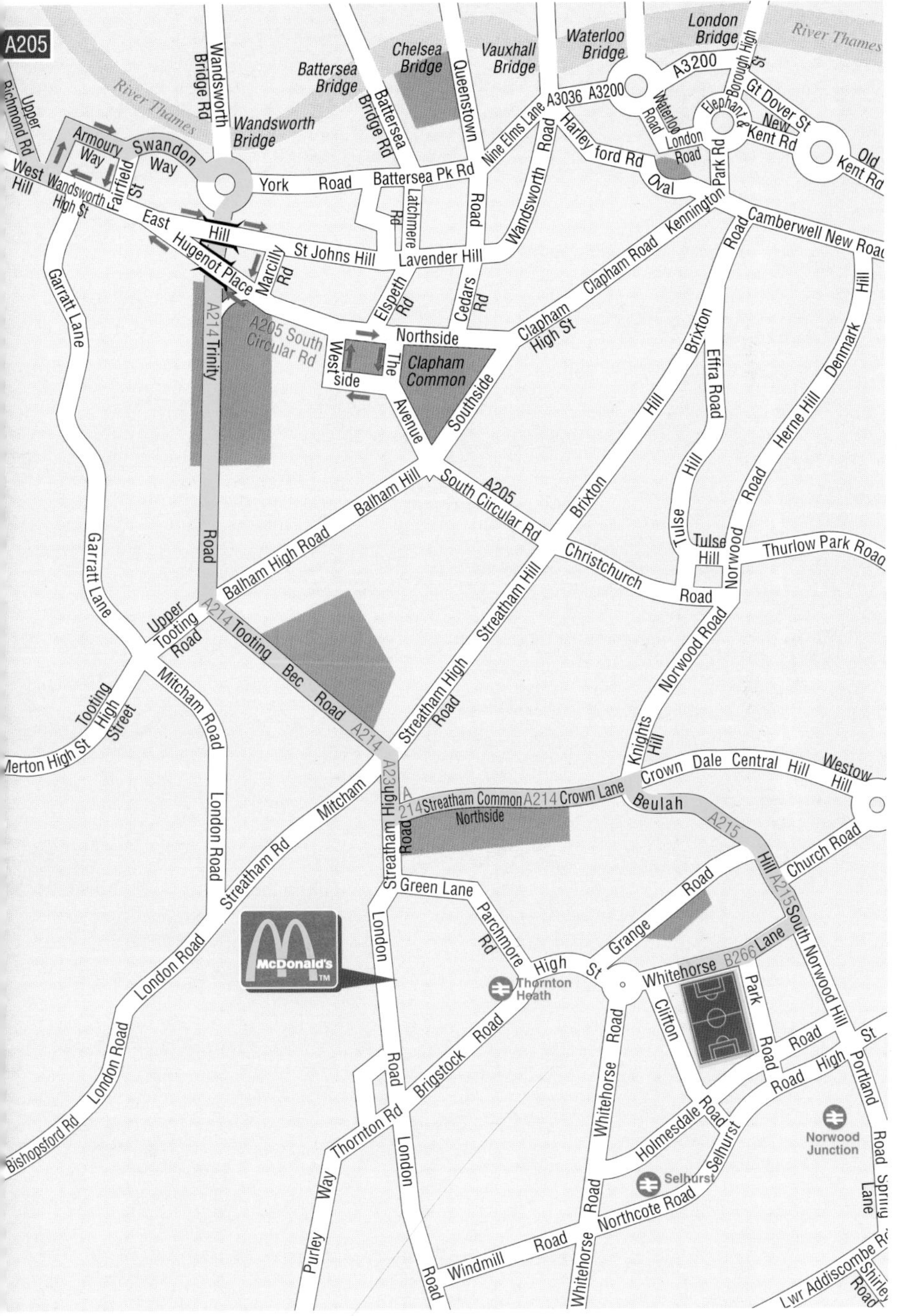

McDonald's™ 939-943 London Road, Thornton Heath, London CR7 6XJ

Mileage Chart

NEWCASTLE
MIDDLESBROUGH
BLACKBURN
LEEDS
MANCHESTER
LIVERPOOL
SHEFFIELD
DERBY
NOTTINGHAM
LEICESTER
BIRMINGHAM
COVENTRY
LONDON
SOUTHAMPTON

	Birmingham	Blackburn	Coventry	Derby	Leeds	Leicester	Liverpool	Manchester	Middlesbrough	Newcastle	Nottingham	Sheffield	Southampton
Southampton													
Sheffield													206
Nottingham												42	162
Newcastle											159	133	320
Middlesbrough										38	128	100	288
Manchester									104	136	67	40	201
Liverpool								33	134	167	103	73	235
Leicester							11	95	154	188	28	68	136
Leeds						97	73	43	62	96	72	35	230
Derby					75	28	87	59	130	165	15	35	157
Coventry				43	11	24	11	99	175	209	50	75	11
Blackburn			122	86	48	11	40	25	101	11	97	63	239
Birmingham		106	19	39	120	43	99	87	174	209	53	79	128
London	11	214	107	107	195	101	205	185	245	276	11	165	76